MOVING CRUCIFIXES IN MODERN SPAIN

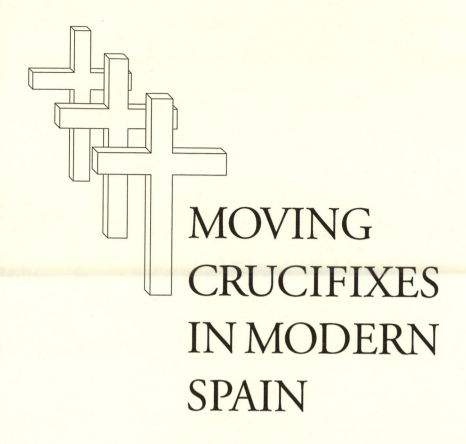

MOVING CRUCIFIXES IN MODERN SPAIN

William A. Christian, Jr.

PRINCETON UNIVERSITY PRESS

PRINCETON, NEW JERSEY

Library of Congress Cataloging-in-Publication Data

Christian, William A., 1944–
Moving crucifixes in modern Spain /
William A. Christian, Jr.
p.   cm.
Includes bibliographical references and index.
ISBN 0-691-07387-2
1. Jesus Christ—Cult—Spain—History—20th century.
2. Crosses—Spain—History—20th century.   3. Spain—
Religious life and customs.   I. Title.   II. Title: Moving
crucifixes in modern Spain.
BT580.S7C47   1992
232.96'3—dc20   91-22089 CIP

Publication of this book has been aided by a grant from
The Program for Cultural Cooperation Between Spain's
Ministry of Culture and United States Universities

Contents

Illustrations

FIGURES

MAPS

Appendix Tables

Acknowledgments

I THANK the following persons for their help with this study: Quintín Aldea, S.J.; Miguel Bergasa; Josefa Berriel Jordán; L. W. Bonbrake; William J. Callahan; Camilo de Grajal, OFM Cap.; Josefina Cedillo; Tirso Cepedal, C.Ss.R.; William A. Christian, Sr.; Zed David; Peter Dinzelbacher; Enrique de Ventosa, OFM Cap.; Idoia Estornés Zubizarreta; William Fackovec; Carlos Fernández; Francisco de Bilbao, OFM Cap.; Candido Galdeano; Eugenio Garrido; María del Carmen González Echegaray; Susan Harding; Cindy Hirschfeld; María José Igartua; Gabor Klaniczay; Thomas Kselman; Benito Madariaga de la Campa; Frank Mahood; Carlos Marichal; Ben Martin; Fátima Martínez Berriel; Josefa Martínez Berriel; Miguel Medina; Ana Elsa Montes de González; Adolfo Robles, O.P.; José Sagasti; José Sales Tirapu; Sheila Salley; Scott Sherman; Guillermo Sierra, OFM Cap.; Janet Stern; Gail Ullman; and Pilar Varela. I also thank the Woodrow Wilson International Center for Scholars, where a first draft was written, and the John D. and Catherine T. MacArthur Foundation.

MOVING
CRUCIFIXES
IN MODERN
SPAIN

FIGURES 1, 2, AND 3. Details of the Christs of Gandía, Limpias, and Piedramillera. Photographs by *Diario de Valencia*, Puente, and the author.

Prologue

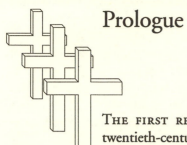

THE FIRST RELIGIOUS apparitions of consequence in twentieth-century Spain occurred in the town of Limpias (Cantabria), beginning on March 30, 1919. There a life-size crucifix, known as El Cristo de la Agonía, was seen to roll its eyes, change its complexion, and sweat after a climactic session of a nine-day mission preached by two Capuchin friars. In the 1920s Limpias became a special testimonial for observant Catholicism not only from Spain but also for pilgrims from the Central European heartland of Christ-centered devotion, from whence occasional busloads still arrive seventy years later.

In this period other crucifixes were seen to move as well—prior to Limpias at Gandía in Valencia (1918), and subsequent to Limpias at Piedramillera and Mañeru in Navarra (1920) and Melilla (1922). This study examines the devotional, social, and political contexts that helped to make these visions credible. Readers who want to know whether the crucifixes really moved or not will be disappointed, as that question is not addressed. Rather the accounts of the visions and the pilgrimages they provoked are probed and sorted to provide a portrait of Spain's Catholics in a time of trial. They understood the visions locally as signs for the new shrines; politically, as divine reactions to current events; and in a wider perspective as part of a progressive, millenarian sequence.

The protagonists of these stories and those who most interest me are the almost anonymous children, women, and men of Spain's cities, towns, and villages who saw the crucifixes move; their parish priests; and their missionary preachers. However, their visions are inextricably caught up in a period of social and political strife, and certain references to the intricacies of political parties and opinion groups within Spanish Catholicism are unavoidable. Spain's political power in the nineteenth century was disputed by supporters of an absolutist monarchy and new middle classes. The century saw three civil wars, a short-lived republic (1873–1874), and see-saw periods of monarchic rule which varied from conservative absolutism to progressive liberalism. Readers are referred to the works of my betters for a more detailed account of this troubled period.

The last of the century's civil wars ended in 1876 with the establishment of an oligarchic constitutional monarchy, in which the two propertied social forces, as the Conservative and Liberal parties, alternated in power and governed through a clientelist spoils system. Elections were openly bought. A major difference between these two parties was their attitudes toward the religious orders, which had been expelled from Spain, their lands and property confiscated, in 1835–1836. The Liberals sought to limit, and the Conservatives facilitated, their reentry and activity in schools and social work.

Left out of power until 1931 were the poor, a great majority of the population. Some of them were politically mobilized. Many Catholic peasants, particularly in the north, the Basque country, and Catalonia, supported a branch of the Bourbon family that promised them certain regional liberties. Known generically as Traditionalists, and more specifically as Carlists or Jaimists, depending on who was their current pretender to the throne, they and their moneyed allies maintained a national network of newspapers. Theirs was *El Correo Español* of Madrid, which first printed the news of the Gandía and Piedramillera visions. Much of the rural clergy and members of certain religious orders were Traditionalists.

A significant portion of the Traditionalist clergy shifted to the Integrists, who broke away from the party in 1886, forming a separate political group with its main strength in the small towns of Navarra and the Basque country. For an organizing principle the Integrists replaced the dissident Bourbons with a kind of theocracy. Their national newspaper was *El Siglo Futuro* of Madrid. They had certain support within the Jesuits, the Capuchins, and in the Venerable Third Order. Like the Traditionalists, they turned up at Limpias. The Integrists were more directly influenced by the clergy, and it is my impression that they had less of a peasant base. Some of them were among the more authoritarian of the industrialists. The special symbol of the Integrists was the Sacred Heart of Jesus, but by 1919 it had become an almost defiant badge of activism for all mobilized Catholics.

For apart from Traditionalists and Integrists, who were regional minorities at best, most of Spain's Catholics were supporters of the established regime and voted for any of a number of factions vying for a conservative constituency. These factions were, more than formal parties, coalitions of patron-client relations built around prominent national politicians like Eduardo Dato or Antonio Maura. There were Liberal Catholics as well, who might be anticlerical, but not necessarily antireligious, organized in similar personalist coalitions. This panorama was further complicated by the emergence of nationalist parties in the Basque country and Catalonia, some of which were markedly Catholic.

The entire tangle of Catholics and right-wing parties and factions was under threat from below in this period, and I have tried to tell the story of these visions from this broader perspective. These visions and their pilgrimages were neither the creation of nor did they become the special domain of a particular political party or a particular brand of Catholicism.

This book is part of a sequence, similar in approach to *Apparitions in Late Medieval and Renaissance Spain*, and closely linked to work in progress on Basque visions in the 1930s. But it is intended to stand on its own as a chronicle of human experience of great intensity, the factors that conditioned that experience, and the sense that was made of it.

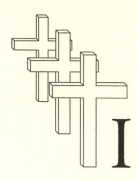

I

Contexts of Belief and Disbelief and the Christ of Gandía

MOVING IMAGES, APPARITIONS, AND THE SEARCH FOR A SPANISH LOURDES

The idea that images might move, weep, or sweat—in some way temporarily become human—was not new in twentieth century Spain or anywhere else in the Catholic world. Indeed, even in the pre-Christian Mediterranean statues were seen to act and react as humans, and these activations were read as prodigious references to current or future events.[1] In Italy the heyday of such occurrences was the sixteenth century, and the statues most involved seem to have been those of the Virgin Mary. While there are documented cases in Spain of such happenings in the fifteenth and sixteenth centuries (an image of Mary was said to have wept in 1520 sixty kilometers southwest of Gandía, at Cocentaina), the majority of cases I have found occurred in the seventeenth century.[2] Most of these involved statues of Christ or crucifixes, a reflection of the new popularity of Christ-centered devotions that accompanied the rise of Holy Week and its brotherhoods.

In Spain the sweating or bleeding of images was a form of hierophany that avoided many of the problems that went with apparitions. Apparitions, as I use the term, were visions of divine figures who communicated messages to their seers. In the wake of heretical movements or dangerous prophets like Savonarola, the Church warned against such independent revelation at the Lateran Council of 1517. Even before this the Inquisition in Spain had begun to investigate laypersons who claimed to have had apparitions. Having a statue that bled or sweated was a much less dangerous way for a town, a brotherhood, or a convent to inaugurate a new source of grace and protection. In such cases there were no potentially heterodox divine messages; there was no human being suddenly elevated to the category of divine ambassador (hence no threat to existing hierarchies); nor was there even a threat to the existing organization of space. The older apparitions had served to consecrate the landscape, drawing cult and attention out of the parish church or the established convents and chapels into the countryside. The activations of statues enhanced not a place, but an image, which was movable. Most of the statues were already in churches, and those in private homes were immediately moved into churches, where they were cherished just like the holy bones of saints. These new sources of grace thus reinforced, and were closely controlled by, the institutional church in its established holy places.

In the majority of the early modern cases for which an investigation was made, there really was a liquid or gelatinous substance of some kind on the image. In these instances there was not, as it were, one seer, but rather everyone who came was a seer, and the investigations were directed at the possibility of fraud on the part of the image-keepers or the person who first discovered the prodigy, at the nature of the substance involved, and at the possible divine significance of the sign, instead of the moral qualities or the emotional reactions of the observers.

Rather than threatening Church authority, these miracles reinforced it. For their content was totally within the acceptable language of the well-rehearsed forms of Christ's passion. These were controlled miracles, worthy of the Catholic Reformation, fit for the kind of devotion that Ignatius of Loyola taught in his spiritual exercises. In the safe paths of the Passion, as Barthes points out, there is no danger of the creative mysticism of Saint John of the Cross or the Quietists.[3] The churches where the miraculous images were placed became popular shrines; these shrines were in towns, under direct clerical control; the interpretation of just what the manifestations portended naturally fell into the purview of the clergy, who could ascribe to them the significance that seemed appropriate.

In fact, while these events clustered in years in which the monarchy or the economy was in trouble (1620, 1640, 1706) and hence may have had

as part of their origin local perceptions of national or international geo-
political ills, they rarely had an impact that was other than local. That
is, at most they might be commented on in letters or be the subject
of prose or verse broadsides published in Madrid or Barcelona, but they
certainly did not enter into what politicians then (and many scholars
now) considered "history." Monarchs, for instance, did not go out of
their way to visit such places. While at first persons from a wider radius
might be drawn to visit the miraculous image, usually within months
these shrines had become rather local, and without exception they are
now of significance for only the village or town in which they occurred.
In some instances all memory of the events has been lost even in the
home town.

It appears that the Inquisition had a chilling effect on the kind of
message-bearing apparitions that had been characteristic of the fifteenth
century, and that in a sense the activation of statues took their place.
Apparitions did not come back into style, however, as soon as the Inquisition began to wane in the latter half of the eighteenth century. One may
attribute this to a decline in religious fervor in general, part of the spread
of Enlightenment ideas responsible for the Inquisition's wane and ultimate extinction. Another reason is the removal of images themselves and
the discouragement of image-oriented devotion by the neo-Jansenist ori-
entation of some of the clergy as manifest in the Synod of Pistoia of 1786.
Indeed, by 1760 even the activations of images were few and far between,
or were accorded so little attention or credence when they did occur that
we have no notice of them.

Apparitions and healing miracles were of prime importance for the
revival of French Catholicism in the nineteenth century.[4] There they
provided a nationwide set of miraculous shrines, fed by a new system of
railways, that reaffirmed the faith of traditionally Catholic regions in a
country increasingly dominated by secular ideas. These events were well-
reported in Spain.[5] In Italy as well there were miraculous events. Statues
were seen to move, weep, or become brilliant in Ancona and Rome in
1796, in Rimini in 1850, and in Prata (Avellino) in 1875–1876. In 1888,
people began to see the Sorrowing Mother between some rocks at Castel
Petroso (Campobasso). Eventually even a bishop had the vision, and now
there is a diocesan shrine at the site.[6] Many of these events were known
in Spain as well.[7]

But in nineteenth-century Spain itself, important apparitions and activations were few and far between.[8] They appear to have played little or no
role in the kinds of missionary revivals led by Antonio María Claret,

Francisco de Paula Tarín, and others that recharged rural and bourgeois religiosity.[9] Nor, with the possible exception of Sor Patrocinio, is there any indication that they played a role in the Carlist Wars, or even in the great mobilizations of Catholics in 1890, 1906, and 1910 to protest Liberal government policies.[10] The symbols called on for these demonstrations were the saints of Spain's traditional shrines and relatively new devotions from outside of Spain propagated by transnational religious orders like the Jesuits, such as the Sacred Heart of Jesus.

The activations of the Christs of Gandía, Limpias, and Piedramillera, and the later apparitions of Mary in 1931 at Ezquioga and elsewhere, thus, should be seen as a kind of revival of older religious strategies, strategies that had not met with particular success in Spain for over a hundred and fifty years, but which were latent in the cultural repertory and were demonstrating an unparalleled vigor in France and Italy. Just how latent these strategies were in Spain is a matter of speculation. In April 1903 there was a striking antecedent to the Limpias visions in the parish church of San Martín de Manzaneda (Orense), where during a Redemptorist mission many persons saw a child with outstretched arms appear in place of the host in a monstrance. In the aftermath of the Limpias activations, writers recalled three other recent Spanish cases: a Christ in the parish church of San Sebastian in Madrid; a Christ which sweated blood around 1907–1909 in a village of the province of Cadiz; and some kind of allegedly supernatural manifestation, whose cult was suppressed, in a shrine in Barcelona.[11] We also know that in 1911 in Seville an image of the Miraculous Mary seemed to open its eyes and work miracles, although the matter was thoroughly suppressed.[12] These vague references lead one to wonder whether, from the early modern period through the late eighteenth and early nineteenth centuries, there might well have been an unbroken series of minor image activations, none of which became very well known, but news of which circulated among Catholics by word of mouth, newspaper reports, or brief mentions in pious magazines.

Returning emigrants and Spanish missionaries brought back accounts of other image activations from Hispanic America. The Jesuit journal *Razón y Fe* carried reports of the visions of three young students in a Jesuit school in Quito who on April 20, 1906, saw an image of the Sorrowing Mary open and close her eyes. Two professors were called, and they saw it too. A very rapid episcopal investigation, including forty witnesses, led to a decree on May 31, 1906, that the visions "could be believed." Later in 1906 there were group visions, much like those at Limpias thirteen years later.[13]

One does not know if the people of Gandía, Limpias, and Piedramillera had heard of these Spanish or American religious events; but they certainly knew about Lourdes. By the early twentieth century, Lourdes was recognized throughout Catholic Spain as a powerful new arena for grace. Indeed, enough Spaniards had been there, and enough well-publicized cures of Spaniards had taken place there, that the search for a Spanish Lourdes was on.

Bernadette's visions at Lourdes, which confirmed the dogma of the Immaculate Conception, occurred in 1858. From the start of major pilgrimages there after the opening of the Bayonne-Lourdes railway in 1867, Spanish bishops visited the shrine, generally on their way to or from Rome. Two stopped in 1870, for instance, en route to the Vatican Council; twelve in 1887, and ten in 1900. While some of these prelates made major detours to get to Lourdes, most were on their way from dioceses in the north of Spain, for whom Lourdes was not far from the border crossing in Irún. Some were on their *ad limina* visit to Rome; others were going to be made cardinals (see Appendix Table 1).

Spanish group pilgrimages, however, were few and far between in the early years. Up to 1904 most of them, like the visits of bishops, were stopovers on the way to Rome. For this period, from most of Spain Lourdes was visited only by the very upper class, like the group of noblemen and wealthy summer residents who went with a Bayonne pilgrimage in 1874, or Queen Isabel and her retinue, who went in 1880. In 1884 a small brotherhood was established under royal patronage in Madrid.[14]

Until the 1880s there is little evidence for widespread lay devotion, and then only in Catalonia and the Balearic Islands. In early 1876 French nuns set up a Lourdes grotto in their garden in Barcelona; but they claimed it was the first in Spain. Four years later there was a magazine in Barcelona devoted to Lourdes; there a sector of the devout was already primed, as it were, by their devotion to Our Lady of La Salette. In 1880 a Lourdes shrine was erected by a parish priest near Figols, in a hilly mining district of the province of Barcelona. It was from Barcelona, in June 1883, that the first Spanish pilgrimage to Lourdes that did not go on to Rome was organized, consisting of 800 persons, including 50 priests. It was followed in the same year by another from Mallorca with an even higher proportion of clergy, 120 out of 615. Early Spanish interest in Lourdes seems to have come through the hierarchy and the clergy, and quite likely as well through French religious orders.[15]

The predominance of Catalans in Spain's pilgrims to Lourdes continued into the twentieth century. Catalans went on two large pilgrimages

FIGURE 4. A reenactment of Bernadette's vision at Lourdes for a postcard, which was sent to Spain in 1905.

in 1887. The first, comprised mainly of Catalans and Valencians, including, the *Annales de Notre-Dame de Lourdes* noted, dukes, counts, barons, and one hundred priests, denounced Liberalism and secret societies; similarly the second, with pilgrims from Barcelona and Gerona, bore a banner reading "Liberalism is a Sin." Pilgrimages continued from Barcelona (1889, 1901), Catalonia in general (1900), and Valencia (1899). But in the entire period from 1868 to 1904 there were just four groups that went exclusively to Lourdes from elsewhere in Spain (national pilgrimages in 1879 and 1897, and two small groups from Asturias in 1901 and 1903).[16]

Major annual pilgrimages from Spain began in the 1904–1908 period, stimulated by two successive fiftieth anniversaries: that of the proclamation of the dogma of the Immaculate Conception in 1904, and that of the visions of Bernadette in 1908. Those bishops who had become Lourdes enthusiasts and whose diocese were relatively close to France took advantage of these anniversaries and their special indulgences to send or accompany contingents.

The prestige of Lourdes was enhanced at this time in Spain by two visits from Alfonso XIII, much to the satisfaction of the shrine chaplains, who described the visits in detail and published his photograph in the

Annales, in pointed reference to their unhappy relations with the Third Republic. In 1905 Alfonso XIII had ten votive candles lit to the Virgin, and went off with a large container of water. He returned with Queen Victoria in 1907.[17]

It was in 1904 that the large Basque expeditions began. They quickly developed a political side, and Basque nationalists held pilgrimages separate from those of the diocese in 1908, 1910, and 1911, until the bishop of Vitoria, Cadena y Eleta, intervened with the bishop of Lourdes to stop them.[18] As with the Integrists before them in 1887, the Jaimists also made expeditions to Lourdes, particularly in 1913, when six thousand went to bring the body of General Tristany, who had died in exile, back to Spain.[19] And doubtless the Catalan and Valencian pilgrimages were not devoid of cultural undertones.

The advent of large Spanish pilgrimages was eased by an important symbolic gesture by Lourdes' bishop, François-Xavier Schoepfer. In 1907 he led a pilgrimage from his diocese to the shrines of El Pilar in Zaragoza and Montserrat in Catalonia.[20] By this year twenty-eight Spanish bishops had signed his petition to have the liturgical office of Our Lady of Lourdes extended to the Church at large; more than half of the Spaniards who signed had been to Lourdes.[21]

The jubilee year of 1908 set a record for Spanish pilgrims to Lourdes until after the Civil War of 1936–1939—over 25,000 in seventeen pilgrimages. It brought the first ever diocesan pilgrimages from Navarra, Santander, Vich, Seville, Jaén, and Burgos.

Subsequently there were regular annual or semiannual pilgrimages from several Spanish dioceses, with an average total of 12,000 pilgrims yearly until the First World War, and 14,000 pilgrims yearly in the period from 1923 to 1930. In 1931, the first year of the Republic in Spain, the pilgrimages ceased, and they remained somewhat reduced until they ceased again during the Civil War (Appendix Table 1).

There is no way to count the Spaniards who went to Lourdes apart from the organized expeditions. At the shrine they calculated that, globally, about twice as many pilgrims came privately as in groups. The proportion going as individuals from Spain was probably lower, and a conservative estimate would be that in the twenty years prior to the visions at Gandía, Limpias, and Piedramillera, that is from 1900 to 1920, 100,000 Spaniards went to Lourdes on organized trips and another 50,000 went privately.

News of cures of Spanish pilgrims provided an added inducement to go to Lourdes. From the nineteenth century sick persons accompanied pilgrimages, but organized "hospital" pilgrimages for the severely crippled or terminally ill did not begin until 1910 (those of Barcelona), 1912 (Basques), and 1929 (Valencia and Valladolid). In 1911 there were two dramatic cures in the Barcelona expedition and one in the Basque group. The Catalans thereupon began to bring with their sick pilgrims dossiers carefully prepared by a medical team in Barcelona, which would serve as proofs for miracles on the French model.[22]

It was in emulation of Lourdes that an effort was made to center Spanish pilgrimages nationwide on the shrine of Our Lady of Pilar in Zaragoza. Such trips were begun in 1880 and scheduled for the 1904 anniversary of the dogma of the Immaculate Conception, as at Lourdes; for the coronation of the image in 1905; and, as at Lourdes, for the jubilee year of 1908.[23] In July 1905, *El Mensajero del Corazón de Jesús* reported that "El Pilar these days has been a real Lourdes ... some might say it should be even greater than that."[24] In his influential booklet, *Lourdes y El Pilar* (1906), José María Azara pointed out that the key to Lourdes' success was its cures, and he suggested ways to bring the sick to Zaragoza, including reduced train fares and the sponsorship of wealthy Catholics. In imitation of Lourdes a hospice was set up at the shrine. In 1908 a major pilgrimage was organized for the centenary of the delivery by the Virgin of Zaragoza from Napoleon's seige. But El Pilar itself was under siege from the French, and its final effort, to set up one big pilgrimage from a different archdiocese each year starting in 1912, lasted only three years.[25]

I interpret the pilgrimage of Cardinal Soldevila and the diocese of Zaragoza to Lourdes in 1920 in order to lay the cornerstone for a monument there to Our Lady of Pilar as a tacit recognition of the supremacy of the French shrine. After much delay the projected monument, for which funds were solicited nationally, was replaced by a simpler altar in Lourdes castle, inaugurated finally in 1934. Similarly, but with less reluctance, Abbot Marcet of the Benedictines of Montserrat went with a Catalan pilgrimage in 1922 to install a statue of the Virgin of Montserrat in the Lourdes parish church.[26]

After 1900 the organization of El Pilar into an active Spanish national shrine (Montserrat, content to be the Catalan national shrine, had no such pretension) was hampered by Spanish devotion to Lourdes. The attempt was made at a time when Spanish trips to Lourdes were becoming regular and large (indeed, the attempt was made for this reason). The relative proximity of Zaragoza to Lourdes meant that the two shrines were competing for the same pilgrims.

As it was, for pilgrims with an opportunity to go to Lourdes, El Pilar had little to offer. The putative visit of the Virgin to Zaragoza, challenged by some Church scholars, to consign the founding pillar of the shrine to

Saint James almost two thousand years before did not have the immediacy of the apparitions of the Virgin to a girl at the Lourdes grotto within living memory. El Pilar did not have Lourdes' international crowds nor the exciting imminence of miracles. Furthermore, as local chauvinism took form in Spain's peripheral regions, El Pilar, with its claim as a national shrine, tended to be seen as a symbol of centralism. For instance, in 1908 twenty-eight parishes in Guipúzcoa, in the Basque country, reported that they sent pilgrims to Lourdes for the jubilee year; only six sent pilgrims to El Pilar.[27]

Up until 1936, the dioceses that sent most pilgrimages to Lourdes were those of Catalonia, Vitoria, Pamplona, and Valencia. Together they accounted for eighty percent of all Spanish pilgrims on organized trips to Lourdes. The Catalan and Basque expeditions, with easy rail routes, were by far the largest. By comparison, the numbers sent from Madrid, Valladolid, or Zaragoza were insignificant, less than one percent of Spain's total. Barcelona was the capital of Lourdes devotion in Spain, acknowledged in the *Annales*. And among Spain's bishops, Catalan, Basque, and Navarrese bishops went to Lourdes the most (see Appendix Tables 2 and 3).

The activation of statues in Gandía in 1918, Limpias in 1919, and Navarra in 1920, occurred in Spain's "alleys" of special devotion to Lourdes, alleys in use since at least the first decade of the century, and alleys in which the need for a Lourdes that was Spanish was most keenly perceived (see Map 1).

The proliferation of visions in a secular France and their increasing success, fed by railways, newspapers, and books, with a literate public, points up a modern side to the apparitions. Both in France and Spain, old cultural forms were revived. But the unexplained events that earlier would have been rather circumscribed local miracles, in the nineteenth and twentieth centuries could be widely disseminated, challenged a rationalist view of the universe, and made access to special supernatural grace a universally available option. Affordable group pilgrimages by train or bus to these international sacred hotspots marked a quantum leap in the accessibility of the sacred, like the leap in access to faith healers operating by television in American households.

These apparitions and the interest they evoked, then, are not a medieval reaction to the modern world. They are a product, part and parcel of that world. The healing water of Lourdes, bottled, labeled, and distributed throughout Christendom (129,000 bottles were shipped out in 1909 alone),[28] was every bit as much a new product as galoshes, baking powder,

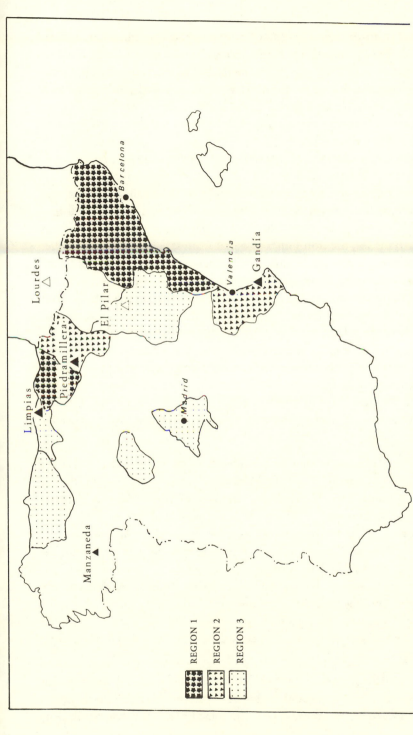

MAP 1. Moving crucifixes and Spanish devotion to Lourdes (based on a count of all Spanish group pilgrims to Lourdes, 1868–1936). Region 1: The Catalan dioceses (as a whole) and the Basque diocese of Vitoria, which each sent more than 30% of the pilgrims. Region 2: The dioceses of Pamplona and Valencia, which each sent between 6% and 10% of the pilgrims. Region 3: The dioceses of Oviedo, Madrid, Santander, Valladolid, and Zaragoza, which each sent between 1% and 2% of the pilgrims. The remaining dioceses sent less than 1% of the pilgrims. The solid triangles represent sites of visions of moving crucifixes. The triangle outlines represent shrines.

REGION 1

REGION 2

REGION 3

or penicillin, in the sense that modern industry, communication, and religious advertising immensely democratized its availability. Some of those
hoping for a Spanish Lourdes were the leaders of the new industrial society, who believed just as much in assembly lines, bonds, electricity, railroads, and hot water as they did in the holy water.[29]

The Socio-Economic Context of Disbelief

The Spain of 1918–1920 was very different from the Spain of the moving
images of the seventeenth century. The First World War had given impe-
tus to Spain's erratic industrialization. Limpias was not far from the iron
works at Ramales, the iron mines of Saltacaballos, San Salvador del Valle,
and La Arboleda, and the booming industrial center of Bilbao.[30] Industry
and mines engendered workers' movements that had national and international ramifications, and in the industrial city and countryside (around
Bilbao, in the mining areas of Asturias, in industrial Barcelona, and in
parts of rural Andalusia and La Mancha), there were well-established sub-
cultures of active disbelief in the Catholic religion. In these areas the majority of males were converts to radical social doctrines, and they equated
Catholicism with bosses.

Sisinio Nevares, a Jesuit active in organizing Catholic unions, assessed
Spain's urban working class, writing candidly in February 1920 to his superiors in Rome:[31]

> They are like pagans who know neither God nor the Church. . . . For ex-
> ample: the workers of Barcelona, Madrid, Valencia, Sevilla, Málaga, Bilbao,
> Gijón, Coruña, Vigo, El Ferrol, etc. and those of other cities and industrial
> and agricultural towns. . . . The world of the workers, lost to our Holy Faith,
> is governed by the doctrines of materialistic communism, which despises and
> combats Religion in the workshop, in the factory, at the political meeting, in
> the cafe, everywhere. The workers, without guides or directors other than
> their very bad leaders, hearing only continuously flattering propaganda, and
> constantly reading Socialist newspapers and books, have come to imagine
> that the Catholic religion has nothing to offer them, that it is a lie, the cause
> of all their misery and the accomplice of the excesses and vices of the wealthy
> capitalists.

Spain also had a small but vocal intelligentsia who did not practice
Catholicism. Their ideas and literature were widely available in newspapers, magazines, and novels. That the socialist, communist, syndicalist,

and anarchist movements, the generation of 1898, and free-minded thinkers like Pío Baroja and Tomás Meabe were at root influenced by Christian principles was no solace to the missionaries, the parish priests, the Catholic propagandists, and the women's organizers active in trying to stop a socio-economic rearrangement of the country as well as the erosion of allegiance to the Catholic Church. Their rear-guard action varied from attempts to form Catholic worker movements or joint owner-worker guilds, both inspired by Leo XIII's *Rerum Novarum*; to rural cooperatives and agricultural banks; to old-fashioned blood-and-thunder revival missions; and to almost magical consecrations of homes, factories, towns, and even the Spanish nation to the Sacred Heart of Jesus.

The fact remained that in the early twentieth century, nonbelief and atheism were live options throughout Spain and were categories in everybody's heads, just as heresy was in the sixteenth century, and witchcraft was heresy in the early seventeenth century. Efforts to stem the tide of disbelief in Catholic populations did as much to establish the category as active antireligious proselytizing. In fact, given the effect of the 1936–1939 Civil War and the subsequent rehomogenization of Spanish culture, there was probably more active anticlericalism and more fervent belief in alternative ideologies in the early twentieth century than there has been since. In the 1980s the major alternative to Catholicism in Spain was indifference; in the 1900–1936 period it was active, often violent, opposition.

The reality of this opposition was plain for all to see and read about. The Basilica of Our Lady of Pilar in Zaragoza was stoned during political clashes on July 17, 1900.[32] Throughout Spain, Benito Pérez Galdós's drama, *Electra*, led to anticlerical demonstrations. On February 12, 1901, the demonstrators in Santander shouted "Long Live Liberty!" and "Down with the Reactionaries!" in front of the Jesuit and Salesian houses, stoned the house of the bishop, and sacked that of the Carmelites. In the same city on November 8 and 9, 1903, after two persons were killed during celebrations for a Republican electoral victory, the residence of the Jesuits and the Workers' Catholic Circle were attacked.[33]

The most salient anticlerical incident in the north of Spain had been the Bilbao riot of October 11, 1903, in which anticlericals coming from a worker's rally attacked a pilgrimage procession in Bilbao that was on its way to celebrate the recently proclaimed patronage of Our Lady of Begoña over Vizcaya. One Catholic was killed, many on both sides were injured, religious images were mutilated or dumped in the river, and the residence of the Jesuits was stoned. A contingent from Santander reportedly participated in the riot.[34] Two years later the Catholic Workers Circle and the parish church were bombed in Ontón, a mining town between Limpias and Bilbao.[35]

The people of the north would also have known about the anticlerical riots of Orense in 1909, and especially of the Tragic Week of Barcelona in the same year, in which dozens of churches and houses of religious were burned, and monks and priests were killed.[36]

To the overt anticlericalism of the early twentieth century was added the most complete labor mobilization in Spanish history. There was a general strike in 1917, and observers in the north were well aware of the ability of local workers to organize local general strikes at the drop of a hat (as they did in Santander on February 2, 1920, to protest the imprisonment of a labor leader). In October 1919 the American consul in Santander reported, "That there is a feeling of unrest here is not to be denied, but this is a condition usually prevailing here."[37]

The depression which fell on the mining districts of Santander and Bilbao due to the drop in demand for iron ore at the end of World War I had not yet hit in March of 1919, when the Christ of Limpias was first seen to move.[38] But even at the height of the war, workers were losing already low purchasing power because of inflation. Subsequently the American consul in Bilbao reflected that the mine laborer's wage, "in periods of great prosperity for the mine owners and operators" had "never been adequate to meet the cost of living on any except the lowest possible scale."[39] On May 2, 1919, two days before the first large pilgrimage to Limpias, working-class women sacked stores in Santander, and demanded from the civil governor reductions in the price of bread, potatoes, oil, and soap.[40] By this time, informed persons knew that high employment could not last. The American consul in Bilbao wrote on April 15, 1919:[41]

> As nearly all of the prominent industrials of this district have enjoyed extraordinary prosperity during recent years, and the usual wage scale was comparatively low, the demands of the laborers have been promptly met and work has gone on with little interruption. However, it is now believed that the point will soon be reached when further wage advances will be deemed impracticable by the capitalists, and as the cost of living is constantly advancing, it will be difficult to avoid serious labor troubles.

The best statistics on strikes in Vizcaya show that the number jumped from at least 36 in 1918 to at least 117 in 1919, when the height of strikes was in April and May. There the period of social pacts worked out between the socialist trade union and the bosses contributed to a dramatic increase in the growth of the anarchist Sindicato Unico.[42]

By the beginning of 1919, on the heels of the Russian Revolution and the apparent demise of the European order, the specter of anarchist and bolshevist chaos loomed large in the minds of Spain's Catholics. An overview of Spain and the world situation at this time in the Jesuit journal *Razón y Fe* was gloomy about the "devastating torrent of social dissolution" of anarchism, and "the worst of plagues, modern bolshevism."[43] For like the United States and Europe, in early 1919 Spain was in the grip of a Red Scare.

In the crisis activists of all persuasions worked to stem the Red tide, according to the *Razón y Fe* writer:

> The publicists of *El Debate*, the agrarians, the Catholic Free Unions and all the other unions that bear that lovely adjective have multiplied their efforts these days, together with Catholic publications, and have given an example of integrity and calm very necessary in the general confusion and the Islamic and morbid indifference that has reigned everywhere. The organization of a civil militia in the case of an uprising of agitators and malefactors is having excellent results. If things continue like this, in a few weeks major trouble will be impossible in Spain, however widespread it may be.

The writer's conclusion was overly optimistic. For in mid-March 1919, a general strike in Barcelona spread elsewhere in Spain. And it was at the time of the mission in Limpias, on March 24, that martial law was declared. For the next three years, all constitutional guarantees were under suspension.[44]

The Christ of Gandía

The socio-economic tension, which coincided in the north with the Limpias visions, affected Valencia earlier. There the wartime constraint on shipping was an economic disaster for the region. Exports of oranges dropped to a third of the prewar level. Lack of gas and coal led to the closing of factories. The result was labor mobilization and political polarization, and in the summer of 1917 there was a revolutionary general strike.[45]

It was in these circumstances that the most immediate predecessor for the Christ of Limpias, the Christ of Gandía, began to be seen as moving and working miracles on June 8, 1918. The Gandía case proved in the long run to have been a crippling precedent for the Limpias visions.

I first read of what happened in Gandía in the introduction to a study critical of Limpias by the Dominican Luis Urbano, who from his post in Valencia was well acquainted with the Gandía episode. He wrote,[46]

> The Holy Christ of Gandía had not yet stopped moving, leaving drops of blood on the bricks of the choir and embracing little girls, with the image detached from the wooden cross; without the Church Authority having pronounced itself on the events, which were discussed in newspapers and magazines and acclaimed by the people as miraculous. Then the suspicion of a proteiform hysteria undermined the stupendous phenomena, and the field of study was changed from theology to pathology. When all this was going on in the Valencian hinterland, the Most Holy Christ of the Agony, venerated in the village of Limpias, the most famous today of Santander, began to move.
>
> The events of Gandía prompted the formation of an ecclesiastical tribunal, which took its evidence and was silent. I believe it will never speak, because it was seen that those events had been the result of sickness and imposture. And since some newspapers had made a great fuss, putting in banner headlines "Miracle! MIRACLE!" it was not prudent to burst these bubbles violently, and indeed they have melted away by themselves.

Another Valencian writing about Limpias, Leopoldo Trenor, also referred to the Gandía episode. "The case of G., a case of ignoble fraud, revealed and condemned recently by the church authorities, fully justified regarding with suspicion and hostility these new prodigies at Limpias."[47]

The newspapers of Valencia shed more light on the initial events at Gandía. They are in general agreement as to what was claimed to have occurred. The version of the alleged seers was first published in the Carlist *Diario de Valencia*.[48]

Four girls who lived in a combination old-age home and orphanage were cleaning the floor of the large choir balcony at 11:00 in the morning on Saturday, June 8, 1918.[49] Pepita, age about fifteen, was washing the floor in a corner, facing away from the altar; Pilar Montes, age ten, and Lolita Sanz, age twelve, were washing the floor in the center of the choir facing the altar; and little Angeles Montes, Pilar's seven-year-old sister, was standing on a bench, dusting a crucifix that was fixed to the choir rail facing the girls, with its back to the altar.

According to these children, Pilar and Lolita noticed two drops of blood on the brick floor and washed them, thinking that Angeles might have scratched herself. But when they were about to ask her, Angeles wanted to get down from the bench. As Pilar and Lolita helped her down she was very pale because, she said, she had seen the Christ on the cross move its head slightly.

She suggested they pray the "Acordaos," but one of the girls said that was a prayer to the Virgin, so instead the three girls prayed five credos to the Five Wounds of Christ. When they finished they saw that the Christ continued to move, and it came down from the Cross and came toward them.

They huddled together, and Angeles gave a little cry that drew the attention of the oldest girl, Pepita, washing in a corner. She stood up and watched the Crucifix embrace the three girls. When they were released from the embrace, Lolita Sanz ran to the door to call the nuns, dragging Angeles on her coattails. Pilar, age ten, was thus alone briefly with the image. She asked it, "What is this, Lord? What do you want?"

The image replied, "I have shed this blood for a reprobate, and I will shed more." The Christ then returned to the cross. Such was the account of the girls.

While this was allegedly happening, there were a dozen persons in the church below, including a Jesuit, P. Oliver, and a canon of the Gandía collegiate church, Angel Hernández. In the home, in addition to the nuns and the residents, there was a carpenter, a worker preparing a telephone installation, and an organist and music teacher, Vicente Miñana. All of these persons, the nuns, and some residents went to the choir to see what was happening. The first to arrive saw the choir railing and the crucifix vibrating as if it had been struck. They noted a bloody sweat beneath the crown of thorns, and a drop descending from the Christ's temple toward his nose. On the bricks beneath the image were two large and one small fresh drops that appeared to be blood. All present burst into tears. And a human avalanche poured into the church, for Saturday was market day, and the market was in an adjacent square.

Only after two hours, at 1:00 P.M., did José Sancho arrive. As the *Abad* of the collegiate church, he was the highest diocesan authority in Gandía. After establishing a modicum of order with the help of the Civil Guards, he convoked a gathering that afternoon of civil, military, religious, legal, and medical authorities, about twenty-five persons in all. He told them that they were there to make sure that the truth was not betrayed and to avoid the invention of legends or frauds, or the frivolous affirmation that a miracle had occurred.

The girls were then quizzed by a judge and examined by the doctors, and they reenacted their vision where it was supposed to have occurred. The doctors examined the liquid, one saying it was paint, and another pronouncing it blood. The church was closed to the public and protected by the police.

Two reporters from *Diario de Valencia* went to Gandía two days later, on Monday, June 10. By Thursday, June 13, when their newspaper first mentioned the event, a Church tribunal had been named and was taking evidence in Gandía.[50] It consisted of the *provisor* of the archdiocese, Miguel Sirvent; the *fiscal* of the diocesan curia, Canon Federico Ferreres; and as secretary, a priest from the Gandía *colegiata*, Pascual Benetó.

At first *Diario de Valencia* held back with its story, pleading its responsibility as a Catholic newspaper ("whose opinion is a norm and a guide for very many consciences"), and declared that it would report fully only when church authorities allowed it to do so.[51] Apparently by Sunday, June 16, this permission had been granted, for the entire front page was taken up with a report on the events, including two photographs of the crucifix and one of the building (Figure 5). Either enthusiasm clouded the authorities' better judgment, or by this time so much had been printed in other newspapers in Valencia and Madrid that what was claimed to have happened could no longer be kept under wraps.[52] As far as I know, *Diario* printed nothing more on the events, in what must have become an embarrassed silence.

In Valencia the only other newspaper I read that picked up the story was *Diario*'s archrival, the Republican *El Pueblo*, founded thirty years before by Vicente Blázquez Ibáñez. Its first mention, under the heading "Miracle!" was on Friday, June 14, 1918, with a cynical commentary on a report that had already appeared in Madrid. It averred that the "miracle" would "serve to confound the impious."[53]

El Pueblo sent reporters to Gandía sometime between June 16 and June 19. No doubt in contact with Gandía's Fraternidad Republicana and perhaps its Socialist and Liberal Monarchist clubs, they tried to smoke out who perpetrated the fraud, and why.[54] They suggested that the "blood" was paint, making fun of the prominent doctor Darás, who had reportedly asserted that since it was "the precious blood of our Lord," it did not have to appear to be normal "animal" blood.[55] And they emphasized how the girls were being protected from questions and seemed to be disturbed by the events.

The culprit fingered by *El Pueblo* was a nun who, fifteen years before in 1903, had been a *cause célèbre* in Valencia when she had fled her free-thinking family to enter a convent. This occurred during a heated election campaign, and *El Pueblo* had organized a protest rally against the clerical wiles that had separated a daughter from her parents. When the rally was over, some of the Republicans went to sing the Marseillaise in front of the convent.[56] This incident came on the heels of a nationally

portentoso de

FIGURE 5. Part of the front page of *Diario de Valencia*, June 16, 1918.

publicized case in Madrid, that of the Ubao family, in which the courts forced a daughter to leave a convent and return to her anticlerical family until she was of age. Pérez Galdós's *Electra* itself was loosely based on this earlier incident. It was therefore a scenario that had been already rehearsed.

The young woman in Valencia, Pilar Izquierdo, had been attracted to the Franciscan Terciaries of the Immaculate Conception in Mora de Rubielos (Teruel), where her father was a pharmacist. But she waited to flee to the convent until she was sent to study in Valencia, and there she entered the order's Mother house.

This order was reorganized in 1876 and was confirmed by Leon XIII in 1902. By 1919 it had twenty-seven houses, seventeen of them in the province of Valencia, and it was beginning to specialize in the care of children who were blind or deaf.[57]

The order also had a house in Madrid where, as Sor Loreto, Pilar was subsequently sent. There, according to *El Pueblo*, she came to be the teacher of one of the sons of Alfonso XIII.[58] *El Pueblo* also claimed that she was of a nervous temperament and "considered herself at times to be possessed by the grace of God, illumined like St. Teresa." It also claimed that she had attempted to work miracles, like trying to change water into oil.[59]

The home in Gandía was run by her order, and she allegedly had arrived there just two days before the visions, which she had concocted together with the Jesuit P. Oliver in order to convert an unnamed, close male relative, possibly her brother Daniel.

This relative was allegedly in the convent on June 8, by her invitation. And according to *El Pueblo*, she had tried to persuade him to see the crucifix *before* the girls sounded the alarm. After the visions she allegedly told him, "See, *you* are the reprobate, can you doubt the power of the divine now?" *El Pueblo*'s reporters, if they are to be believed, could only have gotten this story from Sor Loreto's relative himself.[60]

There was another candidate for the "reprobate." The *Asilo* in Gandía had been founded by a priest, Pascual Catalá, in the 1870s. It was he who obtained permission from the town to use the former Franciscan monastery, famous for the resting place of Beato Andrés Hibernon, persuaded the town to appropriate operating funds, and staffed it with the Franciscan Tertiaries. (Curiously, the two sisters involved in the vision, Angeles and Pilar Montes, were nieces of the head of the order, Sor María del Corazón de Jesús.)[61] At the time of the visions, the home had not for many months received the money needed for operation from the Gandía town government, and *El Pueblo* claimed that about half of its inmates had had to be turned out in the summer of 1917, as they could not be maintained.[62]

This then was a second possible referent for the Christ's words: The "reprobate" was the mayor of Gandía, who did not pay the asylum's costs. This interpretation, implicit in *Diario de Valencia,* was already circulating in Gandía when *El Pueblo's* reporters arrived.[63]

When I went to Gandía in 1983, Sor Loreto and the mayor had been forgotten. Indeed, only the oldest inhabitants remembered anything at all, and even the official town chronicler, a man in his 50s, had heard nothing about it.[64]

What I could piece together from the sisters at the Home during my short stay in Gandía was this: an older girl (who they thought might have been named Carmen) from the nearby hamlet of El Real, and who herself was not a nun, faked a number of miracles, getting two little girls to collaborate with her and buy things she needed by frightening them. She is said to have sent to a painter in Valencia for a substance and put it on the Christ to make it look like it was sweating blood. And she made people think that she herself levitated. The girl gained great power within the order during the events (perhaps by involving the nieces of the head of the order?), and was able to get nuns who did not believe her transferred to other houses. She was proud, "wanted to be more powerful than the Mother General," according to one of the nuns.

Her unmasking in the eyes of the town came when, on an excursion to the beach, she seemed to discover a fish in the sand and claimed it was a miracle. A woman recognized the fish in question, exclaiming "I sold that one this morning!" People concluded that the fish had been planted. The nuns were extremely reticent about the incidents, for "it almost meant the end of the order." They said that the *Abad* of the *colegiata* never believed the girl (his skepticism is clear even in the *Diario de Valencia* account). And they said that the image was subsequently broken up.

The Gandía priest Antonio Martí was about 80 when I talked to him in 1983; he had been a student at the time of the affair. Somewhat abrupt and scornful of the matter, he remembered that when the rector of the Valencia seminary, Manuel Rubio Cercas, tried to question the little girls, the older one would constantly interrupt, although quite explicitly instructed to remain silent. That was enough for Rubio Cercas, who arose, saying, "Here there is no sainthood. The saint obeys." He declared that this was not a case of hallucination, but rather of obsession and sham. (This fits with Urbano's reference to the matter as "pathological," and an elderly townswoman's description of the culprit to me as "malalta"—ill, perhaps mentally disturbed.)

One thing clear from the oral accounts is that the events did not end (perhaps they did not even begin) with the episode of June 8, 1918. According to Urbano, "the Christ was still moving," at the end of March 1919, when the visions at Limpias began. But by June 1919, when Trenor was first asked to write about Limpias, the Gandía events were thoroughly discredited.

For our purposes it is immaterial whether the instigator was Sor Loreto/Pilar Izquierdo or the adolescent Pepita/Carmen. On the face of it, the story of Pilar Izquierdo was too good to be true. For here was a way for *El Pueblo* at once to make fun of the Church and discredit a woman who had remained true to her religious convictions, a traitor to her freethinking family. It was a way to tar the fearsome Jesuits as well. If Sor Loreto had arrived at Gandía only two days before, she hardly had time to find the paint and train the children. And if her brother had a hand in the *El Pueblo* story, then one has additional cause to doubt it. For his intolerant and intemperate letter to *El Pueblo* at the time of his sister's "kidnapping" in 1903 permits one to think him capable of framing her to win a point or win revenge. I am rather inclined to think that, if the *El Pueblo* story has anything to it, it was because Pepita/Carmen creatively incorporated the visit of Sor Loreto's "reprobate" brother into a miracle that was already planned. The girls' initial story in *Diario de Valencia* points to the ringleader being Pepita/Carmen, precisely because of its emphasis on the other three girls, and its explicit description of Pepita's distance from the action.

The question of whodunit should not overly distract us from the larger cultural and social issues at stake. First of all, by 1920 Carlists, Liberal Catholics, and Republicans were all in agreement that it had been a fraud, consciously perpetrated. As we will see, the existence of a liquid on or around the image makes this case more similar to its early modern antecedents, and fundamentally different from its immediate successors at Limpias and Piedramillera. But there is a basic similarity with these later cases in the social and political environment that the "miracle" addressed.

For while Valencia was exceptional in the strength and virulence of its anticlerical movement, the notion of the conversion of reprobates was a preocccupation of Catholics throughout Spain at this time. The editor of *Diario de Valencia*, José Luís Martín Mengod, explained in a background article on miracles that one of the reasons God performed them was "to attract those who do not believe."[65]

Valencia had active, vocal, and prominent Republican, Socialist, and anarchist communities. The lines were drawn in Gandía as well, where we find articles in the Jesuit-inspired *Revista de Gandía* ("Periódico consagrado al divino corazón de Jesús") such as "The Rising Tide," referring to the spread of irreligion and immorality.[66]

The issue of *Revista de Gandía* just prior to the visions was dedicated to the Sacred Heart, in celebration of the fiesta on June 7, with the headline "I WILL REIGN IN SPAIN." On the front page was a poem, "Aspiraciones," by the priest Andrés Martí, which referred to the "proselytes" of "perfidious Lucifer" "in our land." The second stanza read, "We wish that the men wandering and lost/fleeing blindly from the tree of the Cross/would live no longer steeped in impiety/nor close their eyes obstinately to the light."[67] The idiom of conversion of freethinkers by the Cross was around quite precisely at the time of the events.

Gandía was a strategic point for such a "miracle," as the correspondent of Pego (Alicante) wrote to *El Pueblo.*[68]

> Every important religious event in Gandía circulates, makes an impression, and is news for a long time, not only because Gandía is a center for many villages with which it maintains multiple ties, but also because it is an ancient and modern crucible of fanaticism, with the Borgias and with the Jesuits.

For the Left, Gandía, the home of St. Francis Borgia, and the location of the Jesuit Novitiate and Exercise House for the Aragonese province, was a Jesuit fiefdom. But the impious in Gandía had their own newspaper, *Germinal, Semanario Republicano,* which gave as good as it received.[69] During World War I, disastrous for the local economy, these ideological differences were particularly exacerbated.

Whatever the specific local intentions of the children or their putative instigators, the idea of the Christ bleeding for reprobates was understood in wider terms by those who took it seriously whether they believed it or not.

The subsequent visions at Limpias and Piedramillera were quite different from those at Gandía. At Gandía there was a witting, premeditated fraud. At Limpias and Piedramillera, the seers were sincere, convinced that they truly saw the images move. We must take them and their experience more respectfully.

But the context in which the Christs of Gandía, Limpias, and Piedramillera were seen to move, or were claimed to have moved, was essentially the same—a Catholicism experienced as under siege and a devotional inflation due to the resounding success of Lourdes. Both of these conditions helped to make the visions in general, whether faked or sincere, more believable. It was this context of belief that made everyone weep at the Gandía church; it also led people to see the image as having modified its pose or its complexion. And it helped make the girls' story initially plausible not only for the townspeople but also for *Diario de Valencia* and in Madrid *El Correo Español* and *El Debate*.

Whether or not the alleged movements of the crucifix at Gandía were known at Limpias and Piedramillera, 750 kilometers to the north, it was critically important for the later visions that Valencians like Luis Urbano or Manuel Rubio Cercas who would influence their evaluation knew all too well about what happened in Gandía just months before. For them the Gandía episode itself became part of the context, and made even visions which were rather different less believable.

II

The Christ of Limpias: *The Rise and Decline of a New Shrine*

THE RURAL MISSION AS RELIGIOUS AND POLITICAL THEATER

It was during a mission given by two Capuchin fathers, Anselmo de Jalón and Agatángelo de San Miguel, that the visions at Limpias began. In the prevailing mood of social, economic, and ideological unrest, rural missions (and those of the Capuchins were no exception) sought to galvanize the faithful, whether in the more religious villages of the rear guard or on the front lines of socialist and anticlerical penetration in industrial and mining districts. By organizing the parish as a unit and the village or valley as a sacred territory, they undermined the efforts of the opposition to cultivate class consciousness. Temporarily isolating rural workers and intellectuals from their urban allies, the missionaries brought to bear on them the full weight of community religious patriotism.

From 1910 through 1919, eight different orders held missions in the diocese of Santander (see Appendix Table 4). But almost 85 percent of the missions were given by only three of these orders: the Redemptorists, operating out of their house, El Espino, at Santa Gadea del Cid, Burgos; the Jesuits, who had a residence in Santander, but often called on missionaries from elsewhere—Gijón, Carrión de los Condes, Bilbao, or Loyola; and the Capuchins, who had a house near Santoña called Montehano, but who also used occasional visitors from their houses in Salamanca, Madrid, León, and Bilbao. Certain preachers had given enough missions, novenas, fiesta sermons, or spiritual exercises to be well known throughout the diocese (see Appendix Table 5).

In these years the Capuchin missions had a set pattern. Once the mission was contracted and the date set up, usually months ahead of time, the parish would be provided with the mission hymns, at least some of which were generally learned in advance.

On the day of the missionaries' arrival, they would be met by the parish in procession, the parish sodalities with their banners, and escorted to the parish church to the hymn, "A Misión os llama." At the parish church, the missionaries explained the purpose of the mission, and gave a schedule of prayer sessions, association meetings, and age-set meetings for the week. These would vary to a certain extent according to the parish organizations.

On days two through five there would be morning and afternoon preaching or lecture sessions with different groups. Sometime in these days there would be dawn Rosary processions through the town, starting as early as 3:30 or 4:00 A.M., which would end at the parish church with a mass, which would finish at 7:00 A.M. At 10:00 A.M. there would be preparatory sessions, like catechisms, for children, or youths 15 and over, or the Daughters of Mary, or married women, or men. The afternoon sessions would include the Rosary and a stirring sermon, and there might be evening sessions for working men. The various sessions would prepare people for the climactic days six through nine, and the sermons would be set pieces on subjects like the Last Judgment or mutual pardon or blasphemy.

On day six there might be a general communion of the children, followed by a renewal of baptismal vows, with speeches by chosen children. Afterward the children might be served a special treat of hot chocolate.

On the following days there would be the general communion of the male youths, the Daughters of Mary or the female youths, and the married women, in the morning, with Rosary and talks in the afternoon.

Day nine was the climactic day, with the communion of men in the morning, and generally the entire town once more received communion this day. In the afternoon a sermon of perseverance was preached, and a procession held to install the wooden cross left by the missionaries to mark the event and remind the people of their contrition and good intentions. Generally the missionary who carried the cross gave a final speech.

Some missions were prolonged with an extra day in which the town remembered its dead with a requiem mass, a procession to the cemetery, and a sermon among the tombstones.

The Capuchins made available to the villagers their inexpensive mission manual, which included devotional material and mission hymns. In the manual published in 1915 the missionaries are introduced as, more than prophets, apostles. It cites approvingly the example of St. Catherine of Siena kissing where missionaries have walked. In the prologue the reasons for the mission are put plainly: blasphemy and swearing, profanation of the Sabbath, impurities and lewd songs, and hatred and desire for revenge. None of these would be foreign to the everyday experience of Spanish villagers. Everlasting fire awaited those who did not repent, and tears were given as a sign of remorse. Also laid out were a series of ways by which missions could be used to gain indulgences, prayers to be said at different times of the day, an explanation of the mass, an examination of conscience to be made before confession, rules for persevering after the mission, and extra instructions for persons seeking a more than normally rigorous spiritual regimen.[1]

Most of the booklet is made up of the words of hymns, over forty of them. The decadence of hymn writing and hymn singing in present-day Spain might lead one to overlook their importance in the first decades of the century. The visions at Limpias and Ezquioga, the missions themselves, were immersed in hymns. At Limpias every large pilgrimage had a hymn composed especially for it—not only new words, but also new music, and practice sessions were held before the pilgrimage to learn it.[2] There are, therefore, many dozens of hymns, perhaps more than one hundred, to the Christ of Limpias. When I speak to the very elderly who went on the pilgrimages, they can usually remember some of the words and music at a distance of seventy years. Pilgrims to Lourdes also had hymns they learned beforehand, both hymns for their particular expedition and hymns that were popular at the shrine.

Hymns work by implanting in the memory words, and the ideas behind the words, through music. They are a group activity, in which the whole, with harmony, is much greater than the sum of its parts and therefore especially rewarding. There is little compromise in voicing the words—it is a song, a group song, a performance more than a statement. In this way words to hymns can, in fact, be stronger, more explicit, than words one might be willing to speak, as an individual, in public.

In these villages it was generally women who sang in the choirs. Mixed choirs were not acceptable, and there was even some dispute about whether women should sing in church.[3] But some hymns, like "A Misión os llama," were sung by everyone.

The themes of the hymns in the mission manual reflect the services for which they were designed. They are, variously, a confession of sin, an expression of remorse, a plea for forgiveness, a statement of homage, a song of love of God, a pledge of faithfulness, and praises to the Divine Shepherdess, the Immaculate Conception, or St. Francis. There are also militant battle hymns against the impious mob, the world, the flesh and the devil, and quite specifically, the Masons. One hymn sung at Limpias, "¡A Dios queremos!" included stanzas referring to God in the home, the schools ("both primary and normal"), the military, and the government (both the ministries and the king). It ended[4]

> Come on! lively and with bravery
> In the footsteps of our fathers
> We always shout at the impious mob
> We love God, and only God!

In mission after mission, throughout the length and breadth of rural Spain, hundreds of villagers sang similar words, not simply hearing the Capuchins, Redemptorists, or Jesuits pronounce them. It was an immense effort of religious revival, geared not only toward individual salvation but also toward national salvation from the internal enemy, the forces seeking to separate Church and State by following the example of the French or the Russians.

While music and hymns served as mechanisms for the replication of ideas and emotions, it was the missionaries in their talks and sermons who proposed the ideas and conjured up the emotions. They did not sing their sermons, but sermon tone and rhetoric was every bit as far from everyday speech as music. The Capuchins had a year of training in how to preach after they finished theology, *el año de locuencia.* But only the best preachers were sent out often on missions, and their talks and sermons were looked forward to as performances, and judged by their emotional effect.

In the Capuchin missions no effort was spared and much imagination invested in the dramatic evocation of affect. The two missionaries seemed to perform separate socio-emotional roles, a little like the bad-cop, good-cop routine. One of them preached frightening sermons about hell and damnation, and the other emphasized God's goodness and mercy, carrying the cross at the end. The former was like an Old Testament prophet, the latter a stand-in for Jesus.[5]

Anselmo de Jalón, one of the two missionaries at Limpias, seems to have felt more at home in the former role. His preaching is described by the parish priest of Carmona in 1912:[6]

> Who will ever forget the Reverend Father Anselmo, who could be called son of thunder for his tireless zeal, his forthright outspokenness, his organizing genius, his apostolic unction, his impetuous, sonorous, and torrential eloquence so potent it makes the sinner drop like lightning in submission to God. My God, what a *Judgment*, what a Judgment he portrayed for us: A living tableau with all its horrors. In my ears I can still hear the terrified cries of the congregation, the pitiful laments of the children, and the impressive shrieks at the contemplation of the desolating and horrifying Day of Judgment.

Another form of moving hearts was through dramatic imitation of Christ. This seems to have been done by the "soft" missionary. In the procession on the last day, in imitation of Christ's path to Calvary, a Capuchin carried the mission cross. In Carmona in 1912 the people followed P. Joaquín de Solórzano "step by step, and kissed the cross, watering it with their tears. . . . And I saw these 3000 persons," the parish priest continues, "forming a compact group, a strong and dense pack, one unanimous moral body, render a final homage of gratitude to those who did so well, and who left such an agreeable memory. I saw them weep copiously, like Mary Magdalen wept at the loss of her Teacher. Oh divine Religion! I exclaimed at such a tender sight. Oh divine faith, how fertile you are, how many brothers you create, and how sweet are your bonds!"[7]

Similarly, in the final procession at Arredondo in 1913, where Anselmo de Jalón was the other missionary, it was Pablo de Salamanca who carried the cross.[8]

> What happened next cannot be put into words: in and among the dense multitude went slowly the humble son of St. Francis, and when he was noticed a sweet shock came over everyone, expressed with a total silence that inclined the soul to penance and the desire to imitate he who on his shoulders carried the cross of salvation. When P. Pablo got to the platform previously erected, he set up the cross there, and then climbed up onto it and gave a brilliant speech, a model of sacred oratory, which electrified the entire enormous crowd, persuading the people that the cross which saved society

from paganism is the salvation of society today, and will be, more particularly, for our souls. The crowd, which had been so moved in silence until then, spoke with one voice, answering with deafening *Vivas* for the Religion, the Pope, and the faith of the villages.

Just how these "acts" or "scenes" were choreographed depended on the missionaries involved and, doubtless, on their reading of the audience, just as their preaching was inspired and improvised to fit time and place. Mariano de Argañoso, the superior of Montehano from 1913 to 1916, would give his final exhortation holding the cross in his hands, before erecting it, "with such unction and fervor that everyone, without exception, wept abundantly."[9]

In Cabárceno, a mining town, in 1917, P. Anselmo and P. Agatángelo de San Miguel preached their second mission together. P. Anselmo preached the sermon of perseverance, and it was P. Agatángelo, barefoot, who carried the cross, "escorted by the Guardia Civil, and the mayor and the magistrate of the town bearing the lance and the pole with the sponge. When the procession was over, P. Agatángelo, standing on a chair and embracing the cross, gave a moving eulogy of it, giving it a heartfelt kiss."[10]

In this conflictive mining town, the mayor, the magistrate, and the national police cooperated in acting out the Calvary procession in a way that must have heightened the identification of the Capuchin with Christ, and Christ with the working people. Part of the particular impact of the cross-bearing ceremony came with the reversal of roles of the friars. Throughout the week they had been in total control of the town, getting everyone up in the middle of the night, segregating age and gender groups, hearing confessions, and delivering communions. Above all they organized the mental space of the people with their multiple sermons and speeches. They had the floor. The word was theirs and the sacraments were theirs, theirs the keys to heaven, theirs the knowledge of hell. But suddenly at the end, a switch: one of them, barefoot, carries the cross, symbolically humbled, in silence.

There were other role reversals which upset class and age-grade lines. In this same mission, the hot chocolate provided after the children's communion was served, "by seven ladies dressed as waitresses; two photographs were taken of this novel scene."[11] As one can see from these examples, it was not only the missionaries who provided the drama; the parish priest and the townspeople cooperated in the preparation and the staging, and played roles themselves in keeping with, on the one hand, the older traditions of Spanish Holy Week and, on the other, the *tableau-vivant* aesthetic of the period. In this respect the missions were participatory pageants.

There also was a certain amount of staging for the communion of the children and the renewal of their baptismal vows. In Carmona in 1912 the youth of the village "demonstrated their religious enthusiasm and their good aesthetic taste" by the way they decorated the baptistry and their "improvisation of an altar outdoors, next to which nine girls dressed in white, kneeling on prayer chairs and separated from the onlookers by a rectangle formed of foliage and bushes, prayed like a choir of angels by the image of the Virgin, in an ecstatic and majestic pose against an improvised backdrop."[12] Likewise in the mission of P. Anselmo and Agatángelo in Lezaún (Navarra) in 1920, P. Agatángelo prepared the presbytery so it looked "like a garden in springtime well tended by a skilled gardener. It was full of potted plants and flowers, in the midst of which were seven girls dressed in white paying homage to Jesus in the sacrament."[13]

Other orders had their own highlights. For the Jesuits one of them was the sermon of forgiveness, preached toward the middle of the mission, after which parishioners frequently broke into tears in the process of forgiving their fellows. Here it is described in a Jesuit mission in Cabezón de la Sal in 1910.[14]

> It was a very moving ceremony, in which I am not sure what swayed the human heart more—the ardent words of the Missionary, or the unexpected and august presence of Jesus in the Sacrament, or the sobs of the audience that drowned out the voices of the speaker and would have wrung tears out of diamonds. What a tender and consoling spectacle to see how so many souls embrace one another and ask for forgiveness for offenses given and received.

The two missionaries invited to arouse the town of Limpias had previously preached only three missions together, the first in 1917. And after Limpias they preached only two more missions together. They were not, as it were, regular partners. The Capuchins did not usually go out to preach in steady pairs, unlike the Redemptorists. In any event, Anselmo de Jalón and Agatángelo de San Miguel made a very good combination.

They had features in common: they were both about 50 years old; they both became Capuchins rather late, after being parish priests; and they were both effective preachers. In character, however, they were quite different. This is clear from Capuchin annals, the descriptions of their missions, and the memories of elderly Capuchins who knew them.

Anselmo de Jalón is remembered as a "great" or "famous" missionary.

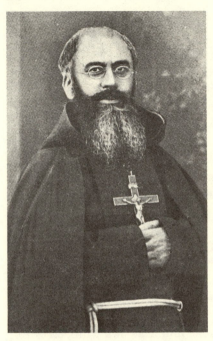

FIGURES 6 AND 7. The Capuchin missionaries Agatángelo de San Miguel and Anselmo de Jalón. Photographs by Labarga in Tomás Echevarría, *Los prodigios de Limpias* (Madrid, 1919).

The "reviews" of his missions in diocesan bulletins celebrate his energy, his vitality, his organizing skill, his determination, and his power in moving people.[15] His obituary at Montehano describes him as a "celebrated and energetic preacher."[16] And preaching was what he did as a Capuchin, not only missions but also novenas, triduos, and fiesta sermons, throughout the north and west of Spain from Navarra to Cáceres to Galicia. Capuchins circulated with permission and sometimes on orders in the triennial reshuffling of posts, from house to house within their order's province, in this case the Capuchin province of Castile. When at any one house, they might be invited to give sermons or missions in other dioceses. By the time of the Limpias mission Anselmo de Jalón, who became a Capuchin in 1903, had preached in at least seventeen different Spanish provinces.[17] The Capuchins I talked to had not known him well; they were students, normally forbidden to talk to those full members of the community who were not their teachers, and I received the impression that in any case Anselmo de Jalón was more removed, less accessible.

Although Agatángelo de San Miguel was slightly older, he had less experience in preaching missions, for he took solemn vows at the end of 1915, when Anselmo de Jalón had been giving missions for ten years. P. Agatángelo's preaching, while softer in volume, was just as effective in moving people's hearts, if we are to believe the parish priests. But in the order he is not remembered for this, but rather for his spirituality. His obituary reads, "Very zealous, exemplary, extremely observant and charitable, he edified all with the example of his virtues."[18] It was not his power but his goodness that stayed with the order after he died.

P. Enrique de Ventosa, now a professor in Salamanca, remembers him as "a man of intense spiritual life."[19] P. Camilo de Grajal, at age 93 the oldest Capuchin in the province, says he chose, like almost all of the other students at Montehano, to confess with P. Agatángelo, for he was "very good, very spiritual, very observant."[20]

P. Agatángelo's charitableness is confirmed in the manuscript chronicle of Montehano. In 1918 most of the house came down with influenza, and two fathers died, in late October and early November. The chronicler makes special mention, unusual for the chronicle, of the "Christian abnegation" with which P. Agatángelo and a Capuchin brother voluntarily cared for their dying comrades day and night. "Seen with the light of faith, it will merit a recompense that God will reserve for them."[21]

Other contemporary observers remarked upon his tenderness, his compassion, his modesty, and his humility. P. Anselmo is described as having a frank gaze; P. Agatángelo as having his eyes normally turned to the ground. P. Anselmo, one day at Limpias, preached in the plaza, and his listeners had to be restrained from carrying him to his quarters on their shoulders. P. Agatángelo, instead of adulation, provoked veneration, and at Limpias people referred to him as "El Santo."[22] As we have seen, P. Anselmo preached the Last Judgment sermon, and as far as I know never carried the cross. P. Agatángelo was usually in charge of the children's communions, and always carried the cross. The two Capuchins represented exceptionally well the two facets of the mission experience and were unusually complementary in style and disposition as missionaries.

THE MISSION AND THE FIRST VISIONS

The events at Limpias had their origin in the spring of 1918 when a wealthy Limpias lady, Carolina del Rivero, heard Anselmo de Jalón preach the novena of the Sacred Heart of Jesus in the parish church. In early 1919 she offered to sponsor a Capuchin mission in Limpias.[23] Anselmo de Jalón and Agatángelo de San Miguel arrived in the town on March 22, 1919.

Limpias is roughly equidistant from Santander and Bilbao, on the bank of the Asón river about ten kilometers from the north coast of Spain. Its parish church is in the small hamlet of Rucoba, but the bulk of the parish population of 1,400 lived closer to the river, and most parishioners in 1919 went to mass at the new chapel of the Vincentian school. The parish priest, Eduardo Miqueli, was 64 in 1919. He had been a faithful subscriber to *El Siglo Futuro* since it was founded in 1875.[24] He was therefore well up on national news from a perspective strongly opposed to social Catholicism in any form. Miqueli had been saddened by the desertion of his parishioners, and had even suggested to the bishop that the parish church be closed.[25] It may be that one of his and Carolina del Rivero's goals for the Capuchin mission was to bring people back to Rucoba on Sundays. If so, they succeeded beyond their wildest dreams.

Following their custom, the Capuchins preached various sermons daily, starting with a Rosary procession at 4:00 A.M. The mission was exceptionally fervent, and all but five "obdurate" males received communion on the morning of March 30. A Capuchin described that scene in *El Diario Montañés*, "The wives, moved at seeing their husbands kneel before the holy altar, wept from consolation, as did the entire town, contemplating so many men . . . receiving communion."[26]

After the act of thanksgiving, when many of those who had received communion were registering with Miqueli in the sacristy to get credit for the obligatory Easter communion, P. Agatángelo preached in the pulpit, giving thanks for the communion, using as his text Proverbs 23:26, "My son, give me your heart." While he was speaking, a small group of girls, ages 12–13, began to see the very life-like, life-sized crucifix on the altar move. In short depositions made eleven days later, two of the girls described what they saw. María Dolores Aldecoa, age 13, saw, "the image . . . open its eyes, raise them, and turn them from one side to the other." Similarly, Angélica Piedra Prado, age 12, saw the image "open its eyes, raise them, and lower them from one side to the other." Between the two of them, these girls named five others in their group who saw the movements.

María del Pilar Palacio y Palacio, age 12, was the first girl to go and tell P. Anselmo, who was hearing confessions near the altar.[27] Only after several girls had done so and P. Agatángelo had finished talking did the two missionaries look at the image. They saw nothing abnormal. In the

FIGURE 8. The Christ of Limpias. The images of Mary and St. John may have served as models for the emotional reactions of spectators. Photograph by Leon-cio Marugán.

meantime others in the church began to see movements, some informed by the children, others doubtless noting the missionaries' own scrutiny of the image. About forty or fifty persons scattered through the congregation began to say the Christ was looking around, was coming to life, and even was sweating.[28]

The mood in the church was very persuasive and very excited. The Capuchins' first reaction was to calm people down and get them out of the area beyond the altar rail reserved for priests and officiants. The people were crying out, "Forgive us, Lord!" and "Have mercy, my God!" P. Anselmo was persuaded by his companion to climb a ladder to ascertain whether there was sweat on the image. He felt moisture on the image's neck, especially under the chin, and told the people so.[29] The two Capuchins and Miqueli, one after another, tried to lead the congregation in prayers, but found themselves so moved that they were physically unable to raise their voices. One of the missionaries drew a group of children who had seen the movements into the sacristy and warned them that they might be called on to maintain what they said they saw in sworn declarations. They held that what they saw was true. They were supported at this point by a respected male parishioner.

At the bishop's request, on April 10 Miqueli asked six adult residents of Limpias, selected from different social classes, men and women, to tell what they saw and felt that day:

Esperanza Mesa Bustillo, ex-schoolteacher, age 40, born in Cartagena:

twice the eyes of the image turned in their orbits from one side to another.

Ana María Medrano Rivero, landowner, age 36, born in Madrid:[30]

the image opened wide its eyes, then closed them, and she noted at the same time movement of the lips of the image, as if it were really a person in agony.

Antonio Martínez Ruiz, farmer, age 41, born in Limpias:

he confirmed with serenity that indeed the venerable image was opening its eyes wider than normal, and gently covered them with its eyelids.

Miguel Goñi Lacunza, farm laborer, age 38, born in Echarri-Aranaz (Navarra):

several times opened and shut its eyes, once shutting them completely.

Manuel Palacio Ulacia, civil servant, age not given, born in Limpias:

for some time he saw nothing abnormal, and finally he saw that several times the image moved its eyes from one side to another, and also downwards.

Manuel Llorente Herrero, landowner, age 47, born in Limpias:

> for a moment he did not see anything, and finally he could confirm how
> five times the image moved its eyes from right to left.

These adults were not all in the nave of the church when the image was
first seen to move. Two men were in the sacristy (probably in line for
communion certificates). One was told of the visions by a niece who was
one of the first seers, and another by a fellow parishioner. A third was on
his way out the church door when told by a youth, who swore on his
mother that it was true.

Some corroborated what they were seeing with those around them.
The civil servant asked the man next to him if he saw anything, and the
man said he too was seeing the image move its eyes back and forth; the
two then looked together and confirmed that they were seeing the same
thing. Similarly, the male landowner, when he went up to the presbytery
to get a good view, found that two girls, ages 12 and 13 (one of them one
of the original seers) grabbed his arm, filled with wonder every time the
image moved its eyes, "and the general impression of all of us was instan-
taneous and simultaneous." The witnesses differ in the number of persons
who beheld the phenomenon, the laborer claiming that everyone in the
church saw the image fully close its eyes once, but the impression left by
the others is that not everyone saw it.

Three of the witnesses mentioned the emotions that their visions produced, as follows:

> It was a portentous thing that brought this witness to a kind of supernatural
> shock (*asombro*), which she noted in the very numerous persons who wit-
> nessed the portent (the ex-schoolteacher).

> Something that brought the witness to a state of supernatural faintness (*an-
> onadamiento*), and she is unable to define her state of mind during such a
> portentous event (the woman landowner).

> This produced in the witness an indefinable impression, like a faintness
> (*anonadamiento*) (the farmer).

In its essentials this first episode at Limpias was typical of subsequent
sightings when groups of persons were in the church. Only some of the
people saw the movements, and different seers saw different things. On
the first day some saw just a back-and-forth movement of the eyes, others
an opening and closing, another a downward movement, and the woman
landowner saw the lips move. In subsequent days, weeks, months, and

the first few years, on the average from 5 to 10 percent of the visitors saw the image move in some way.

In his initial letter to the bishop, sent on April 2, the parish priest had referred to the copious sweating of the image as miraculous. The Santander newspapers on April 8 and 9 described the Capuchin's verification of what they called "sweat." But by April 10 this aspect of the miracle was being played down, presumably by the pious opinion leaders of Limpias. On this day *El Diario Montañés* explained that the sweat "may have a natural explanation, since there is a flat surface which might absorb the vapor of the heat given off by the large number of persons in a closed space. Nevertheless, this effect has not been noted on other festive occasions or in other images which had analogous material conditions." Because Miqueli thought a natural explanation for the moisture was possible, he did not ask the witnesses making depositions on April 10 to testify to it.[31]

It should be noted that this strategy eliminated the one phenomenon that at any point was verifiable—that could be seen and experienced by all present. It was the documented presence of liquids or liquid-like substances on paintings and images in the early modern period that gave consistency and force to the notion of a prodigy and provided the proof needed for there to be a new shrine. At Limpias the decision in the first week to fix the ground on which a miraculous event would be decided on the unverifiable claims of some, not all, of those present that the image had moved in some way or other effectively placed the events in the category of something that could neither be proven nor disproven.[32]

While José María Aguirre Gutiérrez in his daily reports in *El Diario Montañés* was the chief chronicler of Limpias and the main source for all of the many books on the subject, he and other reporters in turn had an important informant in Limpias, Gabriel Fernández Somellera. A wealthy landowner in Guadalajara, Mexico, he had been the leader of a Catholic Social Circle which the Archbishop Mora y del Río merged with the Operarios Guadalupanos of the lawyer Miguel Palomar y Vizcarra to form the Partido Nacional Católico in early 1911. The new party was an attempt by social Catholics to gain popular support under very adverse conditions. Fernández Somellera, the president of the party, was arrested by General Huerta in December 1913 and deported to the Yucatán, and in late 1915 he took refuge in his ancestral home in Limpias.[33] Serendipity placed this veteran of severe anti-Catholic persecution at the center of Spain's first great testimonial miracle of the twentieth century, with a lot of free time on his hands. Known in Spain as a Traditionalist, he kept a scrapbook of clippings about Limpias for the first three years, to which he added diary-type notes of his own from time to time. He also helped the parish priest with a massive foreign correspondence and gave information to reporters and writers.[34]

In his diary he described the effect of the news of the visions on the town:[35]

> Opinion was divided; those of us in the majority believed the portent because of the simultaneity of the vision from different places in the church, the quality of the witnesses from all social classes and conditions, ages, and sex, most of them of good and serene judgment. Others, the intellectual part of the village, denied that there had been a prodigy, speculating that it was an effect of the light, or hallucinations.

There seems to have been some association in the minds of many of the people of Limpias between the activation of their image and Agatángelo de San Miguel, the missionary speaking when the girls first had their visions. One of the girls told a journalist in early April that the Christ first looked at P. Agatángelo, then at the congregation.[36] The Capuchin himself said he had supernatural experiences with the image when alone in the church on nights after March 30, 1919.[37] By April 2, when the parish priest reported the miracle to the bishop, the Capuchin was known as "the Saint."[38] The villagers accompanied him and his companion seven kilometers on their way out of town when the mission was over.[39]

The parish priest at once initiated a *setenario*, a series of seven daily services, dedicated in this instance to meditations on Christ's words on the cross. After the setenario was concluded the matter was broken in the press, first by a note in the diocesan *Páginas Dominicales* of April 6, then by articles in the two Catholic newspapers of Santander on April 7, 8, 9, and 10. On April 12 one of the intellectuals of Limpias who was a disbeliever and a shopkeeper from Ampuero together saw the image move, and it began to occur to people that the miracle might not yet be over.[40]

This idea gained strength from the claims of two persons to have seen the image move *before* March 30. One was a former sexton, an alcoholic of dubious mental stability. He supposedly once told his family he had seen the Christ's eyes move, only to be laughed at.[41] His story could be doubted, but that of P. López, who taught physics at the Vincentian school at Limpias, was more credible. He said he had seen the image's eyes shut in August 1914 when installing electric lights around the image. What he saw caused him to fall from the ladder. He told the sexton, who

said he was not surprised, as others had seen the same thing, and it might
be caused by a mechanism in the image. His superior instructed him not
to repeat what he had seen. He tried to find others who had seen the same
thing, to no avail. But he did check the image, finding no mechanism of
any kind.[42]

The emergence of this kind of post-facto private visionary is common
to almost all major vision episodes in Spanish history. It points up, in this
and other cases, that the possibility of image activation or apparitions is
real to many people at all times. It indicates a permanent "static" of visions, a ground line of unusual perceptions, out of which when the time
is ripe, the more believable visionaries emerge, are selected, and gain public recognition. It is possible that, however ridiculed or silenced seers like
the sexton or the Vincentian were under normal conditions, their experience may have entered the imagination of the kind of children who
began the sightings of March 30, 1919.

In the Limpias case, or rather in the cases of image activation in general, the sightings also exemplify the insufficiency of individual, isolated
witnesses. Only group sightings, plausibly corroborated, will do if a public case is to be made. Such is not the case for apparitions. Single seers of
religious apparitions have been believed, especially if they have a series of
visions over time, if there is a compelling need for divine help, and some
kind of proof, even simply an ecstatic trance in public, can be offered.

Finally, the emergence of the two pre-visionaries, like that of new, subsequent seers, I imagine, helped to consolidate the shift of attention from
the exceptional circumstances under which the March 30 mass sighting
took place, and to focus instead on the immanent miraculous qualities of
the image itself. Given a history of manifestations, the particular mix of
people, time, and intentions on March 30 would become less important;
more important would be the recognition that here was a very sacred
statue, different from normal ones because it had the capacity to communicate with humans and, presumably, help them. In this way the Christ
of Agony was letting its power be known, becoming a shrine image like
the Virgin of Bien-Aparecida, the Christ of Burgos, and Santa Casilda. As
such it required a biography. A miraculous past was quickly found for it,
which involved the protection of Cádiz from a tidal wave in the great
earthquake of 1755.[43] As it became clear that the image itself was miraculous, less attention was paid to the holy missionaries themselves. They
were considered more as auxiliaries in the discovery of a divine intention
than miracle workers in their own right.

But there can be no doubt that the role of the mission in the provoca-
tion of the Limpias visions was critical. That is not to say that the mis-

sionaries had any idea a miracle would occur. Their purpose, as in all missions of this type, was to heighten the emotional level of religiosity in the parish in order in the short run to provoke contrition, confession, and communion; in the middle run to revitalize or freshen up parish devotion and religious practice—perhaps also to propagate Capuchin religious devotions and gain members for their Third Order for laypersons; and probably, in a more diffuse way, to combat or defend against the spread of antireligion. Their procedure of intensive preaching over a period of days was centuries old in Spain, a more institutional and domestic version of the great revivals of Vincent Ferrer in the fourteenth century. The mission was a form of religious saturation, led by preachers larger than life carrying outside charisma, in this case in their long beards and brown cassocks.

Other, lesser strategies served to mark off sets of time during the year for a special religious intensity. The liturgical cycle itself did this, but its times were predictable and planned for in the form of state holidays and family gatherings. In addition, there were the religious times particular to a given place. These were also marked off and built up to by novenas. But the mission, though it sometimes might coincide with a specified holy time (in the case of Limpias with Lent), derived much of its power from being outside that time, an ellipsis, just as the missionaries were from another, outside, conventual world. For those parishioners who were devout, missions were a step toward heaven. For everyone in Spain's smaller, localized societies, the missions were a break from routine, like snow days for American schoolchildren.[44]

In their short span of days, the missions woke people up early, as if they were in a convent, put them through unusual paces, grouped them with their peers by age and gender in ways that made explicit their place in the society and the moral hierarchy, shook them up with a fear of damnation, and softened them with a glimpse of forgiveness and bliss. In this they worked in a slightly diluted way like the closed spiritual exercises that Ignatius of Loyola and the Jesuits made available to select laypeople and clergy. Indeed, missions are best understood as one strategy in a very broad and graduated array of techniques for evoking specified emotions, sharpened over hundreds of years, of which laypersons as well as religious and secular clergy were experienced practitioners. These techniques ranged from evocative prayers to be read silently in church or at home, to more extensive triduos, novenas, or stations of the cross, to the regular liturgy with its eucharistic climax, to dramatic processions of holy weeks, and to sacred dramas in which parishioners acted the parts of saints and sinners. All of them served to sensitize people, take them out of their daily lives, and bring them to feel for Christ's sacrifice and glorification; many of them served to produce the public display of condign feeling.[45]

The heightened sensitivity that the mission drama produced included an openness to the outside, a receptiveness, which made it an ideal vehicle for the propagation of the mission order's saints, devotions, brotherhoods, and procedure. As the orders were generally international in character, often with headquarters in Rome, the missions promoted a certain level of internationalization and Romanization of devotion. Ann Taves has shown the importance of missions in the nineteenth-century United States for the multiplication of devotional techniques of southern European origin, superimposed on the more austere piety of English origin prevalent at the beginning of the century.[46] A study for Spain that followed the evolution of the devotions in prayerbooks in the same period would show a similar influx of French and Italian prayers and organizations.

It was the heightened sensitivity and openness that made the persons who participated in the missions more likely to see and feel religious things that they did not ordinarily see or feel. In the case of the March 1919 Limpias mission, the enthusiasm and intensity aroused were heightened by two quasi-miraculous events. Anselmo de Jalón insisted that the sexton raise a heavy, wrought-iron lamp suspended over the nave as it impeded eye contact with his audience. It was found that the metal support had rusted away, and that in all likelihood it would have fallen on the congregation. During the mission when the church bells were ringing, one of the heavy clappers fell to the esplanade a few inches from one of the boys playing there. These two incidents were, in microcosm, illustrations for the Capuchins' arguments of the imminence of divine judgment and the power of God's mercy. One may presume that they were on many people's minds during the service on March 30 when the Christ was seen to move. But in the abundant literature on the Christ of Limpias, there is little mention of these incidents, and all of that from Capuchin sources.[47] The lack of interest of the press and pious publicists in these events is evidence for the almost immediate shift of attention away from the enthusiasm aroused by the mission and the missionaries to the sacred nature of the image itself and the wider meaning of its activation.

To point up the emotional impact of the mission on its congregation, it is worth recounting an antecedent for the visions at Limpias in rural Galicia in 1903.[48] On April 15 two Redemptorist missionaries from Astorga, Fathers Mariscal and Romero, arrived in San Martín de Man-

FIGURE 9. A procession during a mission by Redemptorists from Astorga in Galicia in the early twentieth century. The mission cross is in the foreground. From Raimundo Tellería, *Un instituto misionero* (Madrid, 1932).

zaneda, a remote rural parish of 170 households in the province of Orense and the diocese of Astorga. They were not well received, even though their order had given missions there twice before. The church bells were not rung, the parish priest did not meet them, nor did the villagers, in part because the town had become deeply divided into two factions. It was, the Astorga chronicler wrote, the worst beginning for a mission in the entire twenty years of the residence.

The Redemptorists were established in Spain in 1879, at first dependent on the French province. They were entirely dedicated to missionizing, which they did in a way somewhat less theatrical than the Capuchins, partly due to the more Jansenist attitude of the French fathers, but also because the order as a whole had explicitly prohibited the kind of dramaturgy that overly stimulated popular sensibility.[49] They placed great emphasis in their missions on the reform of customs, including close dancing, mixed-sex evening spinning circles, and usury.[50]

Nevertheless, like the Capuchins and the Jesuits, their major aim was to provoke repentance and contrition in the form of tears, leading to a good confession. Their famous missionary, Ramón Sarabia, wrote, "The missionary well knows that tears are the indispensible condition to achieve the forgiveness of all sins. That is why before confessions are heard in the missions, an entire day is devoted to the conquest of these tears."[51]

On this day the *Desagravio*, or atonement, took place. It was preceded the day before by a sermon on the Last Judgment.

At Manzaneda the Last Judgment sermon had been ruined by a fire alarm, which had emptied the church in mid-emotion. But nevertheless the next evening, April 20, 1903, the church was filled by people drawn by the prospect of the spectacular candle arrangement they had come to expect for the Desagravio, for which they themselves had supplied the candles. In this ceremony, in contrast to the Judgment, the emphasis is placed on Christ's forgiveness, symbolized by the resplendent exposure of the holy sacrament when the people are called to contrition. It was at this moment that people in Manzaneda had their visions, while P. Mariscal was preaching on a text from Isaiah, "All day my arms are open to my people, which does not believe in me and contradicts me." Given the indifference of Manzaneda to the mission, the text was particularly apropos.

P. Mariscal's exhortation was very much a set piece, and it can be followed in some detail in the order's mission manuals.[52]

> Following our customs, once the Sacrament is exposed a Father from the pulpit directs a fervent speech, exhorting the asking of forgiveness of the Lord. Invite the parish priest, duly forewarned, to ask for it and to intercede for his parishioners. Invite as well the children. Finally, all those present raise their voices and cry out before the Lord.

The manual I cite, published in 1932, was written by a missionary trained in Astorga and active early in the century. It goes on to make suggestions for the speech in question, which it warns, "would be an insult to the spirit of this ceremony if it were a piece of any old sermon. The mercy of God demands here a master stroke." The first outline he suggests appears similar to the one used at Manzaneda:

> *Jesus weeps over Jerusalem.* He visits the city of Jerusalem, garbed in love and pity. How he yearns for its conversion! He cries out, "Convert, Jerusalem, Convert." He well knows its unfaithfulness. He foresees its ruin. How bitter for the heart of a Father and a Redeemer! He weeps.
>
> This scene is repeated. That same Jesus dwells in the tabernacle. He is your neighbor. How he suffers for your salvation!
>
> And what has this town done? How has it responded? (Not with a bitter and menacing tone, but rather with a pained lament describe rapidly the sins of the town, showing how thereby the Heart of Jesus, Father and Redeemer

sacramented, is wounded and injured.) Listen to the laments of your God. What did I do to you? Why have you responded to my love and my blessings with insults and evil deeds?

He does not want to punish. He offers forgiveness. Exposed in the monstrance, he opens the arms of his mercy.

At this moment in Manzaneda different people saw different things. Some saw Jesus as a child with arms outstretched in the place of the host in the monstrance; others saw the same thing, but with his exposed heart bleeding, or holding his hand on his heart to staunch the bleeding. The parish priest saw the arms as attached to a cross. Others saw only the monstrance mysteriously illuminated, "as if there were an electric light behind it." And still others, including the missionaries, saw nothing abnormal at all.

As a result the mission took a sharp turn toward piety and enthusiasm. There was a general reconciliation in the town. And people came from other towns and parishes to the final session of general communion. Pious associations were revived; permission was sought for nocturnal adoration of the Holy Sacrament; and a child Jesus with open arms above a golden chalice was painted on the mission cross.

The similarities with Limpias are numerous: the undercurrent of coldness; the focus on Christ and his rejection; the use of lights to center visual attention; the fact that the seers saw different things, and some people saw nothing; and especially the congruence between what is seen and the theme of an emotional sermon, after a build-up, not just of several days of mission, but more pertinently of many years of internal ideological contradictions and stress.

The greatest difference was in the response of the diocese and the order to the events. The bishop, the Escolapian Vicente Alonso Salgado, sent a notary to take testimony in Manzaneda, where many people declared they saw nothing at all. (At Limpias as well many persons saw nothing the first day, but nobody asked them.) Alonso Salgado thereafter did nothing to ratify the visions; nor did his successors when, after two months, Alonso Salgado became bishop of Cartagena.[53] At Manzaneda one of the missionaries, P. Romero, was left cold by the visions, and did not consider that a miracle had taken place at all. The Astorgan Catholic newspaper published one story about the event, which was reprinted in many Spanish newspapers, and that was the end of it.

The Redemptorists, predisposed against such things, were skeptical. They discounted the events because of the involvement of P. Mariscal, known for his propensity for visionary matters. This contrasts with the great respect the Capuchins had for Agatángelo de San Miguel prior to the Limpias visions, which made them more credible.

A different bishop, a different order, perhaps as well a different kind of town. Isolated Manzaneda had fewer social resources to mobilize, no railroad, and far less access to the media and the influential than did the gentry of Limpias, who were only one step from Santander, Bilbao, Madrid, the king, and the prime minister.

For whatever reason, the critical shift of attention at Limpias toward the miraculous crucifix and away from the missionaries, the mission, and the circumstances of the first visions, never happened at Manzaneda. At Limpias the shift was to the image as a source of grace and to the wider social and political circumstances. At Manzaneda there was no image to shift to that would maintain the vision momentum. And in 1903 there was not the same urgency in the wider political and social situation as there was in 1919. The focus was left on the immediate circumstances of the original visions, which became the determinant, and fatal, explanation.

Some lessons from this comparison are unambiguous. First it shows the power of the mission itself as an emotional theater. In particular it points to the potency of the words of preachers in conjunction with visual stimuli. We will see that time and again during pilgrimages to Limpias, there were group visions while persuasive preaching was going on.

Second, it shows the importance of the response the visions receive. Given a "secret" history of image activations or mission visions, most of which did not gain widespread acceptance, the essential question for social history becomes not why there were visions at a given time, since in all likelihood there were visions at all times. Rather the question is why at a given time were people—whether the church hierarchy, the press, or the public at large—receptive to visions?

THE RISE AND DECLINE OF PILGRIMAGES, 1919–1926

While the fall of the clapper to the Limpias churchyard had the effect of making extraordinarily specific and localized the application of God's providence in that place and time, other aspects of the mission and its miracles pointed outward to the wider world and a broader timespan. The conversion of many of Limpias's men; the fact that the movements of the Christ began when thanks were being given for the conversion, shortly after edifying communions had taken place; the priest's emphasis

that only five men out of the entire population had not received communion; the conversion of one of these five by a vision two weeks later;
all point to a more general context that conditioned the Limpias visions.
It was the context common to the events of Gandía, and indeed to miracles throughout the nineteenth and twentieth centuries in the Catholic
world—the struggle for the souls of men.

In the late medieval and early modern period, the movements of images, like monstrous births, aurora borealis, comets, earthquakes, unusual
storms, or crosses or armies in the sky, were signs, ominous portents of
things that were happening elsewhere or were going to happen. As such,
they called for prayer and penance.[54] This kind of meaning was still
abroad in nineteenth- and twentieth-century Europe, where compilations
like the two-volume *Voix Prophetiques* of the Abbé Curicque related recent signs to French fortunes in the Franco-Prussian War.[55] But in a
world in which belief could no longer be assumed, miracles, the miraculous movements of images, and stigmata like those of Palma Matorrelli,
Padre Pio, and Marie-Julie Jahenny were fiduciary as well as eschatological—proofs of the existence of God as well as signs. True, they had
this value as proof more for wavering believers than for rank unbelievers,
and some Catholic scholars deplored the demand for such news as a sign
of weakness.[56] But there is every evidence that many believers were wavering. It is therefore not surprising that the bishop of Santander's *Páginas
Dominicales*, one month after the Limpias visions began, declared that
while it was unsure whether the Christ was moving as a sign of future
misfortunes, it was certain that the prodigy was "one more proof of the
truth of the Catholic faith," a proof that the bishop knew was sorely
needed.[57]

D. Vicente Santiago Sánchez de Castro knew that his diocese, like
those adjacent—Oviedo and Vitoria—was on the front line of an ideological struggle. In March 1919 he was 67 years old, and he had been
Santander's bishop for 35 years. His episcopal stance was "orthodox, de-
fensive, and moralizing." An assiduous and meticulous administrator, he
visited most of the parishes in his mountainous diocese at least four times,
fomenting the Rosary and the catechism through brotherhoods and congregations. He worried about the effects of secularization—blasphemy,
profanation of holy days, drunkenness, and the division of families caused
by politics, but like most other Church leaders he did not address the
socio-economic roots of this secularization.[58] His response (and that of
bishops throughout Spain) was to mobilize militant Catholics in demonstrations and at election time. The high point of his organizing against

liberal government religious policies was a set of demonstrations on October 2, 1910, at eleven places in the diocese. According to the Catholic press, 76,000 persons were involved, which would have been about a fourth of the total population.[59] As his biographer wrote of the first diocesan pilgrimage to Lourdes, which Sánchez de Castro led in 1908, "The object of the pilgrimage was that which he sought in all public events: a witness of faith and devotion in the midst of a society quite hostile and anticlerical."

The bishop did not conceal that hostility in his *ad limina* visit to Pius X in 1909. Whereas "most of his diocese was believing and submissive," he told the pope, "there are many who were falling away and declaring themselves enemies of religion."[60] By 1919 it was general knowledge that the sympathies of working men in Santander were with the Socialist *Casa del Pueblo*. A Jesuit there wrote in November,[61]

> The ladies, who have unionized 300 or so dressmakers, have come to me and wish to unionize female servants, fishwives, etc. They are ready to do anything and want to avoid for women what has happened with the men—all of whom are in the Casa del Pueblo.

The possibility that the Christ of Limpias might help to stem this apostasy was present in the initial letter of the parish priest, Eduardo Miqueli, to the bishop on April 2. Some of the men who saw the image's eyes move, he observed, were "not those who are pious." The bishop's uncritical enthusiasm was reflected in the notice printed in the diocesan *Páginas Dominicales* of April 6, which stated rather baldly that the image at Limpias "moved its eyes and gave off abundant sweat for some time." It also stated that the activation was believed "in all of Limpias." He had replied to the parish priest instructing him, "not as an official act, but rather as if it were at your own initiative," to obtain signed and sworn declarations from "a couple of witnesses from each class (señores, señoras, children, farmers)."[62]

For a prelate whose strategy was to hold on to his Catholics by having them stand up and be counted, the Limpias miracle was yet another way to mobilize his diocese for a testimony of faith. It appears that, from soon after the first visions, the notion that Limpias could be something like Lourdes for Santander and the north of Spain was never far from anyone's mind.[63]

On April 18, 1919, less than three weeks after the first visions, 300 persons arrived in Limpias from nearby Colindres on foot, the first formal group pilgrimage.[64] On subsequent days the Christ was visited by distin-

guished families from Vizcaya and Santander. Families from Bilbao paid
for the new electrical installation in the church, which was finished on
April 25.[65] On April 27 the bishop's nephew, Jacinto Iglesias, who was
secretario de camara of the diocese, was there planning the upcoming
pilgrimage of Santander; and on April 30 persons from six different
towns, including Santander and Irún, saw the Christ's eyes move.[66]

The Santander pilgrimage of 1,200 persons was prepared with care.[67]
Its procedure became standard for all official pilgrimages. Instructions
were printed and distributed in advance. Pilgrims signed up in Santander's parish churches, and, "to unify, by mixing together, persons from all
social classes," they were given white silk ribbons with medals on them to
wear around their necks. They were also given hymns to the Christ of
Limpias, written for the occasion by a Santander priest, to learn on the
pilgrimage trains.

On May 4, 1919, the authorities of Limpias met the pilgrims at the
station with cheers of "Viva the First Pilgrimage from Santander!" (accu-
rately foreseeing future expeditions). The pilgrims, including many members of religious orders, gathered near an arch decorated with flowers and
national flags, which had a banner reading, "Limpias for the pilgrims."
There the parish processional cross was waiting, surrounded by candles.
Firework rockets were fired, the church bells rung, and there were cheers
for the Virgin Bien-Aparecida, the pope, the bishop, and the Limpias
town government.

The pilgrims then formed a procession on the grounds of the Vincentian school and walked a kilometer to the parish church, led by the banner of the Passionist brotherhood of Santander, then three priests from
Limpias with the parish cross, the Vincentian fathers from the school, the
parish priests of Santander, and representatives of Santander's religious communities. The citizens of Limpias cheered from the roadside,
and the pilgrims sang the new Limpias hymns and a Salve to the Virgin
Bien-Aparecida, passing under a number of decorated arches. At the various points when the procession paused, the pilgrims were assisted by special commissions, one of women and the other of men, comprised of
Limpias's most respected citizens, including Gabriel Fernández Somellera
and two of those who had been called to testify to seeing the Christ's eyes
move on the first day.

Outside the church the pilgrims encountered stands with food, drink,
religious souvenirs, and medals. Inside they heard mass, including a fervent sermon, and then they ate at the inns that had metamorphosed over-
night from village houses. During the meal some pilgrims in the church

saw the image's eyes move, and many came hurrying to try and see it themselves. Twenty of the seers are said to have signed the vision register in the sacristy.[68]

In the first months local pride and enthusiasm in Limpias were intense, fired by continued visions, notably on April 20 when not only laypeople but also nuns from the Limpias girls' school, and the assistant priest of the parish saw the image move.[69] On May 6 nine prominent Limpias men wrote to *La Gaceta del Norte* of Bilbao, declaring they had seen the Christ move.[70] They were outraged when on May 17, someone, probably a clergyman, expressed skepticism or caution about the visions, and were relieved when the following day a Jesuit in Santander spoke out in favor of the visions.[71]

In mid-June, a month after the Santander pilgrimage, the Limpias townspeople reached their zenith in organization. Six commissions were established to receive pilgrims: Reception, Order, Help, Transportation, Information, and Decoration. Commission members could be readily identified by their white and purple badges.[72] The ritual receptions of pilgrimages were taken seriously through the first summer, at least, for when the pilgrimage of Irún arrived by train at two A.M. on August 3, 1919, it was met by one-half the entire town, and accompanied from the train station to the church.[73]

The pilgrimages were coordinated through the Junta de Peregrinaciones Diocesana,[74] and the system of special hymns, medals, and ribbons employed from the start seems to have been modeled on that of Lourdes. The diocese had its own precedent as well, in the three days of pilgrimages on September 6, 7, and 8, 1906, when Sánchez de Castro proclaimed the Virgin Bien-Aparecida patroness of the diocese. Then 18,000 pilgrims marshaled from throughout the province had made the trip to the shrine in the mountains only twenty kilometers from Limpias.[75] As at Lourdes the pilgrimages to Limpias by the various towns and associations were numbered, e.g., the First Santander Pilgrimage, The Third Pilgrimage of the Mariás del Sagrario. And as at Lourdes, every effort was made to have the pilgrimages be demonstrations of enthusiasm that were very orderly.

In the official pilgrimages little was left to chance or spontaneity. Clergy generally visited the shrine in advance of a trip to work out the logistics. Santander pilgrimages were prepared by articles in *El Diario Montañés* with rules for dress and ceremony "in order to make the excursion in the most orderly way."[76] Women were to wear mantillas.[77] The hymns to be sung were specified ("After the procession forms in Limpias, the children will sing 'Bendice, alma mía,' alternating with 'Laudate pueri

Dominum' sung by the priests")[78] and sometimes were rehearsed for several days prior to the trip. In a disorderly world, there was to be no question that these pilgrimages partook of the measure and organization of the just. *El Diario Montañés* admired the Carranza pilgrimage on June 8, 1919:[79]

> In order to plan an orderly arrival, a map was made of the town, showing the points of interest and the distances. The pilgrims went on the two sides of the road in two double files, first the ladies and then the gentlemen. In the center went those carrying the banners, the choirs, and the priests. The step of the pilgrims was uniform, almost rhythmic. It seemed a genius of military tactics had planned the operation like a peaceful invasion.

In these pilgrimages the Catholic people of the north of Spain were putting their society on display.

The rise and spread of the pilgrimages over the first several years were as follows:

April–July 1919. A Christ for Cantabria

Of the 29 formal pilgrimages until July 31, 1919, 16 were organized by parishes, towns, or religious districts, and 12 were made by urban church organizations. Fernández Somellera calculated that by July 31, 1919, between 42,000 and 45,000 persons had come to Limpias, about half in organized pilgrimages and the rest (150–200 per day) in smaller groups. "It is not unusual," he wrote on July 31, "to have as many as 22 masses, and generally there are about 12 these last days."[80]

The pilgrimages were mainly from Santander, Bilbao, Oviedo, and rural districts of the diocese of Santander. The east-west pattern of pilgrimage along Spain's north coast from the Basque country to Asturias was dictated by topography. Communications were more difficult across the mountains to the south, and the centers of population in Castile were farther away. Along the coast was a narrow-gauge railway, which by April 14 had added more cars to its regular trains. Beginning with the Santander pilgrimage on May 4, it organized special pilgrimage trains. Its receipts quadrupled in the summer of 1919.[81]

Many pilgrims arrived by bus. By early May there was daily service from the western part of the province, including Torrelavega, Cabezón de la Sal, Udías, Cóbreces, Puente San Miguel, and Santillana del Mar.[82] By early June 1919, the road to the church was being widened and the town square enlarged to provide parking.[83] (See Map 2.)

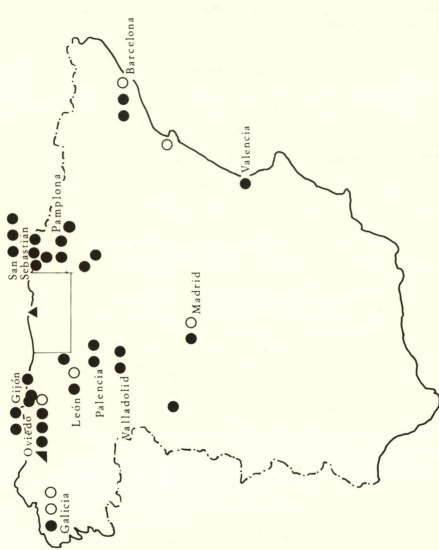

MAP 2. Group pilgrimages to Limpias, 1919–1926. This map of Spain, together with the enlargement on the facing page of the rectangular area outlining the region near Limpias, indicates the places from which groups of more than one hundred pilgrims went to Limpias in three periods (see legend on facing page). It also reveals how the shrine profited from and was limited by railroads and, thereby, topography.

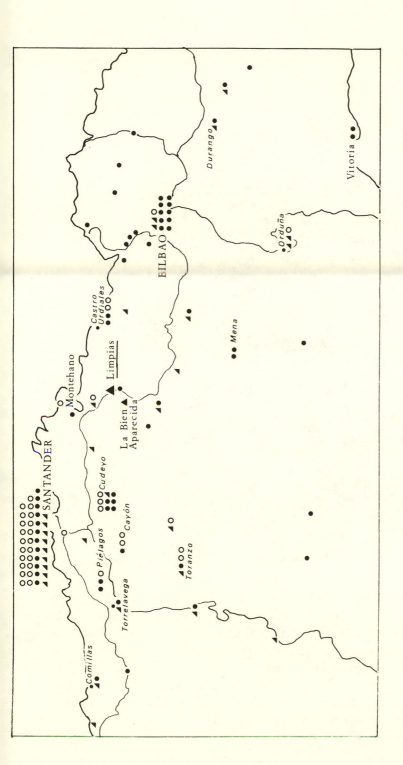

Comillas

Torrelavega

SANTANDER

Montehano

Piélagos

Cudeyo

Cayón

La Bien
Aparecida

Limpias

Toranzo

Castro
Urdiales

BILBAO

Mena

Orduña

Durango

Vitoria

◢ From April to July 1919

● From August 1919 to December 1920

○ From 1921 to 1926

⊢———⊣ 25 km

FIGURE 10.
Pilgrims and
vendors at
Limpias,
summer of
1919.
Photograph
by Labarga
in Tomás
Echevarría, *Los
prodigios.*

Judging from those who signed the vision register, we find that the
pilgrims in this period were equally from rural and urban homes (under-
standing as urban, Santander, Bilbao, Oviedo, and Madrid). Those from
Cantabria predominated (about 70 percent in May, 50 percent in June,
and 70 percent again in July), and fewer than 10 percent came from outside the provinces of Santander, Vizcaya, and Asturias in May and June.
This percentage rose a bit in July, as more pilgrims began to come from
Madrid and Guipúzcoa (see Appendix Table 6).

News of the visions was printed quickly in newspapers throughout

Spain. The story was carried in Madrid's *El Debate* on April 9, 1919. Reporters from *El Debate* and *El Imparcial* of Madrid were in Limpias on June 12, 1919. But the major ongoing source for almost all newspapers was the ample coverage by *El Diario Montañés*.

By May 20, 1919, an increase in the number of houses serving meals had led to a lowering of prices.[84] Some of the souvenir stands belonged to the Irazu family, which operated a hotel and gift shop at the Basque shrine of Loyola. A number of photographers issued postcards of the image and the shrine, and some set up shop in Limpias, taking pictures of pilgrims.[85] Already in 1919 the image manufacturers of Olot (Gerona) were making reproductions of the image, both as a crucifix and as a bust, for sale in the village.[86] Many visitors saw in the souvenir stands, with their high prices, another similarity with Lourdes.[87]

In these first four months, according to the estimate of Fernández Somellera, 3,000 persons saw the Christ move, which would be about 7 percent of those who came. They had the option of registering what they saw in the sacristy, where the first witness register was opened on April 30.[88] A new one was begun on July 5, 1919, with a summary of past events by the parish priest. By August 5, 1919, 400 persons had signed. In the summer of 1919, Fernández Somellera was in charge of the books.[89]

The books were public documents; they were available for pilgrims to read, and seers were making public statements by writing in them. In this sense the statements fulfilled the same role as the votive offerings common to most Spanish shrines: they were proclamations, signed and dated, of the shrine saint's power. Reporters and authors freely quoted from the testimony.

But such statements were more than ex-votos. For in the context of the times, to sign the book was also a political statement which placed one squarely on the conservative, monarchist right. It was another way, like attendance in a formal pilgrimage with medal and ribbon, to stand up and be counted. Because it was a political statement, and because it might entail from skeptics a certain amount of ridicule, signing the book was courageous and added weight to one's claim of a vision. When a man from Lecaroz (Navarra), who came with a pilgrimage of 500 members of the Nocturnal Adoration Society, was told he had had an optical illusion after claiming that the Christ moved, he strode to the sacristy and wrote, "I certify and swear that I saw the Holy Christ of Limpias raise and lower his eyes."[90] The registers, while providing evidence for the miracle, were also by their very existence evidence of the climate of doubt in which the miracle was taking place.

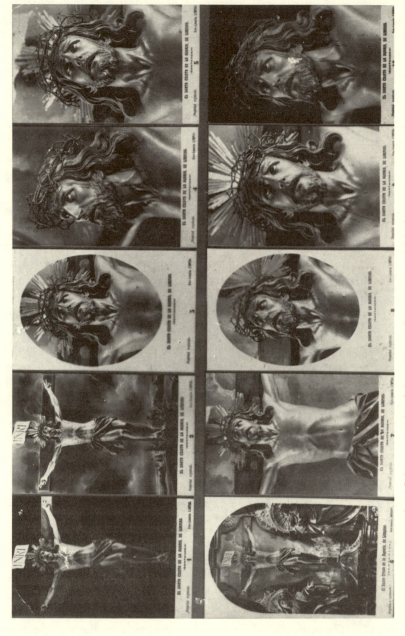

FIGURE 11. A sampler of the postcards of the Christ of Limpias available from Leoncio Marugán.

Some of the seers also felt called to reaffirm their visions in articles or letters to newspapers and magazines. These more literary testimonies were frequently reprinted, and most of them found their way into the many apologetic books that were issued from 1919 to 1922. (At least two of these witnesses, María de Echarri and Joaquín Sicart, were subsequently enthusiasts of the apparitions of Ezquioga.)

In the first couple of months it appears to have been a diocesan strategy as well as a natural result of regional pride to emphasize that the Christ of Limpias belonged to La Montaña, as the province of Santander then, or the autonomous region of Cantabria now, was known. Wedged between two regions with considerably more chauvinism, Cantabria was somewhat slower in establishing the formal symbols of a regional culture than its neighbors. Indeed, the proclamation of the Virgin Bien-Aparecida in 1906 as regional patroness was greeted by the western part of the diocese with some misgivings. Many isolated valleys with intense devotion to a local divine patron felt no allegiance to the distant shrine. But Sánchez de Castro, doubtless drawing lessons from Lourdes, knew that in order to have an effective diocesan mobilization he had to establish symbols and common experiences that would draw his people together. When, thirteen years later, the Christ began to be seen to move at Limpias, the bishop's subordinates did not hesitate to attribute the phenomenon to a kind of reward for the devotion of the region as a whole to the Virgin. Foreseeing that Limpias would be a national shrine, they took pride in identifying it first with all of Cantabria.

When Dr. Santiago Estebanell preached to the Torrelavega pilgrimage of May 25, 1919, he attributed the Christ's motions as blessings for La Montaña's devotion to its patroness.[91]

> Today as never before I feel the grandeur of this Montaña Cántabra, which is, without a doubt, the Montaña of Spain. . . . The Holy Christ has, without a doubt, sought to take advantage of the faith of the Cántabros who love his Mother and so appear to them.

He then called on his audience to bear public witness as Catholics, as devotees of the Virgin, and as regional patriots. Who could have remained seated when he called,

> I want you to make here publicly a solemn profession of your faith and of your beliefs. I want you to acclaim the Christ that has promised to reign in Spain, raising your arm and saying with me: "I believe in Christ the Lord crucified; I believe in the portentous miracles of this our Christ of the Montaña; I believe in the Bien-Aparecida our mother."

The reporter from *El Diario Montañés* added, "An enormous clamor was heard in the church as the voices were raised to acclaim the King of Kings, Our Lord and Father."

The attempt to link Limpias with the still-nascent devotion to the Bien-Aparecida is evident from the instructions given the pilgrims. The following is from the rules for the Cathechistic Pilgrimage in July 1919: "When reaching the road that leads to the shrine from the highway, the procession will pause to greet our patron the Virgin Bien-Aparecida with the diocesan hymn and a Salve."[92] This kind of sacred protocol, which acknowledges a hierarchy and precedence for divinities and presumably reinforces one's notion of the aptness of certain human hierarchies, was subsequently applied to pilgrims from other dioceses as well. Navarrese pilgrims brought October 13–15, 1919, by the Nocturnal Adoration Society of Pamplona were given a printed schedule for their trip with seventeen notes and instructions.[93] Note 7 warns them that, when they reach the road to the shrine, they too will be pointed in the direction of the Bien-Aparecida shrine, and they will sing a Salve "in honor of the sovereign Patron of the Montaña region." Some explanation seems to have been called for, for the note continues, "The Navarrese pilgrimage, like the others that have gone before it, can do no less than follow this pious practice in honor of the Mother of the Redeemer, first, to ask the intercession of the Most Holy Virgin, and then as an act of courtesy to the noble region of Santander, which is going to offer hospitality for a short while." The Navarrese, some of them, would have used similar protocol in some of their own local pilgrimages.[94]

June 1919 seems to have been the month in which the rural doctors of the zone were brought around to believing in the phenomenon, many from a position of curious skepticism. The visions of several of these doctors were reported in detail in Santander and Madrid newspapers.[95]

If there was any doubt about the respectability of the Limpias enterprise, it must have been erased in July. For on July 13 the queen visited the shrine, and on July 30 it was the turn of King Alfonso XIII, accompanied by leading Cantabrian political figures.[96] Before and after him in that first summer, there came numerous families of Spanish nobility. Limpias is close to the fashionable Cantabrian coast, and many of these families summered in the stretch from Santander to San Sebastian. The king had palaces in both cities. In fact, in Limpias itself there were several "palacios" to which wealthy families came in the summer. Within a space of two or three weeks the newspapers named 17 dukes and duchesses, 26 marquises, and 36 counts and countesses who went to Limpias.[97] And in all of 1919 Limpias was visited by at least 12 bishops and the papal nuncio

Francesco Ragonesi.[98] In this period a hymn to Limpias was commissioned from the noted Basque composer in Madrid, Jesús Guridi.[99] Politicians came as well; one of the first was the Traditionalist Esteban Bilbao.[100] With the king had come the wife of the prime minister, Antonio Maura; and Maura himself, who summered nearby, went sometime during the year.[101] All this elite interest confirmed the nationalization of the shrine and the devotion.

August–December 1919. A Jerusalem for Spain

In August 1919 the geographical hinterland widened, in part due to a profusion of articles in national and regional magazines and newspapers. Articles also began to appear in Catholic publications in other countries.[102] There were formal pilgrimages from Irún, San Sebastián, Logroño, Palencia, Valladolid, Cáceres, Salamanca, and Galicia. These trips from far away were mainly organized from cities. In addition there were others from rural church districts and smaller towns in the closer areas of Vizcaya, Santander, and eastern Asturias.

During these five months there were 37 official pilgrimages, with an average size of 400–500. In addition, other pilgrims came at a rate of about 400 a day in August and 300 a day in September.[103] Fernández Somellera calculated that in all of 1919, 110,000 visitors went to the church, and that of these 9 to 10 percent were seers.[104] The parish priest kept statistics of sacraments, and told a reporter that from mid-June to November 20, 1919, 4,280 masses had been ordered, and 15,200 communions administered.[105] From these figures (an average of 28 masses each day) the masses, if all said at Limpias, would have had to have been held nonstop from dawn to dusk. The pilgrimages began to fall off in mid-October, and in all of November there were only 5–6,000 visitors. As the drizzly Santander winter set in, the time for excursions seems to have been over.[106] Mail inquiries did not abate, however. In mid-November Miqueli was receiving about twenty letters daily.[107]

In August there began to be reports of miraculous cures at Limpias, and of the rescue of storm-tossed boats after prayers to the Christ.[108] On September 10, 1919, the village of Fresno de la Vega (León) had prayed to the Christ via a photograph or print and was spared a hailstorm that damaged the crops of the surrounding towns.[109] An article in a Barcelona magazine linked the Christ of Limpias to the new National Expiatory Temple that overlooked the city from Mount Tibadabo.[110] In this period, then, Limpias was incorporated into the preexisting network of shrines and was becoming understood as part of the spatial mysteries of divine intention; as such it was put to use for practical ends of communities and individuals.

The notion of Limpias as the Spanish Lourdes, a center of world pilgrimage, a place where the sick would be healed, had already been broached in articles published in May, June, and July, 1919.[111] Sometime in 1919 a pamphlet was published in Zaragoza proposing a basilica at Limpias.[112] And when the Claretian Tomás Echevarría published his book in October, he took it for granted that there would be a "great national pilgrimage like Lourdes" where an "unnumbered multitude of Spaniards" would enter the "wide doors of the future basilica."[113] The proposal was refined in November when *El Eco Franciscano* suggested that a monastery be appended to the basilica.[114]

As more persons arrived at the shrine and the total number of seers mounted, the visions became more varied and complex. About May 18, 1919, visionaries began seeing blood on the image.[115] On July 6, 1919, Fernández Somellera wrote in his scrapbook, "For some time now the movements of the most Holy Christ of Limpias are ever more varied, for it is not just the eyes and the mouth, but also the head that the visitors see moving. It is more common now for blood to be seen in various places on the body."[116] It was noted that by late August the Christ was most likely to move between two and three in the afternoon, and especially on Friday (presumably because Christ was thought to have died at 3 P.M. on a Friday, and the hour between two and three is when he would be in his agony).[117]

Tomás Echevarría gave in his book an inventory of the variety of visions recorded in the registers.[118]

> There are those who saw him covered with an anguished sweat; those who have surprised him with tears in the corner of his eyes; those who have followed the trickle of blood that ran from his pierced chest; those who contemplated the bloody foam that arose between his lips; those who noticed his eyes when, without a glimmer of consolation, human or divine, they turned heavenward; those who noticed as well that he looked gently at all the observers around him; those who received the divine blessing, given with his eyes, as when with the chalice one turns in the four directions; those who noticed the opening and shutting of the august mouth; who clearly saw the movement from one side to another of the head crowned with thorns; who caught the deep, resigned sigh of the sovereign chest; who even believed that they heard words issuing from his cherished lips.

These are the observations or visions of persons who are acquainted with death, who have seen persons die (a more frequent experience in

1919 than at present), and who through long experience in religious imagination have learned to apply their observations to the death of their Saviour on the cross. The visions at Limpias were possible precisely because this kind of spiritual exercise already existed among the devout. From the very beginning of printed books in the late fifteenth century, handbooks were available for Catholic laypersons that led them step by step and gesture by gesture through the divine agony. One writer on Limpias referred to these traditional exercises as "the contemplation of the torture and the moral and material suffering of Jesus, from his first shiver in Bethlehem to his last spasm of agony on Gólgotha, and very especially in the Holy Hour of Gethsemane." Such exercises involved "accompanying him feelingly and fervently in all of his anguish."[119] For persons used to following Christ's suffering, with the aid of an image or various images, in their imagination, seeing this very lifelike image at Limpias come to life, and die, must have been shattering.

What follows is the description of one such vision, on September 15, 1919. The first excerpt is taken from a letter by a priest from Valencia, Paulino Girbes, which was printed in the *Diario de Valencia* and *El Diario Montañés*.[120]

At five . . . I went back to the church, which was already almost full of people. In order to get closer to the altar, I went in through the sacristy. At that point the bishop of Huesca and a bishop from Ecuador had just arrived. A Passionist father entered the pulpit, recited the Station of the Sacrament and the Way of the Cross; then there was a sermon, preached by the second of the bishops. With what unction! With what fervor! He spoke of the manifestations of the most holy Christ; of the meaning of so many, repeated prodigies it is working in these so calamitous times, when there is so much evil, etc. etc., inciting his audience to a life of faith and to act according to the faith we profess.

When he finished, people recited the Five Wounds, singing some of the mission hymns led by the Passionist father, and while involved in this exercise, with the bishops kneeling in the presbytery, and eighteen priests (I among them) and many laypersons gathered around, we all saw the face of the most holy Christ look sadder, more pale, and more bruised than usual; we saw, and I myself saw as well, the mouth more open. And without completely lowering his eyes, he looked gently at the bishops and to the sacristy, grimacing like someone in his last agony. This lasted a good spell; and when I saw it I started to weep, without being able to contain my tears, and so did the others. The Passionist sang the Parce Domine and then the Credo in a loud voice, and as the vision continued, nothing but groans, sighs, and acts of contrition were heard.

Another priest, Valentín Incio García, from Asturias, was present and described in the shrine register what he saw:[121]

> But what was very noteworthy, and gave me great sorrow, was the very sad and very sweet way he looked at everyone. I could not control myself, I admit, and like me many others began to cry out and declare what we saw. Immediately, all the priests present, those who saw the prodigy and those who did not, together with the multitude that almost filled the church, began to sing the *Parce Domine, parce populo tuo*. And then out loud, with intense fervor, we all recited the Credo twice.

In this case, the visions are framed, as were the original visions and in the first years of the Limpias experience in general, by liturgy, by clergy speaking, and by clerical interpretation. They are capped by witnessing the faith. The meaning for the visions on September 15, 1919, was given before they occurred—the sad state of the world. Christ's eyes were seen to fix on the bishops and the sacristy—the preserve of the parish priest— just as in the original vision Christ was seen to look at the Capuchin preacher.

At Limpias in these visions, Christ's death—a disorder, an interruption in the normal round, an anti-order since he was crucified and rejected— was made the privy experience of believers under pastoral care. The visionaries were not, in the vast majority of the cases, those who, figuratively, made Christ suffer. They were not Socialists, Jews, Protestants, or anticlericals, with very few exceptions.[122] Rather they were the faithful who recited the creed and who wept and suffered along with the Christ they saw. They were sinners, of course, who recited the act of contrition, but they were believing sinners, who had chosen sides by the very act of going to Limpias. For these people, Christ's sacrifice was commemorated in every mass; but at Limpias, more even than in the processions of Holy Week or the new mission cross or the sacred dramas in churches like the descent from the cross, the much-rehearsed sacred scenario was for the seers and spectators vivified, brought to life.

1920. A Second Lourdes for the World?

By 1920 newspaper accounts had provoked interest in Limpias in Europe and overseas. In January letters of inquiry came from all over Spain, southern France, and the countries of Latin America. Letters requesting novenas, medals, pieces of cloth, or postcards, all touched to the image, also brought news of cures by means of these talismans. That month the shrine was visited by 40–50 persons on weekdays, and 80–100 on Saturdays and Sundays.[123] By February 930 persons in all had signed the vision registers.[124]

In April 1920, a member of the second Navarrese expedition wrote approvingly for a Pamplona newspaper that the "unhealthy and cramped" farmhouses where people had been put up in October 1919 had been replaced by "ample and airy hotels, with all the comforts of the modern world." The road into the shrine was being remade, courtesy of the count of Albox, the village's most distinguished summer resident. The church itself had been rearranged to make the most room possible for the pilgrim crowds.[125]

By June 15, 1920, a million medals of the Christ of Limpias had been distributed, and at Limpias there were no less than twenty-three souvenir stands. The correspondence sent to the shrine came first and foremost from Spain, where the main sources were Madrid, Barcelona, and Badajoz, the latter province the site of some well-publicized cures. Of foreign countries the first were Switzerland and Mexico, then the United States and Holland. Over the three months of March, April, and May, 1920, the shrine had received 1,087 letters, or about twelve per day. About a quarter of these letters were from outside of Spain. By then there were at least twenty-two books or pamphlets about Limpias in Spanish. The correspondence in Spanish was handled by the town secretary, that in Latin by the parish priest, and that in French, English, German, and Italian by Fernández Somellera.[126] The relatively high number of letters received in 1920 from countries in which Catholicism was a minority religion, and from Mexico with an actively anticlerical government, point to the apologetic role that Limpias was playing by this time in embattled Catholic constituencies worldwide.[127]

In 1920 the hinterland for formal pilgrimages continued to expand, although the total number was about the same as the previous year. Groups came from Barcelona, Madrid, León, and Valencia, as well as the closer provinces. Illustrious visitors included Cardenal Almaraz y Santos of Seville; the archbishop of Puebla (Mexico); the bishops of Calahorra (three times), Barcelona, Canarias, León, Orihuela, Palencia, Plasencia, Salamanca, Santander, Camagüey (Cuba), Guayaquil (Ecuador), Trujillo (Peru), and Toledo (Ohio); the auxiliary bishop of Valladolid; the Spanish royal family; the Catalan leader Francisco Macià; García Prieto; Princess Alice of England; and, again, Antonio Maura.[128] Alfonso XIII had copies of the image installed in his palace and in that of his children.[129]

FIGURE 12. A personalized souvenir postcard from Limpias, 1920. Photographer unknown.

FIGURE 13. A pilgrimage returns to the Limpias train station. Photograph by José Martínez.

In a formal ceremony on July 18, 1920, Bishop Sánchez de Castro named an official commission to evaluate the Limpias visions, "after consulting his illustrious Cabildo and persons who occupy preeminent positions in the church hierarchy in Spain and having received trustworthy official reports of the wishes of the Holy See." Sánchez de Castro was already ill at the time and died two months later, on September 19, 1920.[130]

The last official pilgrimages in 1920 were in October. One came from Barcelona, another from Madrid and southern Spain. This latter trip was part of a projected new pilgrimage circuit, in which groups were to go to Limpias on their way to or from Lourdes.[131] Package tours were available to individuals on a commercial basis. The Sociedad Española de Turismo advertised excursions including in one trip El Cerro de los Angeles near Madrid, Limpias, Lourdes, and El Pilar.[132] At the end of October there were small groups from Holland and the United States, both of which had been to Lourdes.[133]

In 1920 the project for Limpias as a Spanish Lourdes found other backers, foremost among them the Capuchin Juan de Guernica, who was then based in Bilbao. He was a devotional entrepreneur who had founded the devotion of Eucharistic Thursdays in 1907. In 1920 when it was made a canonical institute by Benedict XV, there were 500 centers in Spain. In February 1920, in *El Mensajero Seráfico*, he floated the idea of a National Eucharistic Basilica of Expiation at Limpias, drawing parallels with Lourdes and Montmartre. He suggested that parish priests who wished to do so could put out collection boxes for this purpose. In April, Guernica suggested that it should be the provincial government, La Diputación de Santander, that should build the basilica. But apparently he had sounded them out, and the diputación considered it too early to make a commitment, as the church had not spoken on the visions.[134]

Already by then Guernica had to combine his proposal with arguments against the skeptical Dominican Urbano. And in May his personal participation in the basilica project was short-circuited by his transfer to Argentina. By November 1920, when he completed his book in defense of Limpias, he had abandoned all hope for a basilica, of which he made no further mention.[135]

Others took up the idea. One was Manuel Cubí, "Capellán penitenciario de El Pilar, de San Sebastián." Cubí, according to *El Diario Montañés*, was the priest "most favored by the prodigious manifestations," which he saw August 18, 1919, September 30, 1919, and as he preached an extemporaneous three-hour sermon on Good Friday, 1920. By then he had purchased a summer home in Limpias, and was assisting the parish priest. The Santander newpaper considered him "the man sent by providence, the one we the devotees of the Christ of the Agony needed, and whom He has provided." With refined tastes in music and art, and independent means, Cubí had big plans for Limpias, which the newspaper did not feel free to reveal.[136]

He apparently decided that the problems facing the development of the shrine were not in Santander, but rather in Rome. So he went there in the Spring of 1920 to lobby and to spread the devotion, distributing pictures, medals, and books.[137]

Cubí turned up again at Limpias in late August 1920, accompanying Benedict XV's special nurse, a friar of the Order of St. John of God. They both witnessed the movement of the image, and said a mass for the health of the ailing pontiff. But we read no more of Cubí's projects, and no more about him as an apostle of Limpias.[138]

The project for a basilica fizzled out in 1920. For in spite of the international interest, the visits by bishops and royalty, and the formation of an official commission, the year marked a turning point for Limpias. There were fewer pilgrimages than in 1919; episcopal sentiment turned against the visions; and there were signs that the Vatican had its reservations.

1921. Recession

In January and February of 1921, observers from the diocesan commission were at Limpias.[139] The flow of bishops through the shrine continued, although fewer came from Spain. Those in 1921 included the archbishop of São Paolo, and the bishops of Ballarat and Córdoba (Argentina). From Spain came the new archbishop of Valladolid, Remigio Gandásegui, who had come before when the bishop of Segovia, and the bishops of Badajoz, Jaca, Málaga, Segorbe, and Osma (Mateo Múgica, later to be bishop of Vitoria when the Ezquioga visions took place). Generally speaking, the Spanish bishops who took interest in Limpias were among those especially interested in Lourdes (see Appendix Table 7).[140]

By July 1921 the floodtide of organized pilgrimages to Limpias had receded. By my count from newspaper reports, in 1919 there were 61 group pilgrimages of 100 or more persons, in 1920 46, and in 1921 only 20. In 1922 there were 6, in 1923 5, in 1924 3, in 1925 7, and in 1926 3. The drop was in part due to the recommendation against group pilgrimages by Luis Urbano, whose skeptical book in 1920 was well received by a majority of Spain's bishops.[141]

But the decline of pilgrimages may also have been due to a cooling of lay enthusiasm. Valladolid is a case in point. This Castilian town had been a center of Limpias devotion, encouraged first by its archbishop, Cos y Macho, who died in December 1919, and also by Pedro Segura, the auxiliary bishop. On December 14, 1919, the Asociación del Santísimo Cristo de la Agónia de Limpias was founded there, along with a monthly newsletter entitled *Manojito de Mirra*. In the first two years the association had had 2,000 masses said in which members received 100,000 communions.[142] Segura was made bishop of Coria in July 1920, but the new archbishop, Remigio Gandásegui y Gorrochategui, was just as dedicated to Limpias as his predecessors, if not more so. A Basque who summered in Liérganes, not far from Limpias, Gandásegui visited the shrine in 1921, and also in 1922 and 1923 when, at least publicly, no other Spanish bishops did. Yet in spite of his interest and the existence of the Limpias association, a Valladolid trip to Limpias was suspended on May 31, 1921, because not enough people signed up.[143] There were no further Valladolid pilgrimages, and only five non-Santander Spanish pilgrimages in the years 1922–1926.

The pilgrimages that did come in 1921, counting even small groups reported in the press, were more local than the two previous years. There were eighteen from the province of Santander, three from Vizcaya, two from Asturias, and one each from León, Galicia, Madrid, Barcelona, and Holland.[144]

The prolific novelist Rafael López de Haro set his novel, *Ante el Cristo de Limpias*, published in September 1921, in the spring of that same year. His descriptions of the shrine routine, the souvenir sellers, and veteran visionaries have a documentary ring to them.[145]

> The sexton ... worked full time touching pious objects to the wood of the cross. He used two long poles, one with a hook on it and another with pincers. Depending on whether it was a packet of photographs or engravings or a bunch of medals or rosaries, the sexton used the pole with pincers or the other one. Once the object was hooked or pinched, he went into the presbytery and, using the pole, made the packet or bundle hit the wood lightly. The owner of the objects observed the contact, and could see that some of the touches lasted longer than others; the sexton would know why.
>
> Lia [the heroine] recalled the episode of the divine Passion, when an impi-

FIGURES 14, 15, AND 16. The second Galician pilgrimage on its arrival in Santander, in Limpias, and the Limpias church in June 1921. Photographs by Guerra for *El Eco Franciscano.* Courtesy Biblioteca Nacional, Madrid.

ous hand lifted to the divine lips a sponge soaked in vinegar and gall tied to the end of a pole.

At the arrival of a train, new spectators watched the image avidly, many with binoculars "pointed at the crucifix in a way completely 'touristic.'"[146]

They went to see it without faith and without awe. For almost all those people, the Christ was a strange thing, and nothing more. Many were there in order to say later in Madrid that they had been there. The visit to Limpias is becoming obligatory for any self-respecting vacationer.

This kind of spectator was not new in 1921. From the very first months of the prodigies there were those, Fernández Somellera noted, who would drive up to the shrine, enter the church for five or ten minutes, and leave saying it was a fraud, a way to get people's money.[147]

Indeed, in keeping with the processional order sought outside the shrine, many observers were concerned about breaches of etiquette and reverence within the shrine. The *Imparcial* reporter present on June 12, 1919, described the church full of persons from 5 A.M. until 9 P.M.,[148]

some seated, others kneeling, many standing, in what are supposed to be the places where the magic vision is most likely, with or without binoculars; and there they spend hour on hour, entire days looking at the Sacred Image. When people believe they perceive some movement they cannot contain themselves and they shout, "Now! Now I see it!"

A Polish writer complained in print to the bishop of Santander about the use of binoculars at the shrine.[149]

Is it permissible in a church and for pious purposes to use binoculars? Would it not be better to save them for other, exclusively profane uses? They must be very far away from Christ, those who, in order to see him, need long-distance glasses.

Fernández Somellera in his diary wondered about the orthodoxy and seemliness of visions of the image moving at the very moment of the elevation of the host after its consecration, causing the officiating priest to break his concentration and look at the statue.[150] He also complained that "people forget where they are in spite of the grandeur of the prodigy, and start talking and discussing in loud voices as if they were in a living room. Occasionally loud arguments break out that are very little in keeping with a holy place."[151]

In contrast was the report of *El Debate* in June 1920 of the Madrid pilgrimage.[152]

> The distinctive feature of the Madrid pilgrimage was its sincere fervor. The devotion and respect of the pilgrims was edifying. It is praiseworthy that no binoculars or other devices were used to examine the face of the image. Last summer we were scandalized to see that truly in this respect abuses were committed.

According to the statistics kept in a new office next to the church, by July 1921 there had been a grand total of 250,000 pilgrims, 130,000 communions, and 26,000 masses in the two years and three months since March 30, 1919. An estimated 10 percent of the visitors had seen the image move, and 2,500 had signed the vision registers. Of the Dutch pilgrimage of May 19, 1921, 14 out of 26 observed the prodigy.[153]

Total visits to the shrine had declined considerably since 1919, but, despite the inevitable presence of tourists, those who did come were more likely to receive communion and, if there were seers, were more likely to sign the vision register.[154]

As the locus for the most recent manifestations of divine predilection for Spain, Limpias in its first years was a natural place for the nation's soldiers to turn for help. General Primo de Rivera, who from 1923 to 1930 was Spain's ruler, had visited Limpias on August 19, 1920.[155] Milans del Bosch, the military governor of Barcelona who caused the fall of the Romanones government in 1919, visited the shrine on August 19, 1921.[156] That year in July Spain suffered a humiliating defeat in the Rif region of North Africa. Two triduos—three-day prayer sessions—were held in Limpias in September and October to pray for the success of Spanish reinforcements and raise money for the soldiers. In early September 1921, soldiers were described as embarking for Morocco wearing the medal of the Christ of Limpias, and among the many published favors of the Christ of Limpias were those of soldiers in Morocco miraculously saved in battle, or who miraculously escaped from captivity.[157] There is a certain parallel here with the interest aroused in the French government and certain French generals by the patriotic religious visions of the Sacred Heart of Jesus during World War I in Loublande by Claire Ferchaud.[158]

By 1921, with the tide turned against Limpias within the Church hierarchy, there was little talk of a basilica. But since much of the laity supported the visions, the basilica idea was exploited by unauthorized enthusiasts or perhaps even confidence artists, who went door-to-door collecting money for construction. They were exposed and denounced, with a touch of lingering regret, by *El Diario Montañés.*[159]

1922–1926. Decline

Benedict XV died in January 1922. Because of visits in 1920 and 1921 by Spanish religious at the Vatican, and by the Nuncios Ragonesi and Tedeschini in 1919 and 1921, the advocates of Limpias believed, perhaps wishfully, that the pope had been sympathetic to their cause.

In any case, in 1922 the decline of the shrine continued. In March much urging in the press was needed to get people to sign up for the annual anniversary pilgrimage from Santander, which was finally canceled because of "bad weather."[160] A pilgrimage from Extremadura to Lourdes in late 1922 did *not* include Limpias, although it did go to Alba de Tormes, Madrid, and Loyola.[161] And in June 1922, even *El Diario Montañés* was forced to concede that the pilgrimages were "neither as large nor as frequent as in the first two years."[162]

In Santander the decline was felt by the merchants. Pilgrim expeditions had spent nights in the town in previous years. But the way they were allotted to lodgings by a fixed rotation at set prices provided no incentive for good treatment. One commentator saw this as a reason for the decline.[163]

From 1923 through 1926 organized devotion was either local or international. There were only eighteen pilgrimages of 100 persons or more, each of them extensively pumped in *El Diario Montañés*. Only two, one organized by the Franciscans in Galicia in 1924, and the other from the diocese of Tortosa after seeing Lourdes in 1926, came from Spain outside the diocese of Santander. Five of the thirteen Santander city pilgrimages were of children in catechism classes.

Foreign interest took up some of the slack. News of Limpias spread out like ripples in a pond, impelled by the publication of enthusiastic pamphlets in various languages. The most popular was by Ewald von Kleist, a German nobleman. By 1922 his booklet had had five editions in German, and others in France, Great Britain, the United States, and Holland. Other Limpias literature was published in Belgium, Austria, Hungary, Switzerland, and Rome.[164]

According to *El Diario Montañés*, letters of inquiry from foreign countries totaled 4,328 by February 1922, with Belgium, Switzerland, and Germany in the lead.[165] There were small pilgrimages from Switzerland and Czechoslovakia in 1922; Belgium and Czechoslovakia in 1923; Venezuela, Colombia, and Scotland in 1924; Austro-Hungary in 1925; and Austria, Hungary, Germany, and the United States in 1926.[166] The special appeal of Limpias to the Swiss, Austrians, Czechs, and Hungarians may have been due to the particular devotion to images of Christ in Alpine and

Central Europe.[167] But almost all came in tandem with trips to Lourdes. Paradoxically, Limpias, which aspired to be the Spanish Lourdes, continued as an international shrine because Lourdes was conveniently close.

In 1924, the opening line of a front-page article in *El Diario Montañés*, "Without a doubt, Faith has not disappeared from the globe," did not refer to Limpias, as well it might have in earlier years. It was the beginning of a description of a diocesan pilgrimage to Lourdes.[168] Limpias had started when pilgrimages to Lourdes had been stopped because of the war. By 1925 Spanish pilgrimages to Lourdes had surpassed their prewar level. The newspaper accounts of Limpias pilgrimages paled by comparison with the certified cures, the international cast of thousands, and the daily drama that Lourdes had to offer.

Statues of the Christ of Limpias are still sold all over Spain and in particular in Galicia, Asturias, and Levante. And they are exported to Latin America, Switzerland, Austria, Malta, and the United States (see Figure 17).[169] For the people who buy them, the Christ of Limpias is one

FIGURE 17. This bust of the Christ of Limpias in the giftshop of a Catholic hospital in New Haven, Connecticut, in January 1991 demonstrates the resilience of the devotion and its spread by means of Hispanic emigrants from the Caribbean. Photograph by Philippe Male.

more holy figure to pray to, like the Virgin of Montserrat, or St. Jude, part of the pantheon of divine helpers. And there is a regular trickle of visitors to the shrine, especially foreigners. But Limpias did not become the Spanish Lourdes.

BEHIND THE SCENES

Why it did not was due to many factors. One is the nature of the vision. By the early twentieth century visions of moving images seen by some, but not all, people were not enough of a miracle. And there were no cures that seemed irrefutable. Perhaps also the death of Sánchez de Castro left the shrine without its most enthusiastic patron. Lourdes itself was undoubtedly too close for comfort.

The intervention of certain church authorities who were not convinced by the phenomena also appears to have been important. One of these seems to have been the Nuncio Francesco Ragonesi. He tried unsuccessfully to persuade Pedro Segura, auxiliary bishop of Valladolid, not to be the first bishop to lead a pilgrimage to Limpias. Segura went anyway in November 1919, and on the trip his sister saw the Christ move.[170] Segura led a second expedition on May 13–14, 1920, and in late June greeted a Madrid pilgrimage to Limpias when it paused at the Valladolid railway station.[171] It is thought that one of the reasons for Segura's demotion to the see of Coria in July 1920 was Ragonesi's revenge.[172] It is also noteworthy that while a few bishops visited the shrine repeatedly, the cardinal primate of Spain in 1919, Victoriano Guisasola y Menéndez, pointedly refused to go there, although he was very close by.[173]

Luis Urbano wrote a critical article in a Dominican journal that he edited in August 1919[174] and subsequently expanded his arguments in the prestigious *Ciencia Tomista*, and finally issued his work in book form in March 1920. His title, *The prodigies of Limpias in the light of science and theology*, was a direct swipe at Tomás Echevarría, whose book had been issued with the title, *The prodigies at Limpias*. Urbano warned the opposition that his study had been stimulated by "indications from very high," by which one might infer the primate of Spain, the nuncio, or even the Holy Office.[175] Note was made in the Catholic press that Urbano's book was presented to Benedict XV by the general procurator of the Dominicans in late August 1920.[176] In his second edition, Urbano pointedly cited the case of Claire Ferchaud of Loublande, in which the bishop of Poitiers had opened a diocesan investigation, permitted the circulation of a new image of the Sacred Heart described by Ferchaud, and the archbishop of Bordeaux had reacted favorably. Nevertheless in 1918 the Holy Office took full control of evaluating the visions and in March 1920 condemned them unequivocally. As Urbano concluded this discussion, "The flames of enthusiasm died out. Mouths were closed. Faith shone in the fog of fanaticism. The beacon of this holy faith was Rome. And the question was concluded. Roma locuuta, causa finita. Let us learn from this."[177] By implication, Spanish bishops should beware of such enthusiasms, for the Holy Office might take the matter out of their hands. There was the inescapable possibility that Urbano was speaking for the Holy Office.

His arguments were repeated and expanded by the English Jesuit Herbert Thurston in *The Month* from August to December 1920[178] and by the American Jesuit Joseph Vaughan in *The Queen's Work* of January 1921.[179]

Urbano was in touch with his fellow Valencian Rubio Cercas, the one who had summarily dispatched the Gandía matter. Rubio Cercas was the most skeptical of clerical writers on Limpias. After a month's stay in which he witnessed forty visionaries, he ascribed all their visions to optical illusions, largely due to fluctuations in the electric current of the lights around the image, or reflections of the red curtain that formed a backdrop to the image, as seen in binoculars.[180]

The Urbano and Rubio Cercas works raised a storm of protest in newspapers, books, and a series of seven articles by the Jesuit Eustaquio Ugarte de Ercilla in the journal *Razón y Fe* from March 1921 to April 1922.[181] The literature for and against Limpias made use of terms and ideas formulated in the previous forty years by French and German psychologists, with additional speculation as to whether the image really moved; whether people really saw it move; whether there were natural phenomena of a similar nature; whether angels may have intervened in the brain to give the impression of movement; or whether, given some of the seers' fainting or shrieking spells, there might be something unhealthy or even diabolical involved. Urbano's cautions also referred to the danger of providing a cause for anti-Catholic mockery.

This polemic addressed two audiences at once—wider Catholic opinion and the Church officials deciding what to do about Limpias. Formally whatever decision to be made was in the hands of the bishop of Santander. He could choose to certify in some way some or all of the visions (that is, declare that they could not be ascribed to natural causes), decertify them, encourage or discourage pilgrimage, or do nothing either way. But the national and international repercussions of any decision were so great that it would have to be backed by the Vatican and the Spanish hierarchy.

Limpias had plenty of visitors from Rome. The Nuncio Ragonesi went sometime in 1919, and already by November of that year there were rumors that Rome had given secret orders to stop the pilgrimages, rumors denied by Sánchez de Castro.[182]

As we have seen, in August 1920 the Spanish nurse of Benedict XV, Celedonio Océn, went to Limpias with the pope's blessing for the parishioners and witnessed the image's movement.[183]

Several Roman visitors were high officials of the religious orders whose local houses were allied with Limpias, as it were. In October 1920, the visitor was a Spanish Franciscan, penitenciario of the Vatican, named José Alonso, who said that in Rome the events at Limpias were being followed closely.[184] The opening of the formal investigation by Sánchez de Castro in November 1920 was said to be with Vatican approval.

On April 18, 1921, the visitor was Silvio de San Bernardo, the superior general of the Passionists, accompanied by the procurator general and the prefect of Peru. "The good fathers confirmed what we had already heard, that everything related to the Christ of Limpias is followed with the greatest interest." They said that Aguirre Gutiérrez's articles were translated in Italian religious magazines, and some of them reprinted in newspapers. "Drawn by this information, this summer many Catholics will come from Rome, possibly among them high dignitaries of the Church, although they may come incognito."[185]

In late June or early July 1921 it was a high official of the Capuchin order, Joaquín María de Llevaneras, the former comisario apostólico of the order for Spain. Born as Joaquín María Vives y Tutó, he had founded the Capuchin seminary at Lecaroz, was the brother of the very influential Cardinal Vives y Tutó, and was allegedly close to Popes Leo XIII, Pius X, Benedict XV, and subsequently Pius XI. He returned to Limpias once more in October 1921.[186]

In September 1921 the Roman visitor was the new nuncio, Federico Tedeschini, a skilled socialite and diplomat, who told the Limpias people how lucky they were to have their town chosen for God's manifestations.[187]

All of this interest naturally raised the expectations of the Limpias boosters. In June 1921 Somellera recorded in his diary the rumor that Benedict XV had a print of the Christ of Limpias by his bedside.[188] It is clear that the many publications that came out in 1920 and 1921 were briefs aimed not only at Spain's bishops but also at the Vatican itself.[189]

It is difficult to know about backstage maneuvering among the papacy (first Benedict XV, then, in 1922, Pius XI), the Holy Office, the nuncios (first Ragonesi, then, in 1921, Tedeschini), the cardinals primate of Spain (first Guisasola, then, in 1920, Almaraz y Santos, and then, in 1922, Reig y Casanova) and the bishops of Santander (Sánchez de Castro in late 1920 was succeeded by Juan Plaza y García, who had been a frequent visitor to Limpias as bishop of Calahorra). Then there were the nation's bishops, some of whom were voting with their feet. Out of the approximately fifty active bishops of Spanish dioceses in 1919–1920, at least seven visited Limpias in 1919, nine in 1920, and four in 1921 (not counting repeat visits). Over the same three years the shrine was visited by nine Latin American bishops, most of them Spanish missionaries, members of religious orders, for whom Limpias was conveniently close to their port of embarkation in Santander. Of bishops of Spanish dioceses, only Gandásegui of Valladolid made public visits to Limpias from 1922 to 1925.[190]

Urbano, or the Church authorities behind him, appears to have convinced some of the bishops to back off from Limpias. When his cautionary study was printed in March 1920 he sent copies to all the bishops. In his second edition, in the fall of 1920, he reprinted excerpts of praise from sixteen of the bishops, and a list of twenty-four others who had congratulated and blessed him.[191] Those praising him included the Augustinians Zacarías Martínez, who had gone to Limpias in 1919, and López de Mendoza, who had granted indulgences to Navarrese pilgrims. Those congratulating him included Ragonesi, the cardinal archbishop of Seville (the primate of Spain from 1920–1922), the archbishops of Burgos and Tarragona (Vidal y Barraquer), and two outspoken supporters of the visions who had encouraged pilgrimages, Manuel González (Málaga) and Pedro Segura.

The only prominent and active church leader failing to respond was the primate of Spain, Cardinal Guisasola. He may be one of the persons whose letters Urbano did not cite "because of the intimate and confidential nature."[192]

Urbano did not sway all the bishops. Even some of those praising him (Alvarez y Miranda of León) or congratulating him (Sánchez de Castro himself, Barberá y Boada of Palencia) subsequently permitted pilgrimages from their dioceses, as did three bishops who did not respond (Plaza y García of Calahorra, Diego y García Alcolea of Salamanca, and Guillamet y Coma of Barcelona). But there was no public battery of episcopal approval for any of the books defending Limpias, whose authors were forced to turn to foreign bishops like that of Pinar del Río in Cuba, who saw the image move and said so in a pastoral letter.[193] It would appear that by late 1920 the balance had tipped against promotion of the shrine, and by the end of 1921 all but the most die-hard episcopal supporters had given up.

In any case the outcome of the formal investigation was the easy course—to do nothing at all. The visions were neither denied nor given credit. The image was not removed; nor were the indulgences it carried even before the visions increased or revoked. I have heard that this laissez-faire policy was only finally decided after a lapse of almost a decade, and that it was confirmed by the Holy Office.

The decision, or lack thereof, has left the shrine as it was, and the visions in a kind of limbo. It also left officially unchallenged the folk belief, first broached in *España Nueva* in 1919, that the image was rigged. This rather silly idea took hold among the most gullible of the incredulous, and is frequently heard today when the subject is brought up. I myself have heard it in Santander, Bilbao, and Tudanca, where I was told in 1969 that "what really happened was that someone was putting water so it came out the eyes."[194] Obviously, if the image had been rigged and therefore really did move or weep, then everyone would have seen, not just a minority of those present.

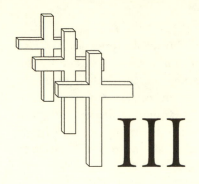

III

The Christ of Limpias:
The Organization of Meaning

PILGRIMS AND ORGANIZERS: THE ROLE OF SECULAR CLERGY, LAYWOMEN, MONTAÑESES, RELIGIOUS ORDERS, AND SOCIAL CATHOLICS

In spite of the Church's caution and ultimate neutrality, it cannot be denied that in the first years the diocese of Santander promoted the shrine.[1] The bishop's nephew was, after all, the chief designer of the pilgrimage model and the motor of ecclesiastical enthusiasm. In a matter of weeks after March 30, 1919, the Christ of Limpias had become a resource for the Catholics of northern Spain, and as time went on the zone drawing on the shrine expanded. The kinds of people and groups going to Limpias and their underlying agendas reveal who were the active Catholics around 1919–1920 and what were their preoccupations. In this respect we have already seen how the miracles were harnessed to the ongoing objective of creating a diocesan identity, symbolically subordinated to the recently designated diocesan patron. We have also seen how Limpias was rather quickly put to use like other shrines to provide cures and control bad weather.

About 60 percent of the group trips seem to have been arranged on the basis of towns, parishes, or broader church districts, without the central involvement of religious orders or lay Catholic groups. People signed up for these trips in their parish churches or with a school teacher. Not all priests wanted to give publicity to Limpias,[2] nor did all who went to Limpias like all that they saw; nevertheless, the involvement of secular clergy in organizing and attending the pilgrimages is striking. There were small expeditions of up to twenty-five persons made up almost entirely of clergy. The dozen or so church district pilgrimages from June to August 1919 generally included fifteen to twenty priests, at least one from each parish. More than forty of the eight hundred persons on the Reinosa pilgrimages of June 17, 1919, were secular clergy.[3] By the end of 1920 the majority of the parish clergy in the diocese of Santander had been to Limpias.[4]

Priests also attended the extra-diocesan pilgrimages, perhaps in even greater proportions. In 1919 72 out of the 475 members of the Galician pilgrimages were secular clergy; in 1921 it was 65 out of 591.[5]

Priests were not only organizers and pilgrims; they were seers as well. At Limpias one of the coadjutors saw the Christ move on April 20, 1919, and the parish priest of Muriedas, Gonzalo Lastra, had a vision on May 11.[6] He later became assistant priest at Limpias. On the Galician expeditions three out of seventy-two priests signed the vision register in 1919, and three out of sixty-five in 1921, a rate similar to that of the lay pilgrims.

Like priests, women also went to Limpias in disproportionate numbers. The Catholic ladies of Santander, eager to organize working women, brought them to Limpias several times. In all, about one in six pilgrimages was mainly organized by women, lay or religious, and most of these were exclusively for women. By contrast, only one in fifteen pilgrimages was made up only of men. In the mixed pilgrimages, which were the great majority, there is every evidence that women predominated.

By the same token, there were more female than male seers. Girls had the first visions, and women may have been less reticent than men in writing their visions and names in the register. In short, so much was there a female predominance at Limpias, that much of the enormous effort to publicize the visions and convince the Church hierarchy was aimed at demonstrating that men, too, were involved.

A month after the visions began, on May 5, 1919, a prominent Bilbaino, Adolfo Arenaza, publicly announced that he had been a seer in a letter to *La Gaceta del Norte*.[7] Avowedly inspired by his example, on the next day nine prominent men of Limpias, including the then mayor and the future mayor, also wrote certifying their own visions. In their letter they referred to Arenaza's declaration as "valiente."[8] I read this in two ways: that it was valiant for a Catholic to declare himself so publicly; but especially valiant for a man to hold himself up for ridicule by publicly announcing he had had visions.

A few men made a virtue out of necessity and argued that the female predominance at Limpias was due to women's religious superiority, and that men had to come around to the faith of women. This was a point typically made in parish missions. The following section of Dr. Santiago Estebanell's speech in Santander in June 1919 in which he justifies his belief in the miracles of the Christ of Limpias, was widely reprinted:[9]

> No, the people's feeling are not a weak force.
>
> All Catholics believed in the Immaculate Conception of Mary many centuries before it was proclaimed a dogma, just as today we believe in the mystery of her Assumption into heaven, even though it is not a dogma. And we believe it because the Church celebrates it, because the people feel it, live it, enjoy it, and believe it. We believe it as well, just as we also believe in the miracles of the Holy Christ of Limpias, because the town where the prodigy took place believes it, and because women believe it, and women are our mothers.
>
> Was it not a woman, what's more, a girl, a poor shepherdess named Bernadette, to whom the Holy Virgin of Lourdes appeared? And now generations of people are continually prostrate at the feet of the Virgin there.

By this logic there were two reasons to believe in Limpias. The first was that the townspeople of Limpias themselves believed. Here Estebanell draws an implicit analogy between *pueblo*/Limpias and *pueblo*/lay Catholics in general, perhaps even rural or uneducated lay Catholics, the ones who were leading the Church on matters of Marian dogma. His second reason to believe was that women believed in the visions. Here he does not refer only to the women of Limpias; that would be redundant. Rather, I think, he refers to the women of the city of Santander (a non-*pueblo*), who, I infer, were rather more enthusiastic about Limpias than the men. His reference to women as "our mothers," a standard rhetorical device in their defense, only underscores that his audience and reference group are assumed to be men. The men needed convincing on Limpias. To hit home the credibility of women, which in 1919 among the clergy clearly needed some defending, he points out the massive devotion at Lourdes, which rested on the credibility of a shepherdess.

A tilt to the religion of laypeople, particularly to that of laywomen, was an essential feature of Catholicism in the nineteenth and the twentieth centuries. At Limpias it was a divine image of a man that was moving and acting, but belief and declared belief in its movements were seen to be feminine behavior.

The Valencian writer Leopoldo Trenor ends the first chapter of his book *¿Qué Pasa en Limpias?* (1920) with a prayer to the heart in agony of the crucified Christ. He calls for a reformation of men, not just in morality, but also in feelings, so they will be more credulous, like children, and more sentimental, like women. In his prayer, as in Estebanell's speech, one sees how hard it was in 1920 to be a devout Catholic man.[10]

> Cure us of our pride and make us children, credulous and simple; it does not matter to us that the know-it-alls make fun of us.
>
> Cure us of our weakness and cowardice; make us strong in pain and selfless in sacrifices.
>
> Cure us of our sensuality; make us chaste and pure, sober and resigned.
>
> Cure the coolness of our intelligence; make us women in our faith and in our sentiments.
>
> Cure us of our weakness of heart and temper us with the fire of your love.
>
> Look at our piety in your Agony, Blessed Holy Christ!

Nowhere in the apologetic literature are statistics on attendance or visions at Limpias given by gender. The visions cited in the apologetic books are overwhelmingly those of men, and the unwary reader might be deceived into believing that the Limpias seers were mainly males. In the six books in which, in the text, many visionaries were named (from a low of 62 to a high of 113), I calculated the proportion of these seers who were priests or male religious, lay men, and lay women (see Appendix Table 8). That of named seers who were priests or religious ranged from a low of 13 percent to a high of 26 percent; that of laymen ranged from a low of 56 percent to a high of 71 percent; and that of laywomen from a low of 3 percent to a high of 30 percent.

It is instructive to compare these figures with those compiled from the Limpias vision registers in order to see how much women seers were played down and males overemphasized. Although the vision registers are lost or (more likely) under wraps, we do have two printed lists of most if not virtually all of the seers who signed the registers for almost four months. The two lists, allowing for misspellings and occasional omissions, confirm each other. During the months in question, twice as many laywomen as laymen were seers, and only 2 percent of the seers were priests. The apologetic books, which presented four times more laymen than laywomen as seers and 20 percent of the seers as priests, were grossly distorting the facts.

The process of elimination of women can be seen clearly in the book *Los frutos de una misión*, which largely consists of articles from *El Diario Montañés*. This book included a complete list of seers up to July 20, 1919. From July 21 on, the author, TMA, included only a selected list of persons with some kind of title, which eliminated virtually all the women (see Appendix Table 9).

The Claretian Tomás Echevarría was quite open about this tactic of "framing out" women from the accounts. He gave long lists of men, he said, because, "unjustly, of course," people might "give little or no credit to the seers of Limpias because they belonged only to the weaker sex, or the pious sex." He himself was not so sure about women as witnesses. "The woman is not ... the person most indicated for testimony about apparitions" unless, that is, men too are seeing them, especially "men who have their heads set firm on their shoulders." In that case, "both testimonies are strengthened."[11]

I have seen only three lists of members of pilgrimages: those of the first and second Galician expeditions, in 1919 and 1921, printed in *El Eco Franciscano*, and that of the first Catalan pilgrimage, in 1920. They confirm what the vision lists implied, that about twice as many laywomen as laymen went to Limpias (see Appendix Table 10).[12]

Numbers and percentages of pilgrims who had visions varied greatly from pilgrimage to pilgrimage. One may speculate why—the preparation of the pilgrims, their particular devotional agenda, their place of origin, the political and social moment, the particular mood at Limpias on the day of their trip, the orchestration and staging of their arrival, and the preaching they heard.

From a comparison of newspaper accounts with lists from the vision register, it appears that few of those who saw the Christ move actually wrote anything in the registers. For the second Galician pilgrimage, the reporter present estimated that two hundred persons (or one in three) saw the image come alive. Even allowing for exaggeration, there must have been far more than the twenty-five who "testified."[13] Those illiterate (more likely to be women) would be less likely to do so, given the trouble of finding an amanuensis. Some people were ashamed of their visions, or at least did not want them publicized in their home town.

The first Catalan expedition, organized through a semipolitical Catholic organization from the most conflictive point in Spain, was avowedly for the conversion and pacification of Barcelona, "theater of envy, hatred, and resentment." One male seer, who saw the Christ smile, at first thought that the smile was meant for him personally, but then reconsidered and decided it was intended for humankind as a whole, "perverse and ungrateful so it will cease to be so before the arm of divine justice falls upon it. I trust that the Christ of Limpias will speak, in the end, clearly, confirming this interpretation."[14]

The priest who organized the trip, Martín Eizaguirre, was pleased with the outcome.[15]

It was necessary that the Catalan pilgrims sally forth from the Limpias shrine emboldened, strengthened in their faith in order to take up the struggle and start a regeneration. Did I hope in vain? Ask each pilgrim; they will tell you that they returned converted into true apostles of the Crucified Christ, ready to preach and give testimony to Christ inside and outside of church, in the home and outside it in the streets and the squares.

In this light, the publication of the Catalan visions had a testimonial aspect. Some of the seers considered it a sacred duty and put considerable pressure on others to make their experience public.

Such pressure was necessary because for many persons the visions were an intimate, private affair. I have friends whose father saw the Christ move when attending a wedding at Limpias. He kept it to himself, revealing it to his family only on his deathbed. There can be no doubt of his sincerity, and there is little reason to doubt the sincerity of the declared seers.

Those seers who did bear witness on the Galician and Catalan expeditions seem to have been a fairly faithful sample of the pilgrims, except for members of religious orders. These signed the register at about four times the rate of secular priests or laypeople, for whom the proportion was five persons per one hundred (see Appendix Table 10).

That so many Galician seers were women was quickly pointed out by the skeptical Urbano.[16] His alacrity explains why in all the extensive Limpias literature there are so few sequences of unselected vision testimony; it was so overwhelmingly female that it would have damaged the shrine's case, perhaps irremediably. In his book Urbano briefly referred to the theological literature disparaging women visionaries and his brief words to the wise, referring to presumption, vanity, and curiosity as vices of seers and typically feminine traits were no doubt for his clerical contemporaries among his most convincing.[17] The threat that women enthusiasts represented to the visions can be gauged by how defensively the

Limpias proponents treated the gender issue, and how hard they worked to find suitable men as seers.

Another category of persons especially interested in Limpias, one that partially overlaps with the categories of priests and women, were Montañeses, or Cántabros as they are now known. For many Catholics from the province, the Christ of Limpias remained El Cristo de la Montaña. At least until 1926, the majority of the visitors to Limpias seem to have been from the province of Santander. And much of the publicity and organization of the pilgrimages can be ascribed to Montañés patriotism.

Their grand marshal, the unchallenged apostle of the shrine and its visions, was José María Aguirre Gutiérrez, a member of the staff of *El Diario Montañés*. Until he stopped writing in February 1926 he lost no opportunity to promote the shrine. At Santander's Catholic daily he was well-placed to do so; and he was the brother of Agapito Aguirre, parish priest at the church of San Francisco, and head of Santander's Franciscan Third Order, a movement closely allied to the shrine.[18]

Aguirre Gutiérrez was tireless in a task that became a personal crusade. He accompanied all the major pilgrimages to Limpias that came through Santander, over one hundred of them. He gave the pilgrimages extensive advance publicity, aiding in the recruitment of pilgrims and raising their morale and expectations. He goaded the city authorities to protect the honor of the devotion and the dignity of its devotees; and he excoriated the Limpias and Santander commercial establishments that took advantage of the pilgrims. Like many other proponents, he appears to have seen the image move himself, on May 11, 1919.[19]

His "slant" on Limpias was a combination of religious conviction and regional patriotism. Anybody or any information in favor of the devotion was grist for his mill, whatever their political or religious inclinations, and in his newspaper he reprinted stories on Limpias from all over Spain. His articles in turn were reprinted in much of Spain's Catholic press, with or without attribution, as well as in Latin America and Italy. I calculate that he wrote over 1,500 pieces on Limpias from 1919 to 1926. For the first years there was generally one article, and often two, in every issue.[20]

His information went out to Montañeses outside the province, and they helped organize the devotion elsewhere. Some of the most effective were priests and religious. The intense Valladolid enthusiasm can be traced in its origin to its Montañés cardinal, José María Cos y Macho, and the Santander Jesuit José de Arri, who masterminded the first Valladolid pilgrimage. De Arri was the brother of a member of the Santander city council, and his sister was a leader of the Marias del Sagrario in Santander.[21] At the start of the visions the Montañés Adolfo Pérez y Muñoz was bishop of Badajoz, which may explain part of the intense interest in Badajoz for the visions. In 1920 he was made bishop of Córdoba, and small groups of pilgrims began to arrive at Limpias with his greetings.[22] Similarly, Montañés Capuchins who headed houses in Salamanca and Madrid brought pilgrimages, and in Valencia the main defender of the visions was a Capuchin Terciary from Torrelavega.[23]

Lay Montañeses also propagated the devotion outside the province. The prolific María de Echarri, whose mother lived in Torrelavega, had several visions at the shrine, and wrote widely reprinted articles in *El Debate* and *El Universo* of Madrid, and *El Diario Regional* of Valladolid. She accompanied the Madrid Franciscan Venerable Third Order (VOT) pilgrimage of 1921, and afterwards gave a talk about Limpias at the Madrid Jesuit house. She was also a devotee of Our Lady of Lourdes, who she was sure had converted her brother on his deathbed.[24] In Cádiz and in Latin America the organized colonies of Montañeses, many with their own publications, were logical channels of influence. Enthusiasm passed easily through the mails and was caught personally on visits from Mexico and Cuba to the homeland.[25]

For instance, in Chiapas in early 1920, a man and his son from Santander distributed hundreds of pictures and novenas, commissioned paintings of the image, and paid for a new altar to the Christ of Limpias in a church in San Cristobal de las Casas. Subsequently pictures of the Christ of Limpias there were seen to be moving, and a number of cures were reported to the home shrine, and reprinted in *El Diario Montañés*. The man, "a veritable apostle of the faith," was supplied with Limpias material by his wife in Cantabria.[26]

We read of a number of these enthusiasts who adopted the Limpias cause, sometimes independent of other organizations. And not all who did so were Montañeses. There was the wealthy Peruvian, Clementina de la Peña, who took eight thousand pesetas of souvenirs to distribute in her homeland;[27] the Sister of Charity who came from Paris for souvenirs for various communities;[28] the priest in Barcelona, Martín Eizaguirre, who gave slide shows and organized two pilgrimages, abetted by a newspaper reporter;[29] and Pedro Segura and his family—his sister a visionary at Limpias, and his brother the head of Valladolid's Limpias sodality, which in turn spread the devotion elsewhere.[30]

When considering these cases one should not give undue weight to the role of individual organizers; that is the bias of Aguirre Gutiérrez, himself an arch-organizer. If he and others encountered a response, it was because for many Catholics in Spain and elsewhere, the events at Limpias spoke to their needs and their preoccupations and fed an appetite whetted by Lourdes. But it is interesting to see by what human connections the worldwide circuit was set up.

It is also instructive to note the degree of involvement of the different religious orders in the pilgrimages and visions. In keeping with their role in the dioceses as missionaries and special preachers, religious were invited to preach sermons, say masses, and lead Via-Crucis and Rosaries in many of the pilgrimages. Many of the pilgrimages, of course, they organized themselves for their sodalities. From accounts in newspapers and apologetic literature one can compile lists of the pilgrimages with which members of religious orders were involved, as well as lists of those religious who had visions. While such lists are inevitably incomplete, they do give an idea of which orders were hot, and which were cooler on Limpias (see Appendix Table 11).

First of all the Capuchins stand out, involved in at least thirty-four of the pilgrimages from 1919 to 1926, or about one in five. Limpias was "theirs" because the visions started in the presence of their missionaries, and because Limpias was close to their house in Montehano. The esteem with which Anselmo de Jalón and especially Agatángelo de San Miguel were held at Montehano before the visions meant that within the order the visions, including those of Agatángelo de San Miguel, were taken very seriously indeed. On April 22, 1919, all of the novices went to Limpias and sang anthems there. On May 13, 1919, early in the morning, a number of the Capuchins from Montehano went "to venerate the miraculous image." Over the next three years no less than eleven Capuchins (from houses including Montehano, Bilbao, León, Madrid, and Vigo), among them the superiors from Bilbao and Montehano, saw the image move and let it be known.[31] Several of these were subsequently chosen as preachers for pilgrimages to Limpias.

Soon after the first visions visitors came from the headquarters of the province in Castille to consider the case, and they considered it favorably.[32] We have seen that Joaquín María de Llevaneras made a special trip from Rome,[33] and in 1921 Luis Amigó y Ferrer, Spain's only Capuchin bishop (of Segorbe), visited the shrine.

Capuchins from Bilbao, Fuenterrabia, Madrid, Salamanca, León, and Oviedo organized pilgrimages of the Venerable Third Order, some of them in conjunction with the Franciscans, and there were at least three trips by Third Order brothers from Bilbao.

Through *El Mensajero Seráfico*, the Capuchins gave the best coverage of Limpias from any order's literature. Information on the shrine appeared in virtually every issue from July 1, 1919, until November 16, 1921, when the subject was rather abruptly dropped. Eight Capuchins published signed articles on Limpias in that magazine or elsewhere. The most assiduous polemicist was Andrés de Palazuelo, a teacher at Montehano when the first visions occurred, and subsequently the chronicler of the province of Castile. He wrote the first description of the mission in *El Diario Montañés* and two books. Juan de Guernica also promoted the shrine and, like Andrés de Palazuelo, stoutly defended the visions against Urbano.

Perhaps it is not irrelevant that Limpias was not the only Capuchin hot spot at this time. Padre Pio da Pietrelcina was said to experience the "transverberation" on August 5, 1918, and his stigmatization on September 20, 1918. The first newspaper article about him was published in Italy on May 9, 1919, but it is possible that word of his wounds could have spread before that within the order. The most influential article about him in Spain was published in *El Mensajero Seráfico* on May 1, 1920, by Laureano de las Muñecas (who subsequently organized a pilgrimage from León to Limpias).[34] Perhaps because of the coincidence with the Limpias phenomenon, attention to P. Pio from Santander was particularly intense. The image at Limpias coming alive in a Capuchin mission, and a Capuchin, like St. Francis, receiving the stigmata of Christ, was not entirely coincidental. Both are evidence of an intense and graphic interest in, and experiencing of, the passion of Christ as part of the devotional ethos of the order.

There is evidence of this in the hymns of the mission manual of 1915, several of which encourage the faithful to imagine, looking at the crucifix, Christ alive on the cross:[35]

Num. 5

Your eyes, where the light is born,
were eclipsed by my frivolity.
And yet they look at me with clemency
and move me to contrition!

Your unmoving lips, a sea of sweetness,
were made bitter by my tongue.
And yet they speak to me with words
that go right to my heart!

Num. 6   For the Procession of the New Cross

Incline,
tall cross, your still arms;
For pity's sake
deprive me not of your sweet embraces
and in tender bonds
tie me here.

Before the visions of Limpias, people already looked at the Christs of
Spain for a merciful glance, words of consolation, and a sweet embrace.
At Limpias the Christ was seen to do all this and more, while in Puglia
a Capuchin became a kind of living crucifix and dispensed spiritual help
to tens of thousands of pilgrims.

If one talks to Capuchins now, they are at pains to emphasize the
amount of schooling they had to undergo before taking solemn vows, and
the relative austerity of the order in regard to miracles and miraculous-
ness. The case of P. Pio, they point out, was, if anything, repressed within
the order. Their friars with long beards were highly learned and trained
religious professionals. They have been accused, they say, of promoting
credulity and superstitions at the Christ of Medinaceli, perhaps the most
popular shrine in Madrid. But all they do is leave the confessional open
for the public to use.

I myself, reading the almost private manuscript chronicle of Montehano, noted the reserve with which the local chronicler retold the Limpias events. He waited for three months to write a two-page account
because, he said, he wanted to do so with prudence, distance, and objec-
tivity. The anguish of the subsequent report, that of the death by drown-
ing of the chronicler himself, Modesto de Azpeitia, when he was attempt-
ing to save two novices, one of whom also perished, is moving evidence
of a community of commitment, love, and spirituality. That the Capuchins of 1919 were the allies of certain religious and political options cannot be doubted. But if one were to take the trouble to separate, ever so
gently, the religious from the political side of their enterprise, one would
find it was by far the greater part.

The Capuchin connection with Limpias was maintained through the
1960s, for Capuchins would go there on the first Friday of every month
to hear confessions.

The Franciscans, a brother order to the Capuchins, also stood out in
their enthusiasm for Limpias. As I understand it, the two orders had more
or less divided up the north of Spain into small districts of influence.

Capuchins dominated in Navarra, Santander, Eastern Guipúzcoa, Bilbao, and León, and Franciscans controlled the VOT in the zones around their convents—most of Guipúzcoa and Vizcaya, and most of Galicia. Relations between the orders were amicable, and Franciscans from Zarauz organized a series of joint VOT pilgrimages in 1920. We have seen that the three Galician pilgrimages run by the Franciscans (the first, in 1919, led by Martín Manterola, the provincial) were large and fervent. Three Franciscans wrote articles supporting Limpias; Fr. A Mariño was a particularly witty, skilled, and discerning opponent of Urbano. At least two Franciscans were seers at Limpias.[36] Franciscans maintained a special association with the passion of Christ since the time of St. Francis and because of their care of shrines in the Holy Land. The number of pilgrimages with Franciscan involvement is striking considering that there were no houses in the diocese of Santander.

The Passionist order, which had come to northern Spain from Italy in the late nineteenth century and had houses in Bilbao and Santander, participated in eleven pilgrimages, not surprisingly, given their devotional emphasis upon Christ's passion. At least one Passionist saw the image move.[37]

The Discalced Carmelites, who had houses in Oviedo, Santander, Soto, and Begoña, were involved in eleven expeditions, often with their sodalities, and Carmelite missionaries spread the devotion overseas.

Redemptorists active in missions in the diocese were asked to be preachers for eleven different pilgrimages from 1920 until 1926. But as far as I know they organized no pilgrimages of their own, and no Redemptorist declared having the vision.

The Santander Salesians brought school classes, and those of Bilbao brought their Archconfraternity of Maria Auxiliadora. Three members of the order founded in 1859 by St. John Bosco, so given to visions himself, saw the image move, including the Superior at Santander.[38]

Some male religious orders had come back into Spanish cities in the second half of the nineteenth century as helpers in urban pastoral care and as specialists in social services.[39] The old parish structure was inadequate in dealing with the heavy influx of immigrants from the countryside, and the state itself was unable to supply the basic needs of training the young and caring for the sick and elderly. The Carmelites in 1899 and the Passionists in 1902 had been called into Santander by Bishop Sánchez de Castro to deal specifically with the social problems and the threat of disbelief posed by the urban fishing community and the dockworkers, respectively. And the Redemptorists were in the process of founding a house in Santander in 1920.[40] Communities of religious such as these served as buffers, interfaces between the society that prided itself on order and the societies perceived as being in disorder. Indeed, it is in their role as front-line ideological warriors against working-class ideas, with houses placed in or on the edge of proletarian zones, that the attacks on religious in Barcelona in 1909 have been understood.[41] There was hostility to them in Santander as well. We read of people jeering and threatening a Carmelite father going to visit a sick parishioner in a working-class neighborhood in 1924.[42] In this perspective, the active participation of these orders in the Limpias events is logical. The movement of the Christ was a powerful argument against disbelief with an attraction that transcended class divisions.

The Claretians did not have a house in the diocese, but they performed a similar function in Bilbao, and in Valmaseda, near Limpias. These communities brought their sodalities twice. Members of the order were active promoters of Limpias through their national journal, *Iris de Paz*. Tomás Echevarría was a Claretian, and his kind of interest was in keeping with the apologetic and combative style of the order's founder, Antonio María Claret, whose biography he had written.

Although they had a school at Limpias, the Vincentians were not central to the pilgrimages. They seem to have kept a respectful distance from the preserve of the parish priest. However, they did participate in several events, and they assisted the curate with technical problems. In addition to Antonio López, the pre-seer, a superior of a Vincentian house in Alcoriza (Teruel) saw the image move. The first prelate to say mass at the altar of the Christ after the start of the visions was the Vincentian archbishop of Lima, Emilio Lissón. The sister order, The Sisters of Charity, accompanied at least four pilgrimages. A reporter remarked that there were nearly always some of them at the shrine.

Dominicans were somewhat cooler to the phenomenon. While members of the order accompanied six pilgrimages, they organized only one, from Oviedo. There was no official Dominican presence at the opening of the diocesan inquiry. Of all the orders in the diocese, only they and the Vincentians were absent.[43] It could be that Limpias, like Bien-Aparecida, was seen as a threat to the venerable Marian shrines kept by Dominicans at Las Caldas and Montesclaros. But Dominican coolness may be more related to the order's tradition of science and learning, and the application of Thomas Aquinas's hard rules about miracles. Within the conservative contours of the early twentieth-century Church, the Dominicans were relatively progressive, as was their journal, *Ciencia Tomista*. It is not surprising to find them taking the lead in questioning Limpias.

Furthermore, a measure of ancient rivalry with the Franciscan orders cannot be ruled out. It appears this rivalry was quite alive in 1919. Students at Montehano would *patear*, stamp their feet beneath their desks in disapproval, when their teacher, Agapito de Sobradillo, introduced certain Thomistic notions he had learned from the Dominicans in Fribourg. He told them how the Dominicans there had looked down upon the Capuchins.[44]

Nevertheless, some Dominicans were deeply affected by Limpias. Nolasco de Medio (1856–1928) in Oviedo wrote a substantial rebuttal of his fellow Luis Urbano. On his deathbed his last act was to kiss an image of the Christ of Limpias.[45]

One senses a certain reserve toward Limpias in some Jesuits as well. In 1919 the Society of Jesus was preeminent among the orders in Spain in scholarship, wealth, and general prestige, with houses in all of Spain's major cities. No major new devotion in Restoration Spain could get very far without at least tacit approval from the Jesuits.[46] In the diocese of Santander they were very active in rural missions, and operated the Pontifical Seminary in Comillas.

We have seen that as early as mid-May 1919 Antonio María Flores, a Jesuit based in Santander, gave the visions a critical boost by declaring that "it would be imprudent to deny them," and that in July 1919 the Jesuit devotional magazine from Bilbao, *El Mensajero del Corazón de Jesús* took the judgment one step further, saying "it was not rash to believe in them." At least one Jesuit, P. Nogara of the Bilbao house, saw the image move.[47]

Jesuits were the second order, after the Capuchins, in participation in pilgrimages to Limpias. About one in six pilgrimages had something to do with them. A number of Jesuit superiors and teachers visited Limpias from Deusto, Orduña, Oña, and Comillas, and so, in July 1920, did Andrés Machado, the Jesuit bishop of Guayaquil, Ecuador.[48] In Santander P. Jambrina founded a Brotherhood to the Christ in Agony in 1919, and many prominent men joined.

Nevertheless I think I detect a certain distancing. In the case of the Santander Brotherhood, its purpose, like that of Valladolid, does not seem to have been to promote devotion to Limpias as much as to capitalize on it. The subjects of the lectures or sermons at its meetings, which were held in Santander, were more general devotional or socio-political issues, and as far as I know it did not organize trips to the shrine. It also seems to me that those Jesuits who controlled the great Marian congregations—The Apostolate of Prayer, the Daughters of Mary, the Luises, the Brotherhood of San Estanislaos—used Limpias as a rallying point less than they might have. In the first six years I know of only seven trips by these congregations. Was there a reticence communicated by or through the Jesuit order? Although three Jesuits wrote in support of Limpias, in particular Eustaquio Ugarte de Ercilla in *Razón y Fe*, the Jesuits Gründer, Vaughan, and Thurston wrote key articles of caution.[49]

It is also possible that the Christ of Limpias was seen as distracting attention from the Jesuit-controlled Sacred Heart of Jesus. Some of the literature about the Christ of Limpias from more liberal sources contrasted its Hispanic austerity to "devotions . . . which speak to things agreeable to our present psychology—which is, more than feminine, effeminate, and effeminate in part because of these saccharine devotions."[50] The novelist López de Haro was even more explicit.[51]

> The frivolous, theatrical devotions, in gaudy pastels, are going to disappear. The syrupy images are going to be withdrawn, these Christs with a face like a tenor in an operetta that issue forth on floats with rubber tires that have a hidden set of batteries; and in their place the lovely, proud, and tragic images of the crucified Jesus will come back on the shoulders of the faithful.

The Sacred Heart of Jesus by 1920 was a symbol of conservative Catholicism, and it is not surprising that these writers took advantage of the movements at Limpias to take a poke at an image they resented because of what it stood for. What role, if any, this symbolic opposition might have played on the part of the Spanish Jesuits is less clear. In any case, prominent defenders of Limpias like Tomás Echevarría and Leopoldo Trenor denied any conflict between Limpias and the Sacred Heart, and indeed, explicitly linked them. The Capuchins at Montehano were just as enthusiastic as the Jesuits in promoting the Sacred Heart, and certainly would have seen no conflict between the devotions. For one seer, Consuelo Salvat y Deu of Barcelona, the question was resolved mystically:[52]

> What was my surprise when I raised my eyes and saw, not the Holy Christ on the Cross, but a splendid, resplendent, brilliant white image that I recognized as the Sacred Heart of Jesus, which I contemplated for several minutes after which it disappeared and I once more saw the Holy Christ on the Cross.

Nuns were less prominently involved in pilgrimages than male religious, or at least the newspapers took less notice of them. Mention of nuns is made in relation to eleven pilgrimages. The Sisters of the Poor regularly brought their charges from the old age home in Santander. A number of orders brought their students on school excursions, or alumnae reunions; and a new order, the Damas Catequistas, brought a group of male workers. As with male religious, many nuns visited Limpias in small groups, not necessarily as part of pilgrimages, sometimes as with the Redemptorist Oblates in 1919, with visiting superiors of the order. The Daughters of the Cross operated a girl's school in Limpias, and on April 20, 1919, several of them reportedly saw the image move.

In addition to the third orders and sodalities of religious orders, two lay associations dedicated to the Eucharist and the presence of Christ in churches held annual pilgrimages for several years to Limpias from across the north. The Marías del Sagrario was founded in 1910 by Manuel González for women to revere the sacrament and take care of churches. González himself, as bishop of Málaga, visited Limpias in September 1919 and August 1920.[53] Groups from his organization, much given to pious excursions in general, made five trips in the years 1919–1923.

The Nocturnal Adoration Society in Spain was founded in Madrid in 1877 in the Capuchin church of San Antonio. Some of the most dramatic visions at Limpias occurred to its members in their all-night vigils there. Groups went to Limpias from Santander, the Basque country, Navarra, Palencia, and Madrid.

Finally, there were group trips from the organizations of Social Catholicism, especially from Santander. An effort was made to have this miraculous, agonizing image fortify the resolve of the small minorities of Spain's working people who belonged to Catholic unions, through interclass pilgrimages. It is in the descriptions of these pilgrimages that, reading between the lines, one surprises the general perception of class warfare. For instance, in the description of the first Santander pilgrimage, barely a month after the first movements on March 30, 1919, it was pointed out that the emblems worn by the pilgrims "brought together persons from all social classes."[54]

Interclass mingling was clearly unusual, as was explicit acknowledgment by workers of fealty to Christ. The use of Limpias in this latter respect was in line with the recent fashion of "enthroning" images of the Sacred Heart of Jesus in the workplace. The reporter for *El Diario Montañés*, not long before the miracles, had "witnessed the edifying spectacle of workers proclaiming the Social Reign of Jesus Christ" by "enthroning the Sacred Heart of Jesus in their workshops" at the ironworks of Ramales, a town near Limpias. On June 8, 1919, "with a fervor equal to that shown at the feet of the Sacred Heart that looks over their work from its throne, we saw the people of Ramales . . . prostrate at the feet of the Christ of Agony."[55]

A week earlier there had been a pilgrimage of two hundred Santander dressmakers. As in other parts of Spain, they were organized by upper-class ladies into the Sindicato Católico de la Inmaculada. Fernández Somellera wrote in his diary that "they came for a day of fun in the country. They entered the church for a few token devotional acts, and many of them experienced the prodigy." Fourteen fainted, one of them asking "for forgiveness in a loud voice, offering to be better in the future."[56]

Shortly afterward it was the turn of the working women from the center run by the Damas Catequistas in Santander. At Limpias, the restaurant owners,[57]

> wanted to give preferential treatment to the Lady Catechists and Instructors, but although they thanked them for the offer, they gracefully declined so as not to distinguish themselves in any way from their workers and students. What a beautiful spectacle of Christian democracy! Some of them, I happen to know, have eaten at the table of the King and Queen.

The pilgrimage of 250 miners from the Allier coalfield in Asturias included a parade in Santander on September 28, 1919. "Only in the shadow of the Cross," the newspaper commented, "can the solution to the problem that most bothers our statesmen be found." At Limpias, "owners and workers, obeying their parish priests, listened to the voice of He who also was a worker in Nazareth, in his divine command, 'Love one another.'"[58]

For a great pilgrimage of female tobacco workers, fish-sellers, and dressmakers on July 11, 1920, there were preparatory sessions in a Santander church to learn the pilgrimage hymns, led by society dames. The reporter accompanying the expedition of 660 workers saw on the train "distinguished ladies . . . affectionately conversing with the humble pilgrims as if they were their lifelong friends," and later reciting the Rosary together. After the day's mass, lunch, and the Stations of the Cross, led by a Passionist father, the pilgrims "gave a moving demonstration of their faith, asking that there be placed in contact with the venerable image a variety of photographs, medals, rosaries, pieces of cloth, and other religious objects that they acquired for this pious purpose." The reporter confessed, however, that "not a few obstinately resisted believing the evidence of the prodigies attributed to the image."[59]

The period of 1919–1921 was the apogee of the Catholic women workers' unions. In 1921 there were estimates of 20,000 members nationwide, a modest total.[60] The national spokeswoman and organizer, María de Echarri, herself twice saw the Christ of Limpias's eyes move. She and her union had helped achieve, at least on paper, eight hour days for women and brought to public notice the exploitation of women workers.

OPPOSITION AND RIDICULE

Not all women workers were Catholic, however, and most industrial workers were not. Limpias was a testimony of faith precisely because there were so many people who did not believe in God. And of course, those people did not believe in Limpias. It was because he did not want to expose Catholicism to ridicule that P. Urbano urged caution on Limpias's defenders. "They are reading us with a hundred eyes, ready to criticize us with a hundred tongues. And we should not complain about this, because it will serve to increase our care, sharpen our judgment, and weigh our reasoning."[61]

Within Spain and in Urbano's Valencia, opposition to Limpias increased in proportion to its popularity among Catholics. The *Mercantil Valenciano* attacked Limpias, and was answered by a Capuchin from Cantabria in the *Diario de Valencia*. In August 1919 an article in the Madrid newspaper *La Humanidad* by Julián Fernández Piñero agreed that for the injustices of the world and for the First World War Christ ought to be weeping, but not the image of Limpias, which he saw as the domain of those who work and profit from wars and exploitation. The second half of his article eloquently attacks the social base for the Limpias events, as seen from the Left.[62]

> Now you ask me, my skeptical friend, did the Christ of Limpias really weep?
>
> Consider this; Christ, in these four years of tragedy and crime that the war has lasted, has had many reasons for weeping, and I believe that tears of blood have flowed from his eyes.
>
> I believe that Christ will weep and has wept; but not the sculptured Christ of Limpias, displayed on an altar with the flames of candles, the sparkles of jewels and the smoke of incense.
>
> The Christ who has wept and who weeps is the one who preached an ineffable human brotherhood and filled his heart with the love of everyone and suffered the sorrow and the injustice and the persecution of the powerful.

This Christ wept tears of blood when on the fields of battle the imperialist mania destroyed the crops and the shrapnel rendered the furrows sterile, and children were immolated in their schools and women in their homes, and thousands of men were cut down by anger, and cities were blown down by red hurricanes of fire.

This Christ wept when he followed the armies to the killings and saw men pursue each other like animals in the bowels of the earth and in the green abyss of the waters and in the blue serenity of the skies.

This Christ still weeps in the homes of the women widows and the children orphans, in the cells of the offenders and in the wards of hospitals and in the patios of asylums and in the houses of the workers without bread and in the shacks of the farmworkers without hope.

The Christ that weeps is the one who braved the dangers of the sea in a boat of humble fishermen; but it cannot be this Christ of Limpias, for whom the shipowners of the North, who got rich by risking their crews on smuggling expeditions, compete to offer banknotes as alms.

The Christ whose eyes weep continually for the pain of humans is the one whose left hand never knew what his right hand was giving; the one who was caressed by the hands of a woman sinner; the one who was the friend of Mary the humble and Martha the competent; the one who cured with his hands the wounds of lepers and walked barefoot in the dust of all the roads of mankind.

But it cannot be this Christ of Limpias, to whom the councils of Catholic ladies organize pilgrimages in motorcars, handing out their alms with great fanfare, proclaiming in newspapers their works of charity, and protecting, humiliatingly, the woman who is adulterous.

The Christ who weeps is not the one carved and painted in the church in a village in Santander.

The one who truly sheds tears of blood is the Christ of fraternity and justice who is still nailed to the cross of all human inequalities.

And above all, the one who weeps is the Christ, spiritual, suffering, and true, whom all of us carry crucified in our hearts.

The Christ of our feelings that find no response; of our sorrows that no one consoles; of our thirst for love, for liberty, and for beauty that goes unquenched.

And the truest, most ardent, and bloodiest tears are those that were wept by this good and just redeemer that all of us would like to be, but who is held crucified in our soul by the cruelties of life and the injustice of mankind.

Some of this opposition, in less refined form, could be heard in Santander as well. Three months after the Limpias visions had started, for many people they were a laughing matter. On July 2, 1919, under the headline "Intolerable!" we read in *El Diario Montañés* the following note:[63]

> Several respectable persons have come to us to protest, with just indignation, about certain songs which involve in a way more than disrespectful the venerated name of the Most Holy Christ of the Agony. These songs, which at once offend deeply the religious feelings of the people and give reason to doubt the people's good breeding, can be heard these days, especially after a night on the town or at fiestas. It has come to the point where in one traveling booth, set up in some of these fiestas, skits are acted out that constitute a veritable ridiculing of religion. It is further reported to us these profanatory scenes have been observed impassively by agents of authority. And that is intolerable.
>
> As soon as we heard about these songs and acts, we informed the civil governor, who, as we imagined, was properly outraged, and took good note of our protest, which was the first he had heard. He promised he would punish vigorously anyone, whoever it may be, who committed the scandalous acts reported. To this end, Sr. Páramo today will give the necessary orders to the agents under his jurisdiction, as he is disposed to require from them the most rigorous obedience to his orders to avoid the recurrence of these intolerable acts.

Aguirre goes on to ask for the participation of the mayor and the citizenry and promises to denounce any recurrence. But, as with the mission hymns, once it is incorporated into rhyme and song, it is hard for an idea to die.

On September 10, 1919, 350 pilgrims from Oviedo, organized by Carmelite fathers, and in particular by the brother of the Capuchin missionary P. Anselmo de Jalón, made their way in procession from the Santander railway station to the Carmelite church through the center of town. But it was not a happy occasion, for instead of carrying their own luggage, they unwisely entrusted it to the enemy. Read the outraged reports of *El Diario Montañés.*[64]

INTOLERABLE

(for government authorities)

As we said before, the Asturian pilgrimage went from the railway station to the Carmelite church by way of the Avenida de Alfonso XIII and Paseo de Pereda.

The passing of the pilgrims was watched respectfully by the many persons in this busy area at that time, and the men took off their hats when they saw the banner.

But this engaging scene, which revealed not only the religious sentiment of our town but also its awareness of the duties of hospitality, almost went unnoticed, spoiled by the truly gross brazenness of a group of sooty women of the kind who load and unload coal on the docks. They formed a kind of impertinent escort for the ladies who came in the pilgrimage, encircling them for the better part of their trip—from their start on the Avenida de Alfonso XIII all the way up to the Calle de Lope Vega—with the most provocative of attitudes.

When the pilgrim ladies sang, those disgraceful women tried to drown out their voices by countering the words of the hymns with scurrilous songs alluding to the cause of these pilgrimages.

And it did not suffice that in order to avoid these filthy songs the pilgrim ladies fell silent, for then on male and female pilgrims alike, and the religious Fathers as well, these wretches showered the grossest phrases of their crude repertoire.

When the lieutenant wanted to intervene, he saw that it would be counterproductive, because the women who so impertinently were besieging the pilgrims were also carrying some of their baggage in exchange for a tip.

It may be that one of the scurrilous songs the women coal-loaders sang is one still repeated in Santander and Bilbao in the 1980s when the subject of the Christ of Limpias is raised.[65]

El Santo Cristo de Limpias	The Holy Christ of Limpias
dicen que suda, que suda;	they say is sweating;
lo que sudan son los cuartos	what are really sweating
en el bolsillo del cura.	are the coins in the priest's pockets
Eso es verdad	This is true
porque lo he visto yo.	because I saw it myself.

That this level of working-class bumptiousness existed in Santander in 1919 is proof that the movements of the Christ of Limpias occurred in a troubled environment, were immediately read as speaking to that trouble, and from the very start for many people on both sides the pilgrimage was a "testimony of faith" like the political pilgrimages against liberalism, the enthroning of Sacred Hearts in houses, towns, and workplaces, and, particularly, the National Enthronement of the Sacred Heart, read by Alfonso XIII at the dedication of the great monument outside Madrid on May 15, 1919.[66]

What Did the Christ of Limpias Mean to Convey?

It was an open question just what the image meant by its motion, just how it was speaking to time and place. The ambiguity of the mute sign, the gesture without words, has certain advantages, in that each observer can read into it *ad libitum* general or private meanings, or both. Throughout the first years there was in every book and every major article about Limpias speculation as to the divine intent.

One of the very first analyses of the possible meanings of the events was published in Bishop Sánchez de Castro's semiofficial weekly, *Páginas Dominicales*, on April 27, 1919. It laid out possible divine intentions:[67]

the announcement of unknown misfortunes
calls to receive divine grace
the conversion of sinners
rewards for one or another virtue

"All speculation," it said, "was fruitless," aside from what the weekly had indicated at the very start, "that the prodigy at Limpias is an extraordinary display of God's mercy, and one more proof of the truth of the Catholic faith."

Most of the subsequent interpretations of the Limpias phenomena fell within the options mentioned above, placing more or less emphasis on one or another category, and specifying what virtues were being rewarded, or which sinners were being called to grace and conversion, from what particular kind of sin.

For instance, Agatángelo de San Miguel declared three months after the first vision that his first fear was that the activation of the image "was the prelude to a great chastisement for the abomination of Mankind like the one that occurred a few years ago in Martinique, which was also announced through the mouth of an image."[68] Perhaps he was aware of the collections of prophecies of divine chastisements published by L'Abbé Curicque, or those compiled by his fellow Capuchin in France, Marie Antoine Clergue, with titles like *The Great Pope and the Great King*.[69] In any case his fear was predictable, since for hundreds of years the activation of images, especially in imitation of the Passion, was considered a bad sign.

By the time Agatángelo de San Miguel made this statement, he knew about the vision of a girl who had heard the Christ say, "Parce Domine, parce populo tuo" (Forgive them, Lord, forgive your people). Word of this message, which was not initially reported in the press, circulated among pilgrims, and confirmed the idea that Spain or the world was ripe for a chastisement.[70] But it also encouraged the notion that the Christ was moving precisely to avoid it, by interceding with God.

Similarly, P. Agatángelo was persuaded that "all proceeds from the mercy of God, which is so infinite that it has not yet been exhausted in spite of witnessing so much evil, and which desires at all cost to make the world recover from its blindness." That is, he believed that the Christ's activation, while still a warning, was meant as a sign that there was still time to repent and take remedial measures, avoiding the great chastisement. He thus experienced the vision at Limpias like one of his own missions writ large, with the Christ acting as the missionary who warns of punishment and holds out the possibility of redemption. The congregation of the Christ of Limpias was not a village, but all of Spain, or all of the world.

That the Christ was moving in response to the troubles of Spain or the West in general was doubted by none of the interpreters. For the *El Diario Montañés*, the visions occurred "in these times of frigid indifference and a shocking corruption, of shameless cynicism and gross insults to Religion."[71] For a Madrid priest, the movements of the Holy Crucifix attracted Spain's attention "in this supreme hour of social hatred, raw sensuality, and mad Bolshevik avarice."[72]

The noblewoman Soledad Ruíz de Pombo similarly linked immorality and politics. Writing in *El Debate*, she held that the movements of the Christ were in response to the sinful dance of the nonbelievers, in spite of the tragic backdrop of the First World War.[73]

> A vision forms in the back of the mind, which dares to ask the cause of so much anguish. . . . The world appears all soiled with mud and blood; on the bloody soil are dancing endlessly impious men and immoral women. In this horrible dance, the beat is marked by hatred, as the seven deadly sins sing their songs. And each round in the dance marks a crease of horror in the agonizing face of Jesus. In the meantime, in the little church of Limpias resounds a murmur of prayers, in response to a voice that speaks of penance.
>
> And the world goes on and on in its mad race. The warning is in vain, so many times repeated, that seeks to put some shame in women. Respect for themselves, guarding the treasure of their natural beauty, and being careful of their decorum. Respect for others by not putting temptation in their way and removing the stones of scandal from their path. Deaf and blind to preaching and prodigies, "They have eyes and do not see, ears and do not hear." And like

them the men, also insensible to all that is not egotism, pride, and sensuality. And the tide rises! And the war, latent, is mining, always more deeply, the foundations laid by harmony and order. This is, without a doubt, why the Christ of Limpias has renewed its agony.

Writing in the same newspaper in 1921 Juan Bautista Ayerbe summed up the reasons for the Christ's movements as "these times of struggle, apostasy, immorality, and social disorder."[74]

Tomás Echevarría in his book published in October 1919 was more specific. He interpreted the movement of the Christ's eyes as related to "the winds of the syndicalist hurricane" that in March 1919 were "blowing in all the corners of the nation" and "sought supreme concessions from the monarchical regime." By implication, the Christ was moving to defend the monarchy of Alfonso XIII.[75]

If the causes of the Christ's movements were the sinful state of the world and its political corollaries, just what effect the divine intended from Limpias was less clear. There were those like Agatángelo de San Miguel who hoped it would cause people to repent and thus avoid a catastrophe. The Madrid priest Federico Santamaría Peña, wrote that "Limpias has come to be the pickax that demolishes the works of Renan, Strauss, Voltaire, and the other rationalists who over time with the help of the Jews have caused so much harm in so many souls."[76] As we have seen, there were intermittent reports of the fulminating conversion of scoffers, sinners, Socialists, or the odd Protestant at Limpias.[77] But any hopes that Limpias might lead to the mass conversion of the unfaithful were quickly seen to be unrealistic, and generally observers held out more modest goals for the divine intent.

For instance, a Santander preacher implied that the purpose of the activations was to establish a powerful shrine, whose effects spread mysteriously, not unlike radio waves. "Go to Limpias, where my Son has set up a source of the supernatural, a luminous volcano with supernatural rays, a nucleus of mysterious spiritual forces, a bower of Catholic faith."[78]

It was this last idea, a bower of Catholic faith, that others emphasized. The pilgrimage of Limpias, said *La Atalaya* at the start of the visions, "can be edifying for those who have not yet lost their faith."[79] Rather than convert sinful dancers or syndicalists, or promote the harmonic unity of all mankind, the movements were a resource in the ongoing struggle. They were intended to strengthen, encourage, and reward the faithful. Indeed, wrote "A Spanish believer in Limpias" in *El Debate*, that is why the movements occurred in Spain. "Spain can boast of having been once more chosen by God for the demonstrations of his glory and his love.

Spain as a nation is perhaps unique in not having been roped to the yoke of universal apostasy."[80] Christ moved at Limpias not to convert those who had committed apostasy in Spain, but rather as a reward because so many Spaniards had not done so. "Christ wants," wrote Ayerbe, "no doubt, to draw us to Cantabria to remind us of his sorrowful Passion and death, to be adored, to renew the faith, and to grant his pardon and grace."[81]

Similarly, to the questions "Why are you weeping?" and "What do they mean, my God, these glances that turn toward the believers and make the unbelievers tremble?" Soledad Ruíz de Pombo suggested, "Do these glances mark in the air the sign of the Redeemer, and thus bless the Catholic flock, represented by the faithful gathered there?"[82] As she suggested, the idea that Christ was appearing to and for Catholics was reinforced by the reports that the image had looked especially at a preacher or bishops present.

Perhaps the most exalted version of this idea came from the Santander seminary professor, Valentín de la Torre, who had been a diocesan observer at the shrine in the summer of 1919. In his long exposition about Limpias inaugurating the seminary term on October 4, 1919, he drew an analogy between the reconquest of Spain from the Moors, led by King Pelayo from Asturias, and the role of Limpias in the twentieth century.[83]

> Today a new wave, not of scimitars [as with the Moors] but no less terrible, invades our dear Fatherland. Is the Holy Christ of the Agony from our dear corner of La Montaña destined in the eternal decrees to save our beloved Fatherland and detain the flaming sword of the avenging angel that spreads death and desolation everywhere?
>
> Holy Christ of the Agony, Save Spain!!!

Here was no formula for the conversion of unbelievers, but rather for their military conquest.

Some of those who saw the image movements as essentially directed to Catholics understood them as endorsements of particular devotional choices. Juliana Armas, a resident of Barcelona, saw Christ at Limpias bright and smiling, and considered this support for her apostolate in favor of devotion to the Holy Spirit.[84] Bishop Manuel González seems to have seen the Christ move, and understood the movements as a call for attention to the Holy Sacrament, as with his Marías del Sagrario. "What I thought I saw at the altar of Limpias was principally this: Jesus *crucified* asking the world for an alms of compassion for Jesus in the *Sacrament*" (his italics).[85]

Similarly, the seer Leopoldo Trenor, who was an enthusiastic promoter of P. Mateo Crawley's movement to enthrone the Sacred Heart in people's homes, understood the movements of the Christ of Limpias as an endorsement of devotion to the Sacred Heart.[86] Yet another seer took his vision as a call to a vocation of expiation "for the sins of contemporary society, especially blasphemy," and became a Capuchin.[87] He joined the house in Bilbao, where Juan de Guernica, who as far as I know was not a seer, understood the visions as related to national expiation and his own Eucharistic Thursdays movement.[88]

Others interpreted the movements as Christ's remonstrations to certain kinds of Catholics, as if he were taking sides in their internecine disputes. For instance, the idea that Christ moved to bring people away from syrupy, effeminate devotions (like the Sacred Heart, one may assume) was first printed, only two months after the movements started, by the radical Social Catholic Maximiliano Arboleya Martínez in his Oviedo newspaper.[89] He quoted an Asturian noblewoman as opining that the Limpias manifestations of anguish and agony served "to remind us what we have all been forgetting in order to cultivate devotions very much in style, that do not speak to us of sorrow or torture—they serve to remind us of devotion to the Crucifix . . . (as in) the tough, manly, solidly Christian times of our ancestors." Arboleya Martínez was the most outspoken opponent of Integrism in Spain; he took as his models Belgian and French priests with close contact to the working class.[90]

In fact, he was right in the sense that the Limpias visions did provoke a renewed interest in the devotion to Christ's passion, as in the Stations of the Cross, or the Five Wounds. There was also an increase in the number of missions in the diocese.[91]

Similarly, in one of the few mentions of Limpias in the Liberal *El Cantábrico* of Santander, a writer wondered whether the Christ might be moving in distress at the devotional hypocrisies of Catholic conservatives, "those who enthrone him in their houses or in El Cerro de los Angeles with great fanfare and ostentation," "Pharisees," "gossiping beatas," and "the enriched and the begloved."[92]

Conversely, more conservative Catholics saw the Christ as moving out of anguish at the posture of liberal Catholics. It was in liberal households that writers like "Emma" in the *Diario de Navarra* saw a dangerous laxness in morality, an erosion of religious custom, and a breakdown of patriarchal authority. At Limpias, she held, "God was showing himself offended, perhaps dissatisfied, for the barren results of his Redemption." While she mentions the unbelievers, assassinations, and civil unrest, she blames much of it ultimately on the pagan climate created by "modernistic" Catholics.[93]

> He appears to an infinitude of persons of all kinds and does not show himself grand in the splendor of his glory; not at all. He appears afflicted, agonizing, as when the Herods and the Pharisees crucified him, showing the very holy wound in his side. . . . Because the world that now stands before his most holy eyes is no better than in pagan times . . . the fury of unbridled vices, which carry with them universal excesses in all areas of life and in all of is aspects. Do we not see much of society discontented, unbelieving, and with an unquenchable thirst for vengeance that produces the repeated crimes and assassinations which shock the world and frighten good and peaceful folk, alien to all these social changes. . . . When do we see, as we used to some years ago, the head of the family gather all his children and servants, irrespective of age and sex, to recite the holy rosary every night?
>
> But why should we worry about that old hat, say the many families with modernistic religion, who proclaim themselves fully practising Catholics, of course, while showing demurely their indecent arms up to the shoulder, scandalous legs even above the knees at age fifteen or more, and shameless cleavage in front and behind in the imperial style . . . even married women, next to their worthy spouses. And off they go boldly to church and even receive communion, as if they were going to the altar of Vesta, or to worship Venus or Bacchus. Is not this a fact, a sad reality? It seems like they are anxious to recuperate the times when women were repressed and abused!!!!
>
> It would be more Christian and sensible for a woman to preserve with dignity the home in which the Virgin Mary lovingly placed her. Mary is the example of the submissive daughter, the model spouse and mother, at the highest level of perfection. She inspired order, modesty, and diligence in the home, with a holy economy.

Emma's references to liberal Catholics also applied to the Liberal party that intermittently governed the country. If the liberal Catholics were the Pharisees who crucified Christ, the Liberal governments of Romanones and his ilk were Pilate, as in one of her final phrases, "Why shouldn't Christ appear afflicted and agonizing, as in the time of Pilate?" She was not alone in her judgment.

Tomás Echevarría understood Christ's movements at Limpias as a very concrete intervention against the Liberal government in power at the end of March 1919 in order to allow, with the Rightist government of Antonio Maura, the consecration of Spain to the Sacred Heart of Jesus. His analysis draws both on the specific instant in which the eyes were first seen to move and on the political moment of Spain as a whole. He takes the fact that the children saw the eyes move when the Capuchin was preaching on the theme, "Son, give me your heart" as a metaphoric reference to the need of all Spaniards to install Christ in their hearts and a concrete reference to the upcoming dedication of the monument of the Sacred Heart of Jesus at El Cerro de los Angeles outside of Madrid.

But, he argues, the Liberal government of Romanones then in power would have prevented Alfonso XIII from dedicating Spain to the Sacred Heart. The Limpias visions occurred at the critical moment of syndicalist strength, right after martial law had been proclaimed. Shortly thereafter, on April 15, 1919, Romanones resigned, "giving way to a government that almost all of us considered better." Echevarría considered it a divine portent that Antonio Maura, "the man most despised by those miserable aroused masses" was named to lead "an ultra-Right government."[94]

Echevarría's interpretation, which seems to have been consonant with that of the original Capuchin missionaries, may have been based in part on the visions of the assistant parish priest of La Bañeza, León, who walked 260 kilometers toward Limpias in five and a half days in early August 1919. He wrote that he saw the Christ of Limpias take on an expression of relief in the midst of his anguish, and then seemed to understand the words, "El Cerro de los Angeles" and "Thank you, my God."[95]

All of these writers interpreted the movements of the Christ of Limpias in terms of their own social, devotional, or political agendas. The nationalization of the devotion in a matter of weeks left a localist interpretation behind, and only at first was special importance given to Limpias itself as a place, Cantabria, or a specific moment. Rather, all came to agree on the importance of a general time and place. The time came to be understood generally as recent times, and the place understood generally as Spain, or even the West. That is, as the interpretation was made in a broader context, time and space were considered less specific and more representative.

For a minority of observers, in the prodigies of Limpias there was a deeper eschatological meaning, something they discerned in the apparitions and the miracles of Lourdes as well. For them, Limpias was one more sign of the end of time and the Second Coming. As such, needless to say, their position represented an extreme transcendence of time and place.

For some of these Spanish Catholics, the rampant secularism of Western European society was itself a sign of the end of time. On the fringe of this current was the visionary priest Pedro Valls, who in 1915 went quite far out on a limb by publishing a pamphlet without ecclesiastical censure entitled *El Apocalipsis en 1918*. In it he combined prophecies from the theosophist Annie Besant, the Book of Daniel, and nineteenth-century French sources to show that sometime between 1911 and 1928 the Teacher of Teachers would come and settle accounts not only with "civil society, skeptical and atheistic" but also with sectors of the Church who worshipped false Christs.[96]

But there were many other millenarians, inspired in part by the Chilean hermit and astronomer, Manuel Lacunza (1731–1801). His posthumous work, *The Coming of the Messiah in Glory and Majesty*, had editions in Cádiz (1813), London (1816, 1826), Tarragona (1822) and Mexico.[97]

The main Spanish millenarian theorist of the 1920s was a canon of Jaén, Cristino Morrondo Rodríguez.[98] In addition to Lacunza, he cited as the other "modern" sources two Franciscans, Francisco Tiburcio Arribas and Francisco Toribio Martín, and a Claretian, José Ramos, as well as three Chileans. Morrondo's work was published serially in *La Semana Catolica*, where it rather took over the space previously dedicated to Limpias, as the visions there lost their novelty and official Church encouragement. It is fair, I think, to deduce that at least some of the same kind of people interested in Limpias were interested in wider eschatological issues.

Other writers on these matters in *La Semana Catolica* were Pedro Romero and Alfonso Sarrablo y Palacio, all in the period from March 1923 to September 1924, when someone called the magazine to order, and an "advisement" instructed readers to disregard the articles that had been published. This tradition continued like an underground stream, swelled by the affluent of yet another millenarian Chilean, into the 1930s, when it nourished the enthusiasm of the supporters of the visions at Ezquioga.[99]

While this line of literature was not countenanced by the more thoughtful Catholic publications (one does not find it taken seriously in *Razón y Fe* or *Ciencia Tomista*), it seems to have held a great attraction for certain members of the religious orders, and cathedral and parish clergy. It fit in with one of the more esoteric interests of the Carlists, the idea that a Great Monarch would arrive in the here-and-now and set things straight. A plethora of literature along these lines was published in Valencia by José Domingo Corbató from 1903 to 1912.[100] Eventually his prophecies, together with those of the Mother Rafols, were brought out during and at the end of the Civil War as referring to Francisco Franco.[101]

Another way in which the public was "softened up" for matters of prophecy prior to Limpias was a series of pamphlets, some of them thinly disguised political propaganda, which used prophecy and revelation to explain and predict the outcome of World War I. This literature was not necessarily apocalyptic, although it cited many of the same prophets as the millenarians, but rather it addressed the particular needs of people in wartime. Some of it was translated into Spanish, and, thereby, the notion of revelations referring to present events was especially in the air in the period 1915–1920.[102]

So there was a certain public prepared, as it were, for the divine secrets of Agatángelo de San Miguel in 1919. In his original letter to the bishop of Santander, subsequently printed and reprinted all over Spain, the parish priest of Limpias, Eduardo Miqueli, implied that there was a secret side to Limpias to which the very spiritual P. Agatángelo was privy. "I believe that *el santo* as they call P. Agatángelo, must know something, for, when asked by a pious lady, he answered, 'Here something portentous has happened,' and he remained every day prostrate before the devout image."[103]

This paragraph virtually sent P. Agatángelo into hiding. When Teófilo Martínez Antigüedad went to Montehano shortly after the Limpias mission, P. Anselmo was cordial and open, but P. Agatángelo was skittish. "He is a little suspicious and tries to escape from the public, fearing that the curious would come to try and obtain revelations, which these good and prudent religious refuse to make, principally to keep the malicious from distorting their casual participation in the events, and because they can add nothing to what is in the public domain."[104] This prudence extended to the Montehano community, for one Capuchin remembered that P. Agatángelo had an unspoken rule not to talk about the Limpias events.[105]

But he did have something, rather a lot, to reveal, and because of Miqueli's letter, people knew it. He may have let on something to someone in the order, for the first article on Limpias in *El Mensajero Seráfico*, written sometime in June 1919, encouraged speculation about a deeper, wider meaning for the Christ's activation.[106]

> Will the Holy Christ of La Montaña speak to reveal his will and the concrete purpose of such prodigious events, as the Holy Virgin spoke to Bernadette in the grotto of Massabielle? Are we at the end, or just at the beginning of a series of marvels that our most adored Redeemer proposes to execute in that happy place?

The writer went on to hope for Limpias as "a center for world pilgrimage, a permanent center for miracles, and the splendid site of supernatural life." But he mentioned something else, the hope that "the social reign of Christ over the entire world, and especially Spain, might become more real and effective."

Already in late May an article by a Santander doctor and Lourdes devotee, Antonio Gutiérrez de Cossío, in *El Diario Montañés* had used some of these same phrases, suggesting that the Christ "may speak like the white Virgin of the rock of Massabielle." "Who," he wondered, "will be the privileged soul with whom He communicates?" And he speculated whether the apparitions and miracles of the Virgin of Lourdes were not "precursors for the coming of the Messiah . . . precursors once again for the reign of Christ." If that were the case, then these similar phenomena at Limpias might mark "the beginning of the social reign of Christ."[107]

The idea of a social reign of Christ was close to the hearts of the Capuchin and Franciscan orders. The VOT had been revitalized as a kind of sodality in the 1880s, with the mission of "preserving civil society from worldly corruption." In addition to its more spiritual side, the VOT was to serve as a bulwark against "the modernist spirit, in its three main forms—insubordination, immodesty, and sensuality."[108]

The hymn of the VOT specified an enemy: the Masons, portrayed as evil plotters along the almost paranoid lines that Léo Taxil exploited.[109] In the hymn the Masons prepared "secret machinations with infernal means"; the lodges "sharpened their knives to finish off the Church"; "proud freethinkers shrank from the light of heaven and trusted only in science"; and all were foiled by the combined efforts of the sons of St. Francis.[110]

While freemasonry was not as intense an issue in 1919 as it had been in Taxil's heyday (it was revived in the 1930s as a bugaboo), the VOT still had plenty to worry about, and it adopted the Sacred Heart as one of its vehicles for the attempted sanctification of the secular world. It was a Jesuit, Bernardo de Hoyos, who received the revelation on May 14, 1733, from the Sacred Heart, "I will reign in Spain, and with more veneration than elsewhere." But in the early twentieth century it was the devotion of conservative Catholics in general.

The idea of enthroning images of the Sacred Heart in households, factories, town halls, and monasteries was spread by Father Mateo Crawley Boevey, a religious of the Order of the Sacred Hearts, a relatively small order with only four houses in Spain. But in his tireless tours in Spain, starting in 1914, he was seconded by the Unión de Damas Españolas del Sagrado Corazón de Jesús, founded in 1908, and the Obra de la Entroni-

zación del Divino Corazón en los Hogares, founded in 1914. Both organizations were presided over by nobility.[111]

The Capuchins were almost as involved in the Sacred Heart devotions
as the Jesuits. For instance in June of 1917, 1918, and 1919, the Integrist
Circle of Santander made an excursion to Montehano to celebrate the
feast of the Sacred Heart. On this day and the nine days before it, the
Capuchins fanned out through the diocese preaching novenas and sermons. The Sacred Heart was enthroned in the monastery.[112]

In Madrid, the enthusiasm of the VOT, who were mobilizing for a
national monument to celebrate the Eucharistic Congress of 1911, combined with that of Father Crawley, and a group of devout laypersons,
who had succeeded, with the encouragement of the Society of Jesus and
the Vatican, in having Spain consecrated to the Sacred Heart in the presence of Alfonso XIII in 1909 and 1911.[113] A joint effort, transcending devotional agendas, was made to build a national shrine to the Sacred Heart
of Jesus, which in March 1919, at the time of the Limpias visions, was
virtually complete. We have seen how Tomás Echevarría considered the
divine purpose of the visions at Limpias to be the dedication of the monument. But this strain of observers went farther—they saw in Limpias
the dawn of the social reign which the monument symbolized.

In late June or early July 1919 Agatángelo de San Miguel told some
Asturian priests that there was a deeper aspect to the prodigy which he
could not reveal. He believed that the visions would continue and that
the Christ of Limpias would eventually speak. His remarks were first published on July 27, 1919, and rapidly reproduced in newspapers in Pamplona, Palencia, Lugo, and in a Capuchin publication in Murcia.[114]

They added another facet to the pilgrimages, a new incentive for attending. Who knew who would be the one to hear what the Christ of
Limpias wanted? A "rectification" was published on August 24, 1919, in
which it was asserted that the published interview contained inaccuracies.
But the rectification can only have fanned the speculation, as it left open
the possibility that there was indeed some secret message that had not
been released: "What occurred in the first and later manifestations of the
Christ of Limpias will in due time be made public, if it is thought necessary and appropriate."[115]

As late as the Spring of 1921 the belief that the Christ would speak was
still being held out (in this case by a Franciscan, Angel Diéguez, who
himself became a seer) as an incentive to get people to sign up for the
Second Galician Pilgrimage.[116]

There is no doubt that God is manifesting himself in Limpias. In my mind,
what is happening at Limpias is the forerunner of something very important
and extraordinary. God does not work these wonders to entertain the curious. . . . We have been assured that Christ already spoke to someone very dear
to him, and that he promised to speak in a way that everyone would understand when a certain pilgrimage went there. . . . Will ours be the fortunate
pilgrimage that Christ is awaiting to make his voice heard? We must make up
our minds: We have to go to Limpias!

The proposal by a doctor in May 1919 that people bring the sick to
Limpias to be cured found an echo in another revelation by Agatángelo
de San Miguel, this one in September 1919 to the effect that cures would
soon become known. *El Diario Montañés* considered this news prophetic,
as it preceded the news of Limpias's first major cure, that of a priest from
Castro-Urdiales.[117]

At the same time, P. Agatángelo apparently let it be known that other
images would begin to become active, although this was off the record.
This second part of his interview was made public in May 1920 when
indeed another crucifix, this one in Navarra, began to move.[118]

All this prophetic underside of Limpias, and its rapid reception by
certain commentators, points to a continuity between early twentieth-
century Spain and the eschatological interpretation of prophecies and
miracles in nineteenth-century France. The apparitions and miracles at
Lourdes, and the apparitions and prophecies elsewhere in France were
understood as signs of a new age, which was at the end of time.[119] It is
this idea that underlies the reactions of some of the Capuchin and Franciscan commentators to the Limpias events, helped along by the secrecy
and the off-the-record hints of P. Agatángelo.

In May 1920 "Fr. B. María de E." provided the readers of the Capuchin
El Mensajero Seráfico with one of the key texts predicting the coming of
a new age—the prophecy of Madaleine Porsat—under the title, "The
coming of the Reign of Mary." According to Porsat, whose message was
first published in 1866, the Marian Age was a preliminary to the coming
of Christ. "Mary comes to make a place for her Son in the triumphant
Church. Here is the Immaculate Conception of the Kingdom of God
that precedes the coming of Christ."[120]

It was in the context of this kind of eschatology, never fully discredited
or repudiated in the Church, that some of the clerical commentators
"read" the events at Limpias, together with the consecration of Spain to
the Sacred Heart, as a progression from Mary as precursor to the coming

of Christ himself. Limpias was the sign of a shift from the new Marian age, confirmed at Lourdes, to the age of Christ.

How much this millenarian enthusiasm involved significant numbers of laypersons can only be a matter of speculation. Certainly it affected certain lay organizations, like the VOT, closely allied to the Franciscans and the Capuchins, where, as in Esteban Bilbao's speech at Limpias in June 1921, there was great emphasis on the Great Promise to Father Hoyos of the Sacred Heart.

This sense of mystery, of mystical progress of Catholicism, was in a curious way similiar to the very modern notions of the secular positivists—of history as progress, or even of history as the inevitable playing out of internal contradictions of the Marxists. It is symptomatic, I think, of a historical period in which it was especially difficult to practice a simple, devotional Catholicism, aimed at personal or familial salvation, without regard to the "salvation" of the nation or the situation of Catholicism internationally. The Catholic of the north of Spain was willy-nilly thrust into this wider arena, however remote and rural the location.[121] The diocesan mobilizations against Liberal education laws, the thorough coverage of the countryside with missions, and the aggressive ideological competition of unions and freethinkers meant that collective political-religious issues and solutions were part of everyday Catholicism. And among the more optimistic solutions, with its share of takers, were the more providential ones discussed here.

The obverse was no doubt also true. The polarization of ideological options led to a clerical rigidity that no doubt forced the apathetic or the lukewarm to choose sides. On the front page of *El Diario Montañés* of May 31, 1922, was the entire judicial sentence condemning a citizen of the city to five days in jail and fifty pesetas in fine, plus costs, for not taking his hat off to the Holy Sacrament in the street even though a priest asked him to.[122] This sentence was handed down in a city where substantial segments of the population were indifferent to religion; it could not but help to push that indifference toward hostility, with all the wider sociopolitical implications that hostility entailed.

The millenarian interpretation of Limpias contrasts with older kinds of Catholic (or even pre-Christian) interpretations of prodigies as anomalies announcing anomalies—disasters or big changes in weather, harvests, disease, war, or royal succession. That was P. Agatángelo's first fear—that the movements announced a cataclysm, and the first alternative suggested by the diocesan commentator—"the announcement of unknown misfortunes."

But both interpretations were rather out of date in 1919, and more common were the options presented previously, summed up by the Jesuit Ugarte de Ercilla in July 1919.[123] He reassured his readers that what was happening at Limpias was nothing new. "God has worked these graces, so it seems, in a number of images." The effect of these events, he said, was "to get the attention of the distracted, convert not a few sinners, excite the faith in many hearts, promote the cult of sacred images, and, more importantly, augment the love of God." It was this blander, more restricted kind of meaning that predominated.

It is my impression that the more spectacular interpretations, whether eschatological or catastrophic, were restricted to a limited circle of pilgrims and observers. While a majority of the clergy might be aware of them as options, they kept them on a back shelf in their minds, much as, in the 1980s, the idea of the visions of Fatima announcing a new age was at best a minority interest.

An Overview

One thing that distinguishes the events at Limpias from later moments of mystical enthusiasm in twentieth-century Spain is their formal, choreographed nature. The pilgrimage processions, beginning just twenty days after the first visions, were as organized as those of Corpus Christi, heavily decorated and ordered with etiquette.

Limpias, or at least the Limpias we have access to through press and propaganda, was less spontaneous than other superficially similar events. From shortly after the start it became a pet project first of the diocese and the Santander lay Catholic militants, then also of those of Bilbao, and then, quickly, of the nation's monarchy and nobility. The Conservative wing of Spain's ruling class took Limpias to heart. This was an urban elite with potent organizing power through a *de facto* alliance with certain religious orders. As early as June 18, 1919, a reporter for the Liberal newspaper, *El Imparcial,* noticed the turn the phenomenon was taking, in a guarded article. "To none of the people in the village are to be attributed these unexpected events and it is a great injustice to accuse them of collaboration in political-religious schemes or speculative motives."[124]

The spread of the pilgrimages is evidence for this urban, elite tone and direction. The pilgrimages were organized first from cities, and then from the countryside. They spread by leapfrogging regions to their capital cities. I think in part the reason for the quick formalization of the Limpias events, aside from the prior example of Lourdes, was the presence in the village itself of a cultivated, politically alert, and organizationally adept upper class, the kind of people who commissioned the original mission, widened the roads, formed the welcoming committees, and answered the mail.

Once the modality of the pilgrimages was set, they became a showcase for the most vital organizations of northern Spanish Catholicism—children, women workers, the agricultural union, active parishes, religious sodalities in their organizational prime, all paraded in order, singing, from the train station to the shrine. They went not just willingly but also obviously. They were labeled with ribbons and medals so that others on the train or in the streets of their home place would know they were pilgrims to Limpias, enthusiasts of the Christ that in the midst of Spain's troubles was moving.

It was a pilgrimage center that in its first, exciting years had as an important facet the notion of "us" as opposed to "them." If it was immediately read as a proof of the Catholic faith, it was because a proof was needed for unbelievers. A Galician pilgrim, Dolores Silva, ended her testimony, "I certify this for the greater glory of God and the conversion of the unfortunate incredulous."[125] A canon of Lugo, Cesar Abellás, summed up this attitude in a sonnet to the Christ of Limpias written at the shrine. In it he refers to the Galicians on the pilgrimage as "la gente mía," my people, the best people on earth, the people with heart, piety, tenderness, faith, adoration, and love. He contrasts these good people *here* with the "impious people" *there* (*there* being the city? Barcelona? Andalucía?). The people *there*, the "them" of Limpias, are people "of a thousand blasphemies," people with "stiff necks and hard feelings," "the most vile people on the globe."[126]

ANTE EL CRISTO DE LIMPIAS
    (postrada Galicia a sus pies)

        Nos, populus ejus
        Nosotros, el pueblo suyo
                  (Psalm. 94)

Del Calvario apuraste en tu agonía
El cáliz del dolor de los dolores,
Cuando de mil blasfemias los clamores
Llegaban hasta Tí, de gente impía.
Qué consuelo te diera en aquel día,
—Oh Jesús, oh Amor de los Amores—

Escuchar los acentos, los rumores
Que hoy a Tí suben, de la gente mía!
Allá, el pueblo más vil que el orbe encierra
El de dura cerviz y entraña dura,
Todo protervia, ingratitud, malicia.
Aquí . . . el pueblo más bueno de la tierra,
El pueblo-corazón, piedad, ternura . . . .
Y fe . . . y adoración . . . y amor . . . GALICIA!!

Caught up in the hurly-burly of political strife, or the sexual politics of plunging cleavages and daring hemlines, or the religious politics of competing orders, Integrism or Liberalism, the Sacred Heart and the Crucifix, Catholic writers and pilgrimage preachers felt free to speculate why the Christ was moving. It is harder to know what was on the minds of the people with more local and less conflictive preoccupations. For many of them, we can deduce from the description of vows, the purchase of talismans, and the recounting of cures, Limpias was in part a new shrine, one where the divine touch was fresh and new, and the power all the more powerful because it was visible and could so palpably move people's hearts.

In this sense Limpias was of a piece with the general revival of Spanish holy places that took place at the end of the nineteenth century. Valvanera, Nuria, Montserrat, El Pilar, Guadalupe, all fell on hard times in the early nineteenth century. As in France, but with some delay, Spain's shrines were revived and once more served as immense batteries of grace. Limpias became one of them.

I do not have access for the more intimate meaning of the visions to the visionaries themselves; those vision testimonies reprinted in apologetic books are too heavily selected and edited to be representative.[127] In addition, the events occurred just beyond the threshold of useful living memory. However, there are enough recorded accounts for the similar visions at Piedramillera in 1920 to allow speculation, at least, on the movements, not of the images, but of the seers' hearts.

FIGURES 18 AND 19. Alfonso XIII consecrates Spain to the Sacred Heart of Jesus on May 15, 1919, from *Estrella del Mar*, 1920. Courtesy Hemeroteca Municipal, Madrid.

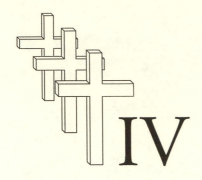

IV

The Christ of Piedramillera

IT WAS IN September 1919 that Agatángelo de San Miguel had predicted that additional images would begin to move.[1] About eight months later, on May 14, 1920, the parish priest of Piedramillera (Navarra) wrote his bishop, "as of the 11th of this month at 11:00 in the morning, our village has become a second Limpias."[2]

By then many people had gone from Navarra to Limpias, both on individual trips as well as on three group pilgrimages. A group of thirty went from Estella, twenty kilometers from Piedramillera, on August 23, 1919, and four of them saw the Christ move.[3] Groups from Estella also participated in the larger Navarrese pilgrimages organized by the Nocturnal Adoration Society in October 1919 and April 20–21, 1920.[4] The latter trip took place only three weeks before the Piedramillera visions began. It included Nocturnal Adoration chapters from Lodosa, Cirauqui, Legarda, and Los Arcos, all towns near Estella and Piedramillera.[5] The Piedramillera priest, Pedro Arrastio, had been to Limpias. And the Limpias visions had been extensively reported in Pamplona's newspapers. On May 8, 1920, three days before the new visions began, Anselmo de Jalón and Agatángelo de San Miguel, the very missionaries who had sparked the Limpias visions, began a mission in Lezaún, about thirty-seven kilometers northeast of Piedramillera.[6] (See Map 3.)

Piedramillera was a nuclear village of four hundred inhabitants, located in the most Carlist zone of Navarra. In 1920 those who owned land lived well, producing grain, olive oil, and meat; the many who did not had to look elsewhere for wages much of the year. Piedramillera is not far from the Ribera, the zone of Navarra along the Ebro of latifundia known already in 1920 for its religious indifference and radicalism.[7] Even Los Arcos, just twelve kilometers to the south, is considered by the people of Piedramillera as a place of "little faith."[8]

In contrast, Piedramillera belonged to the devout part of Navarra whose depressed rural economy, zealous parish priests, and large families supplied Spain, Latin America, and the Far East with a disproportionate number of priests, nuns, and missionaries. The numerous religious communities located in Navarra served as recruitment centers for these vocations. Around 1920 Navarra ranked third nationwide among provinces in the number of religious per 10,000 inhabitants (77), after adjacent Guipúzcoa (131) and Alava (102). Santander (43), ranked 15, was far behind.[9] Each village developed a special affinity for certain orders, which was handed down from aunts and uncles to nieces and nephews. In recent years the young men of Piedramillera, for instance, have become Trinitarians, and the women Redemptorist Oblates and Sisters of Charity.[10]

In 1920 Piedramillera made pilgrimages to at least two shrines. One was San Gregorio in nearby Sorlada, visited once a year in May for protection against crop pests. The sacred relic of San Gregorio, encased in a silver head, still in the 1990s comes to the village every year so the people can pour water through it to sprinkle on their fields. Grasshoppers were a particular danger in the region, and in fact there was a minor infestation not far away the year the visions began.[11]

The other shrine visited by Piedramillera was Our Lady of Codés, about fifteen kilometers to the west, notable for cures of diseases. The visit in 1920 was on May 15, in combination with the other villages of the Berrueza valley. The shrine was revived by a new brotherhood in 1904 and from 1912 to 1917 was a center for spiritual exercises for the district population, led by Jesuits from Logroño.[12]

Like most villages in Navarra, Piedramillera also hosted every year the visit of the sacred image of Navarra's most popular shrine, San Miguel de Aralar. Villagers may also have had devotion to Our Lady of Puy in Estella.

There was no major shrine to Christ in Navarra,[13] but at one of the most active Navarrese shrines, that of San Francisco Javier, there was a crucifix said to have sweated blood every Friday in 1552, the year Francis

Xavier died in China. So the early modern tradition of the activation of statues was, at least vestigially, alive in Navarra in 1920.[14] Piedramillera's lifelike crucifix, in a lateral altar of the nave of the parish church, was probably associated with the village's Cofradia de la Vera Cruz, a brotherhood common in the zone, originally of flagellants.[15] One of the few villages in Spain where flagellation continued in this brotherhood, San Vicente de la Sonsierra, was not far away in La Rioja.[16]

What with the spiritual exercises of Ignatius Loyola at Codés (in which the Passion is vividly remembered), the Javier tradition, and the village brotherhood of the True Cross, there was in Piedramillera and its district a special concentration of religious imagination on the details of Christ's death.

As at Limpias, the vision at Piedramillera began with a group of girls, here slightly younger, ages eight to ten. I spoke to one of them, María Muneta, in August 1982.[17] She recalled that they had been accustomed to visit the church, on the outskirts of the village, recite a Station of the Cross, and kiss the crucifix every day during the school recreation period. On May 11, 1920, there were about a dozen girls in the Christ's chapel on the right hand side of the nave, and one, Martina, said, "It seems like he's opening his eyes." María Muneta told me, "But the rest of us did not see it. But Martina insisted, 'It's true, it's true!'" Other villagers told me that there were two girls, not just one, who first saw the eyes open, and that their names are on the church bells recast in 1921.[18]

Newspaper reports in 1920 said the visions began when one girl who had been assigned as a penance in confession to kiss the foot of the crucifix was too short to reach it, and the Christ stretched out his foot to her.[19] This appears to be an embroidery on the original event, as neither village eyewitnesses nor the priest in his letter to the bishop mention it. It is possible, however, that the girls' visits to the crucifix were connected to imposed penances.

At the time the girls were in the church, Pedro Arrastio was coming up the hill to the church in order to give the children preparing for their first commmunion a catechism class. As he wrote the bishop three days later, "they told me on the way, and I replied with a smile of disbelief; but what was my shock at seeing the Holy Christ with his right eye open and his left one part way open, when I always, looking from different positions, had seen him with his eyes closed!"[20]

The children ran out, weeping; presumably with the permission of the priest the church bells were rung; and the villagers came in from the fields. The priest wrote, "The news spread like wildfire through the village, and by afternoon through the surrounding villages, and from that

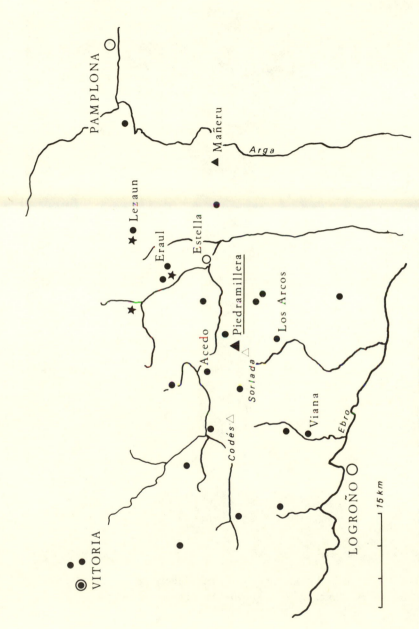

PAMPLONA

Mañeru

Arga

Lezaun

Eraul

Estella

Piedramillera

Acedo

Los Arcos

Sorlada

Codés

Viana

Ebro

VITORIA

LOGROÑO

15 km

MAP 3. Zone of devotion to the Christ of Piedramillera, 1920–1921.

124

FIGURE 20. A composite photograph of Piedramillera and its Christ, displayed in many homes. Photographer unknown; copy by Miguel Bergasa.

FIGURE 21. Detail, Christ of Piedramillera, 1982. Photograph by the author.

time on this church, always so empty because it is detached from the village, is now always to be found with people from all these villages, and it is said that many see it move its eyes and lips. Here it is as in Limpias—some see and others do not when all are looking at once."

By the third day (May 13, 1920) one of the visionaries was from sixty kilometers to the northeast, the village of Echauri near Pamplona. Nevertheless, Arrastio delayed writing the bishop until, he said, he could be sure that something serious was happening. But since on May 13 many people "entirely trustworthy" had very clear visions, he told the bishop briefly what had happened and requested instructions. The villagers had asked him to start a novena on May 15 that would terminate on the holiday of Pentecost Monday with a special preacher. They also asked him to take the miraculous crucifix out in procession. Anticipating even larger crowds, he also asked permission to say mass outdoors.

The bishop, the Augustinian Fray José López de Mendoza, replied at once urging caution and denying permission for the novena, processions, or outdoor masses.[21] But before his letter arrived the priest wrote again, on May 15, 1920, even more excited. "This village is beside itself, extremely upset." The seers, he said, "were not only willing to swear by what they had seen, but even to give their lives for it"; at night he could hardly get them out of the church. Arrastio rather desperately requested an observer from the diocese who could report directly on what was happening. On that morning the priest and some of the villagers had gone on the pilgrimage to Our Lady of Codés, and on their return at 4:00 P.M. he found that very many people had seen "the miracle." By then, he said, over a hundred persons had had visions, at least one person from each of the surrounding villages. Many fainted, whether "women, children, or strong men, as at Limpias" and one village youth who had seen it several times had become very withdrawn, and the village was afraid he would get sick. On that day a girl from Acedo was cured of St. Vitus Dance at the church.

The bishop replied at great length, advising extreme circumspection, but suggesting that a register of the most notable visions be kept in case it was needed some day.[22] This second letter had not yet been received when the priest wrote again on May 18, 1920. By then the first novena had been canceled, but another one, to the Holy Spirit, possibly one made annually prior to Pentecost, had begun. The visions continued, "to all classes and conditions of persons—to some as soon as they enter, to others later; to some with a sweet and loving look, to others sad and anguished, and to yet others, severe; there are some men and boys from the village who almost always see it; and some are so scared that now they do not dare to go and look at it. What is happening here is indescribable." The priest had allowed his parishioners to spend the eves of two feast days in the church all night, at their insistent request. The fainting continued, and some people had to be taken to the pharmacy.

The parallel with Limpias had been heightened by the arrival on May 17, 1920, of the original Limpias missionaries with about three hundred persons at the conclusion of the nine-day mission in Lezaún. The Capuchins had expected to be met processionally and to be able to address their mission congregation inside the Piedramillera church, as would have happened in Limpias. But by then the Piedramillera priest knew his bishop would not approve, and hence the Lezaún procession had to disband, and the people enter the church as individuals.[23]

Arrastio in his May 18th letter asked the bishop that, as at Limpias, a set fee of five pesetas be placed for masses; that he be allowed, as at Limpias, to pay for postage to answer the letters he would be sure to receive out of alms given to the Christ; that the testimony of seers be taken down; and that a new account book for the alms be opened. He was totally convinced of the miraculous nature of the events and again asked for a special emissary. Another priest later wrote the bishop concerning Arrastio that he "at all costs wants this to be real, and so he is more gullible in believing the repeated testimonies."[24]

This latter priest was in fact the bishop's special emissary, Miguel Atienza of Acedo. But Atienza did not send his skeptical letter for two weeks, after he had observed the happenings at Piedramillera and thought about them. In the meantime, on May 24, a miracle register was started for those cases the parish priest deemed significant. I found it forgotten in a closet of the uninhabited parish house.[25] After a May 24 vision, some others were recorded retrospectively—not the first ones of May 11, 1920, but some as early as May 13. The last vision described was on February 23, 1921. In all, forty visions of twenty-eight visionaries are mentioned, mostly in the first month of the visions.

All of the visionaries, and all of the priests or laypersons mentioned in the limited diocesan correspondence on the matter, lived in the triangle formed by Pamplona, Logroño, and Vitoria, which includes parts of the provinces of Alava and Navarra. The spread of news from this zone was limited by the control of the bishop over the Pamplona press. No articles about the matter were printed in the two principal Catholic newspapers, *Diario de Navarra* and *El Pensamiento Navarro*, to the dismay and disillusionment of the priests and believers.

Outside of Navarra there was a brief mention in *El Diario Montañés* on May 27, 1920, probably with information supplied by the Capuchins, and in *La Semana Católica* of Madrid on June 12, 1920, but neither of these sources gave the name of the village, Piedramillera. Both wondered when the bishop of Pamplona would speak on the matter. The only substantial articles I know of were published in the Traditionalist *El Correo Español* of Madrid, from Navarrese correspondents in Estella (May 28, 1920) and Viana (June 22, 1920), which Luis Urbano reprinted in his second edition.[26] But these mentions were not followed up in the national press, possibly after contacts with the diocese, and the Piedramillera visions, without publicity in Navarra other than word of mouth, tapered off gradually in the next two years.[27]

Only the occasional item in Pamplona newspapers or the diocesan bulletin indicated that anything unusual had happened: that two Capuchins, one of them Anselmo de Jalón, preached a novena in Piedramillera October 9–17, 1920;[28] that a philanthropist from Bilbao, Victorina de Larrinaga, was donating basins for holy water, candelabras, a lamp, and other liturgical paraphernalia for the church, as well as paying for the recasting of the church bells, in December 1920;[29] and that a great fiesta, announced with prospectuses, was held in 1921 to celebrate the anniversary of the "memorable 11 [of May]," in which the new bells were christened, the cathedral choir sang, a Jesuit and a Redemptorist from Pamplona preached, and large numbers of priests and laypersons attended.[30]

Arrastio, who had only been in Piedramillera on an interim basis, was replaced by the titular parish priest, Luis Lambea, on February 17, 1921.[31] Lambea does not appear to have been so keen on the visions.[32] After his accession there is only one more testimony in the registers, and the only way to follow the continuing decline of devotion is through the parish account books.[33]

More than sixty years hence, we cannot know who all the seers were at Piedramillera nor all of what they saw. I could find no seers in the village who would describe their visions, and even if they did, it would be at an enormous distance in years and intervening history. Villagers told me of one woman who had been a seer, but when I talked to her she more or less denied it, embarrassed. The people of Piedramillera, proud of their Christ, are nevertheless unsure about the orthodoxy of the miracle, confused and hurt by the rejection they received from their bishop. Furthermore, even Piedramillera, a rock-solid Catholic hamlet that in the last decades had provided the Church with "a regiment of nuns," as one villager put it—about twenty—and six to ten male religious, has been touched by the decline in religious fervor of recent years.

From the 1940s until the 1960s the village had a stern, righteous priest, Don Nicanor Ursúa Sanz, who every year had everybody up at 6:00 A.M. for the entire month of October saying the Rosary before they went off to work in the fields. And every year, May 3–11, they still hold a novena in honor of their Christ; and every year, they say, it rains. But along with the rest of Spain, Piedramillera is less sure of its religious allegiance. A woman sitting on a doorstoop, commenting on the miracles, said, "Now people say, even some from the village, that they were fooling us with so much confession, so many masses. What do you think? I think we lived better then." And as in the rest of Spain, several of the male religious from

Piedramillera have left the religious life. "Rebounds (*rebotados*)" was the name for them in the village in 1982.[34]

So the memories are less firm than they once were. The woman who may have been a seer finds it hard to remember—her mind is very bad, she says. She remembers well, however, the blind and mute woman from Los Arcos who was cured after putting an offering in the alms basket, and who spoke to people from her mother's balcony. When the Los Arcos woman reached her home town, Pedro Arrastio wrote his bishop, "many people went out to greet her, and then they visited her in her house, where the most pathetic and moving scenes took place, for on that day she saw for the first time several of her children."[35] According to the miracle register the woman, Theodora Blasco y Lana, age 36, had been blind and mute for nine years, and was cured on June 6, 1920, when she touched the feet of the crucifix. Her signature is clear and steady in the book.[36] It was her cure in particular that impressed the Viana correspondent of *El Correo Español*.[37]

So aside from certain salient cures, the movements of the Christ are hard to document fully now. Of the hundreds, perhaps thousands of seers, only twenty-eight are recorded in the miracle register, those considered most trustworthy by the priest. There is no sense in taking them as representative. There are no children under thirteen or adults over sixty-four; there are nine married men, but only three married women. Nor can one assume that what they are given as seeing is representative of what was seen, or even of what they saw, but rather what was chosen to be recorded. For example, villagers still remember that some people, certain children, saw the image sweat, but there is no mention of sweat in the witnesses recorded.

What is recorded is highly revealing, nonetheless, for it is a measure of what the priest found important, not just as proof of a miraculous activation but also as evidence for divine intervention. What is also recorded, this mainly in letters to the bishop, is people's reactions to these visions, information critical for the ecclesiastical discernment of the spirits involved.

The miracle register shows the communication of feelings to the seers—divine pleasure, anger, or sadness—and the reactions of the seers—becoming heartened, sad, or afraid, often accompanied by fainting. The priest's description of these *síncopes* or fainting spells as "the same effects as in Limpias" is telling. For in 1920 there was a lively polemic about the Limpias visions that hinged in part on this very aspect.

The ancient criterion for discernment of spirits by the feelings of the seer
was that while the initial reaction might be one of fear or terror, it would
quickly shift to sweetness and harmony if the vision were divine. Press
reports of visions at Limpias, and Somellera's diary as well, showed that
many people swooned away in their visions and had to be carried out. For
the Dominican Urbano, the swoons were signs that the visions were not
divine; supporters of Limpias tended to minimize the fainting, or deny
that it occurred at all.[38]

At Piedramillera one of the three arguments against the validity of the
visions by the bishop's consultant, Miguel Atienza, was precisely that
many visionaries fainted:[39]

> I believe that these effects of fainting should not be experienced if the event
> were miraculous. For if it is miraculous, doubtless God works it to demon-
> strate his mercy and goodness, which should arouse in us feelings of sweetness,
> open-heartedness [*ensanchamiento*], peace, tranquillity; and even if the first
> impulses that God wanted to excite were of terror (if the favored person is a
> sinner) yet I believe that the favored person should reflect that God does not
> wish to frighten with this, and from the moment in which they do not know
> how to overcome their first impulses and reflect on this, I think it is all the
> result of subjective sentiment, and not objective and real.

The vision listed first in the register was by Juan Galdeano y Arana,
married, age thirty-four, from Eraul, about thirty kilometers to the northeast in the Yerri valley. It was his neighbor, Raimundo Galdeano, who
paid for the Capuchin mission in Lezaún, and later in 1920 brought the
Capuchins to Piedramillera.[40] On the morning of May 24, the Eraul parish priest said one mass and assisted at another in the Piedramillera
church. After the second mass he noticed a group of men from his parish
and asked them if they had seen anything. They pointed to Galdeano,
who was still shaken from his experience, and he told his story haltingly.
The Eraul priest urged him to dictate his vision; Galdeano disappeared
and was located only after an hour. The Piedramillera and Eraul priests
then took him to the rectory, where the Eraul priest wrote the vision
down. A measure of the importance attributed to this vision is that both
priests at once sent accounts of the vision to the bishop.

The Eraul priest noted that Galdeano "is polite and good, does not
drink wine or liquor, and is very industrious." Galdeano told him this:[41]

> I arrived at the church when you were saying mass at half past eight and
> you were finishing the consecration. I looked at the crucifix and I saw it as if

it were alive, with its eyes open. He looked at you and at the altar with a happy face, and stayed that way all through the mass. When the mass was over he——died! [When he said this he was very moved and tears ran down his face.]

After receiving communion and giving thanks, I again entered the chapel, and I saw him with his eyes open and directed at those who were going out of the chapel. [During all this time I felt very upset.] After the bells rang for High Mass I saw him again with his eyes open, and he looked at three young men who were on the steps of the chapel.

The mass began and the choir had barely begun to sing the Kyries when he opened his eyes again and looked at all the people without fixing on anybody. During the consecration he became happy and smiled, looking at the priests and the altar. Then I became happy and felt better [*me ensanché algo*], and he remained that way until the communion, and then I did not see him anymore.

After the second mass, when he was leaving the church, Galdeano said to the other Eraul men, "I don't know why we ever fail to hear mass if we can help it." During the mass he told his friends what he was seeing, and even that the Eraul priest was looking at the crucifix and must be seeing it too, but neither the friends not the priest saw the image as alive. Galdeano was the only seer in the church.

When the Piedramillera priest wrote the bishop with Galdeano's account, he reported what the Eraul priest had told him. "Galdeano was very shaken, as is the case with the immense majority [of seers] who for a good while cannot talk, only weep, with a hiccup that lasts a long time."[42] Arrastio added a postscript that showed how little he understood the bishop's reticence about the phenomena: "PS: It seemed a good idea to me to print up this testimony to send out with the parish seal to those who ask for information. What do you think? Let me know."

Christ smiling made Galdeano profoundly happy, it heartened him— "*me ha ensanchado el corazón.*" But this was not his only emotion. When the image on the cross died, and when it was directing its eyes to those leaving the chapel, or later watching the three youths or looking vaguely over the congregation, Galdeano felt "*mucha emoción.*" I have translated this as "very upset," because it must have been an emotion that was disheartening and sad, for Galdeano wept when telling of the death, and contrasted that emotion to his later becoming heartened. It was this sense of being overcome and weeping that stayed with him after his visions were over. There is an implication in the vision that since Christ did not smile when looking at the congregation, the three youths on the steps of the chapel, or the people leaving the chapel, he was not happy with them, and that attitude was communicated to Galdeano's heart. Later at the house where he was staying, Galdeano refused all food.[43]

In the midst of his agony, the Christ of Piedramillera seemed to be judging those around him, and Galdeano seemed to feel judged as well, although the image apparently never directly looked at him.

There were ample precedents at Limpias for this interpretation of Christ's glances. One young man from Estella, Edilberto Herrero, had gone to Limpias three times before the Piedramillera events started, each time seeing the Christ move, and by March 1920 he had entered the Capuchin order. On March 1, 1920, he wrote, "[The Christ of Limpias] does not appear to like the way some persons enter and leave his holy temple, for he looks at them, whenever they come in or go out, with a severe and angry expression."[44] This kind of interpretation is in fact part of the religious upbringing of almost all Spanish Catholics, who as little children are instructed to behave well in church as "Christ is watching you," generally referring to a crucifix.

At Piedramillera several seers saw the Christ look directly at them. Margarita Echevarría, a widow age thirty-seven from Zufía, fifteen kilometers away, saw the image open and shut its eyes several times in a fifteen-minute interval on May 28, 1920, "sometimes with a sad look, and only once with a happy look which it directed at her directly," while she was saying the Stations of the Cross.[45] While the "plot," as it were, of the Piedramillera Christ's movements were his agony, mirrored in the "plot" of the mass, there was a "subplot" as the Christ singled out congregations, groups, or individuals for meaningful glances. Of the twenty-eight seers recorded by Arrastio, eighteen saw the image looking at people; two saw the image lower its arms from the cross and try to embrace them; and sixteen saw the image looking at them in particular. The seers characterized the expressions of thirteen of these looks. The numbers are too small to be significant, but the general pattern is that the looks of Christ were sad (*triste*) when directed at men or at others (seven cases) and happy, sweet, or loving (*dulce, alegre, cariñosa*) when seen by women directed to themselves (three cases) and when looking at a priest saying mass (one case). There are only two exceptions to this pattern. In short, the Christ seemed to be pleased with the women and the priests, but displeased with the men.

One Piedramillera woman, age thirty-two and married, saw the Christ smile every time she entered the church.[46] She may be the same woman villagers still recall as having seen the image open its eyes whenever she entered the church until she died.

In any case, the persons recorded or remembered as incredulous were all males. Two villagers in 1982 recounted the case of a youth from Los Arcos who tossed a coin at the image:

A young lad came—and you know, the young people, they're so—and he said, "Open your eyes, open your eyes, let's see if you open your eyes now [with the disrespectful *tu* form]!" And he threw a small coin at it. But he fell down in a swoon [*desganado*] and they had to carry him out, and it took a while before he revived.

Similarly, in the miracle register, a bachelor age twenty-six from Santa Cruz del Campezo in Alava wept when he saw the Christ "open its eyes and mouth as if he were dying" even though "he had entered the chapel laughing and making fun of what he had heard about the Holy Christ." On another visit three weeks later he had to be carried out of the chapel when he fainted afer the Christ opened it eyes and looked at him directly.[47] In all, four of the seers in the miracle register in addition to Galdeano had their own reactions (as opposed to the reactions of the Christ) recorded. All were men, three of them unmarried. Three fainted, one for six hours, and the fourth was *acongojado*, anguished. The Viana newspaper report gave another case, that of Francisco Fernández, known as "Rorro," who broke out in a cold sweat and started to faint when he saw the Christ move its eyes and blink.[48]

On the one hand, the friendly, happy, sweet and loving looks that some of the women and priests received may reflect a more intimate, familiar relationship with Christ. When Edilberto Herrero told the Christ of Limpias he was consecrating himself to Him, the Christ smiled and Herrero's "soul was flooded with sweetness."[49] The notion of a good, merciful, and sweet God was popular at this time in France, and such an attitude on the part of Christ was expected by the bishop and, as we have seen, by his adviser Miguel Atienza. The men, by this reasoning, would not receive smiles because their relationship with Christ was more distant and formal.

But the gender difference reflected in this testimony, I think, more especially reflects an internalized sense of sin, and perhaps even of sinful disbelief or doubt. The Christ looking at people without expression, or sad, or severely, while in his agony on the cross, is looking at the people who have crucified him. Even in Navarra and Alava, where male attendance at church has traditionally matched that of females, the younger males were having doubts. Perhaps just as many women were fainting as men, just as many women feeling guilty; if so, at the very least the priest's choice of visions to record reflects a general perception of the backsliding of men and the need to counteract it with these salutary examples.[50]

How it was that younger men could be backsliding (or should be seen thus) in faithful Navarra may be explained in part by their temporary emigration elsewhere. Navarra had remained steadfastly agricultural, and those without land had to look elsewhere for work. Between 1900 and 1938 Navarra had one of the highest rates of emigration for all of Spain, an excess of 65,626 emigrants over immigrants, which counterbalanced the natural growth of the population, constant at about 300,000 persons.[51] From Piedramillera some went up to the mountains of Guipúzcoa as charcoalers.[52] We have seen that one of the original seers at Limpias was an agricultural laborer from the Navarrese town of Echarri-Aranaz.[53] And some went farther afield. Outside of rural Navarra, the emigrants were exposed to other ideas and habits. "This is a village in which at age eighteen they all emigrate to California, whence they return ten or twelve years later in a dismal spiritual state," wrote the parish priest of Oroz-Betelu in 1920.[54]

It was in the light of this kind of moral danger that Pedro Arrastio wrote down the miniature morality plays that some of the visions seemed to be. He would no doubt have subscribed to the analysis of the Viana newspaper correspondent who wrote:[55]

> For the believer, who carries as his lantern the history of the Church replete with prodigies and extraordinary signs, what is said about the Holy Christ of Piedramillera seems most natural; that to a materialistic and indifferent society, the Lord seeks to bring his love through proofs that transcend natural forces.

The bishop, Fray José López de Mendoza (1848–1923), was dealing with the same problem of a materialistic and indifferent society, but on a broader ecclesio-political level. A distinguished canon lawyer at the end of his episcopal career, with no ambitions for higher office (he had turned down the archdiocese of Burgos), he seems to have made up his mind on Piedramillera relatively quickly and by his own lights.

In 1920 he was seventy-two years old. He studied canon law for three years in Rome, later teaching at the Augustinian seminaries at Santa María de la Vid and El Escorial, where he was the vice-rector. It was after a successful set of sermons in the royal chapel that he was nominated bishop of Jaca in 1891 and promoted to Pamplona in 1899. While at Santa

María de la Vid he called together a village whose citizens had been lax in making Easter confessions and warned them that God would punish them. Soon after, a hailstorm hit the village territory, sparing the lands of adjacent villages.

In spite of this kind of hieratic sternness, in the diocese of Pamplona, he and the Augustinians in general were held to be liberals, in part because of his support for social Catholicism. He never backed away from a conflict, persisting in pastoral visits to towns like Mendavia where he had been placed on warning, even if it meant leaving in a shower of stones. At one point he even prohibited the reading of the Catholic *Diario de Navarra* because of its attacks on him. The Integrist sector of the diocesan clergy denounced him to the Vatican, and in 1906 he renounced his see in a personal letter to Pius X. After an interview in Rome, the pope refused his resignation, and the diocese made peace with him. His twenty-fifth anniversary as a bishop in 1916 was celebrated with much fanfare. It is not surprising that he did not yield to popular or clerical pressure in the Piedramillera episode.[56]

From the very start López de Mendoza understood the significance of Piedramillera not primarily for the seers and local region, but on a national and even international scale in the fierce ongoing war for men's souls. The priests of Piedramillera and Limpias saw the movements as divine interventions to fill empty churches, to preserve the just and convert the unjust, and to demonstrate to the unbelievers of the Ribera or the industrial suburbs of Bilbao or the nearby skeptical pharmacist that Christ is real and the Church, the priests consecrating hosts, are his representatives. But López de Mendoza was worried that this would be one intervention too many. Regardless of whether the people of Piedramillera saw the Christ move or whether the Christ was really moving, he seemed to say to Pedro Arrastio, it would not be strategic to give the movements publicity. While we have only one of the bishop's letters to Arrastio, actually a first draft, it is clear from Arrastio's replies, other correspondence, and the fact that the ban on newspaper coverage was never lifted, that the bishop's attitudes as reflected in this draft did not change.[57]

On the one hand he agreed that, if the visions were authentic, their purpose would be "for the just to sanctify themselves more and more, for the lukewarm to become fervent, and for the sinner, if there are any, to convert truly to Our Lord God." In the case of the youth who had become introverted and melancholy, and others like him, the bishop told Arrastio to counsel him that "what has happened are not chastisements of the Lord, but rather great mercies, and that they should examine well

FIGURE 22. Fray José López de Mendoza, the bishop of Pamplona at the time of the Piedramillera visions. Courtesy Teodoro Alonso Turienzo, O.S.A.

their consciences and purify them for a good confession, and that way they will enjoy the delights and mercies which the Lord by these marvelous means has sought to communicate to them. Tell them all that if these marvels are true, Our Lord God seeks through them to incite us to penance and improve our Christian life, as he did in Lourdes and in part in Limpias as well, but that for [this purpose the marvels] are not necessary, and we should do this in any event according to the Lord's commandments." This then was his pastoral advice—how the priest should speak to his parishioners, relieve their anxiety, and get them to place their trust in a loving God. López de Mendoza sought to relieve people's fear of a chastisement, whether personal or collective, and his advice reflects more modern, less "Jansenist" or rigorist conceptions of a God who is stern and punishing.

This pastoral counsel, however, was an afterthought in his letter, an appendix. The body of the letter concentrated on the strategic inopportunity of the Piedramillera events. It is worth quoting at length, for it reflects general opinions in the Church and does much to explain the context that proved receptive to the vision episodes of 1918–1922.

If then the church, governed by the Holy Spirit, has always thought it necessary to proceed with such scrupulousness in matters of such transcendence for its own good and the good of its children and in order to avoid, as far as it can, even remotely supplying arms to its enemies to combat it, ridicule it, or despise it, you will understand that now it must extremely augment this prudence because of the incalculable number of its enemies, who combat it with satanic zeal in all fields and dispose of all human means for achieving the ends they propose, which they will not achieve because the Church is a divine work and has ensured by its divine founder the triumph over all of them: "Portie inferi non prevalebunt adversus eum."

While this is infallibly so, so also is it, as experience teaches us with total clarity, that incredulity has made numberless conquests among the children of the Church, and that even among those who have not separated from her, it has succeeded in cooling the faith and relaxing Christian morality in a large part of them, so that they are now fertile soil for the extension of its conquests. And this is the very powerful reason which counsels a redoubling of prudence when it comes to events such as you describe in your two letters.

Furthermore, I believe that the events of Limpias are for Spaniards a new and powerful argument that counsels extraordinary caution and prudence.

You know that for the last two years, more or less, the press has reported the extraordinary things that have been testified to by persons of all classes, genders, conditions, and ideas, some of them especially convincing witnesses because they are men of science or hold ideas contrary to our religion.

Well, in spite of so many and such exceptional witnesses who make depositions in favor of events that they say they have witnessed in Limpias, the incredulous make fun of them, ridicule them, and even among Catholics there are those who hold that all can be explained naturally, and that in no way can these events be considered miraculous.

This being the case, would it be prudent if in a remote corner of Navarra similar events were announced that had only been observed by simple and pious folk? Would this not give weapons to the enemies of religion to continue their attacks on the people of Limpias and the people of Piedramillera? Would it not confirm those Catholics who in good faith believe that all can be explained naturally? This is the special argument which obliges me to counsel prudence and more prudence.

This letter may be slightly disingenuous, for it is possible that López de Mendoza himself was one of those Catholics who "in good faith" believed that Limpias "could be explained naturally." Or at least he might have begun to have his doubts. Although he had granted indulgences to the Navarrese expedition of October 1919 he did not do so in the Spring of 1920, and he seems to have been convinced by at least some of Luis Urbano's arguments. For in response to the first edition of Urbano's book, and therefore probably before the Piedramillera visions began, he had written Urbano this carefully expressed encouragement, "In my opinion you have achieved your goal of defending the faith against its detractors and instructing the believers. May God grant you much time to publish even better things, and for that receive the blessing of your most devoted."[58]

In any case he was perfectly prescient about the negative effect of the Piedramillera visions on Limpias. In spite of his prudence, news of the visions leaked out, first by way of Santander, and then through the Madrid Traditionalist press. And Urbano indeed seized on the information, adding an appendix on Piedramillera to the second edition of his book. Urbano pointed out the inconsistency of publicizing the visions at Limpias and suppressing news about those in Navarra.[59]

Furthermore, in the May 28, 1920, articles from Estella about Piedramillera that Urbano reprinted there was passing mention of yet another crucifix in the Navarrese village of Mañeru, about forty kilometers east of Piedramillera, halfway to Pamplona. There again, it was reported, children, three of them, saw an image move.[60]

And using the Urbano second edition, other Catholic doubters like the Jesuit Joseph Vaughan mentioned the Piedramillera visions to show that Limpias would hold Catholics up to ridicule. "Soon Protestants will be talking of a Spanish plague of winking, blinking and nodding crucifixes."[61]

If the Limpias question had not subsided by 1922, doubters would have had still more ammunition, for on May 25, 1922, the Fabra news agency reported that in Melilla an image known as the Christ of the Prisoners was weeping and "showing clear signs of extreme anguish and agony" during a novena in the church of the Purísima.[62] Melilla, a Spanish enclave in North Africa, served as the base of operations in the Rif War. Since devotion to the Christ of Limpias was taken to North Africa by army officers and conscripted soldiers, and since the Limpias shrine was

Un Cristo milagroso en Melilla

Ante todo, ruego á todos
los que estas *Cositas* lean,
no tomen lo que á contarles
me apresuro, á irreverencia.
Como verán, me limito
á acoger lo que comentan
con fervoroso entusiasmo
gentes sensatas y serias,
entre las que predominan,
según mis informes, *ellas*.
Aseguran las personas
piadosas de referencia,
que una imagen de Jesús
que de antiguo se venera
en el templo que hoy los fraíles
Capuchinos regentean,
vierte con frecuencia lágrimas
y los ojos abre y cierra
cuando los fieles acuden
en demanda de clemencia,
por las culpas y pecados
que por fuerza, aquí en la tierra
cometemos todos, todos.
¿Quién en el mundo no peca?
El milagroso suceso
á que aludo y que recuerda
el registrado hace años
de Limpias en una iglesia,
ha dado lugar ya á muchas
animadas controversias
y son también muchos, muchos
los notables que se aprestan
á comprobar tan extraña
como prodigiosa nueva.
¿Es un exceso de fe?
¿Un visión? Allá esas
personas que lo pregonan
y aseguran sin reservas.
Yo, como digo al principio,
me limito á daros cuenta
de lo que dicen y afirman
gentes piadosas y serias.

                    P. PILLO.

FIGURE 23.
Poem in *El Telegrama del Rif,*
Melilla, 1922.
Courtesy Biblioteca Municipal,
Melilla.

used by families of soldiers besieged in the Rif struggle, it is not surprising that later, when many of these same soldiers were being held captive for ransom, family members in Melilla should see an image move as at Limpias during a novena preached, once again, by a Capuchin.

Given a climate of war between belief and disbelief in which "a large part" of Catholics themselves were in doubt, the terror of many of the more casual seers makes more sense. It may be that by 1920, when there were vocal, alert Spaniards in known geographic enclaves or given social locations who rejected traditional Catholic culture, what Pedro Arrastio, Miguel Atienza, and José López de Mendoza were reading as an old-fashioned sense of sin or guilt on the part of the seers might in addition have been an internalized fear or awareness of giving in to the other—the other new, "materialist" society. For "sinners," if they define themselves as such, are a part of Catholic society, perhaps a necessary part, certainly an integral part. But just as in the Middle Ages there were Jews and Moors, in 1920 there was another category outside the just/sinner dichotomy, the unbeliever. With the energy of the hierarchy focused on stopping the spread of disbelief, sin itself could be seen as the first step to disbelief, just as doubt was sinful.

Epilogue: *The View from Eraul*

ERAUL IS A grain-producing village near Abárzuza in the Sierra de Urbasa of Navarra. In 1920 it had about 270 inhabitants who, like those of Piedramillera and Mañeru, spoke Castillian.

Curious about how a man from there, Raimundo Galdeano, came to sponsor missions by the Limpias Capuchins both in Lezaún and Piedramillera, and how another Galdeano, Juan, from the same village had visions in Piedramillera, I went to Eraul in July 1988. There I was directed to Cándido Galdeano Echevarría, a very hale eighty years old, who turned out to be the nephew of Raimundo Galdeano and the son-in-law of Juan Galdeano Arana, the seer. It seemed perfectly natural to him that someone, at long last, should come inquiring about his uncle's missions. What he told me linked together the visions at Limpias, Piedramillera, Ezquioga, and La Barranca in the experience of one family.[1]

Raimundo, his uncle, was born about 1868, had no children and was widowed for the last decades of his life. He was a restless, self-sufficient man, always on the move with his burro. He cooked for himself and kept house for himself, after a fashion. He decided to dedicate whatever he earned from his farming (he owned a less-than-average size farm, was neither rich nor one of the poorest in the village) to sponsoring missions, particularly those of the Capuchins of Montehano, where he had a relative, P. Pastor María de Eraul.[2]

From 1934 to 1942, the last eight years of his life, he lived with his nephew Cándido, who therefore had ample opportunity to hear about his uncle's great spiritual hobby. Cándido understood that his uncle had sponsored no less than thirteen missions, and remembers a thick packet of letters from the Montehano Capuchins dealing with the practical arrangements.

Cándido recalled the names of some of the villages where the missions were held. And in the diocesan bulletin one reads reports of others. Some are given in the manuscript chronicle of the Montehano monastery. And in three cases it was specified in print that Raimundo Galdeano was the donor. We can identify eight of these missions for sure; all are within a thirty-five kilometer radius of Eraul (see Appendix Table 12).

This series of Montehano missions began in Larrión, adjacent to Eraul, in September 1918, even before the visions at Limpias. By that time Agatángelo de San Miguel and Anselmo de Jalón had become sufficiently successful in Cantabria for them to be recommended by P. Pastor María to his relative in Eraul. The Montehano Chronicle in 1917 remarked on the "very surprising success" and the "extraordinary attendance" at their first two missions together, in the mining towns of Villaverde de Trucios and Cabárceno.[3]

It is clear from the description of the 1918 mission in Larrión from the diocesan bulletin of Pamplona that the two friars made a deep impression. It is reported with admiration that they arrived having crossed the Urbión mountains from Alsasua, barefoot, as an act of penance.[4] The distance was thirty-five kilometers.

Their arrival in Navarra was unusual in other respects as well. Almost all the missions in the diocese (there were an average of nineteen per year reported in the bulletin from 1914 to 1933) were by missionaries from houses within Navarra, especially the Redemptorists (from Pamplona), the Capuchins (from Estella, Pamplona, Lecaroz, Sangüesa and Alsasua), and the Jesuits (from Pamplona and Javier), but also Vincentians, Claretians, Carmelites, and Passionists (see Appendix Table 13). At most missionaries might travel from adjacent Guipúzcoa and Vizcaya (above all those who preached in Basque) or Logroño.[5] In these years Agatángelo de San Miguel and Anselmo de Jalón were virtually the only missionaries who came from farther away. For them it was particularly unusual, as they were operating outside their Capuchin province of Castile, in a brother district where there were already many Capuchin missionaries.

So that if the second Limpias was in the zone near Eraul, it was no coincidence. For there was in that district a kind of "warm-up" with two prior missions at Larrión and Zudaire (in September 1919) by the Limpias missionaries. These contacts help to explain the early and enthusiastic participation from the zone in the Limpias pilgrimages. And we have seen that a third mission had been in progress in Lezaún when the Piedramillera visions broke out. Furthermore, it is not impossible that P. Agatángelo may have communicated to his Navarrese listeners his conviction that other crucifixes would begin to move.

Raimundo Galdeano was not the only nor the first person in Eraul who sponsored missions. A Capuchin missionary, Bernardino de Eraul, was the superior of the Capuchin house in Estella. He persuaded his parents, Veremundo Galdeano and Mercedes de Barrena, to leave all their money for periodic missions in Eraul.[6] The missions were held under his supervision beginning in 1916 and continued every six years up to 1934, at least, with missionaries from the Estella house. Bernardino preached missions himself in other area villages, and at this time there was yet another Capuchin missionary from the hamlet, Cristobal de Eraul.[7] So that little Eraul had a special affinity for missions.[8]

Pious bequests for missions, in any case, were common at this time. As in Eraul, there were missions every six years in nearby Artavia. In Garzaín there were missions every four years, endowed by the man who had been its parish priest for fifty years. And there were similar arrangements in Arroniz, Arellano, Ardanaz, Irurzun, and El Pueyo.[9]

Raimundo's efforts were exceptional in various ways. He paid for many missions. He paid for them in the villages of others. And those he paid for were particularly expensive, 450 pesetas, according to his nephew, no doubt because the preachers had to be brought from so far away (at first from Montehano, and later from El Pardo, near Madrid).

As I explored these matters with Cándido Galdeano, it seemed that almost the entire chain of visions in the north of Spain from 1919 to 1934 had touched Eraul and his family. He did not know whether Raimundo, his uncle, had ever gone to Limpias, but he did know that his own grandfather, Raimundo's father, José María, went there. One of the two friends who accompanied him, Fidel Unanua of Abárzuza, saw the Christ's eyes move, and Cándido remembers Fidel pantomiming the movement of the eyes as he shared the memory with Cándido's grandfather around the hearth on winter evenings.

As for Piedramillera, Cándido himself went there with his father and two other villagers when he was twelve years old. The trip by horseback took six hours. In Piedramillera they stayed with cousins of Cándido's mother, who was from nearby Learza. Cándido vowed he would give all fifty céntimos he carried with him to the Christ if he saw it move. He did not, and he gave only ten. But while he was in the church, a group of women did see it move. His father-in-law, Juan Galdeano (who was no close relation to Raimundo), maintained to his death the truth of his own vision.

One of the last missions Raimundo Galdeano paid for was in Lizárraga, probably in 1931 or 1932.[10] Perhaps to pay the missionaries, he went to the village on horseback, and while he was there he met the many Lizárraga children who in those years were visionaries. With one Lizárraga girl he went to Ezquioga, and there he observed her in trance.[11]

In part due to Raimundo Galdeano, the spirit of the visions at Limpias was kept alive in western Navarra, where it was reproduced in Piedramillera and Mañeru, and was later subsumed in the visions of Ezquioga and their Navarrese sequels. Eraul was exceptional because of its Capuchin connection and its refined taste for missions, but even so there were many hundreds of villages and towns in the north of Spain that followed the sequence of visions with interest, and whose inhabitants traveled long distances to be witnesses.

A view of the visions from Eraul, rather than from the vision locus itself, produces different insights. One has to do with the relation of communities and missionaries. This relation is not just with a particular order but also, within that order, with particular missionaries. Just as Raimundo Galdeano, even before Limpias, had taken a liking to Anselmo de Jalón and Agatángelo de San Miguel, so in villages across the north particular missionaries developed a following in particular places, and were called back time and again for sermons and novenas.

The significance of this for the Limpias pilgrimages is that, due to the previous preaching of the two missionaries throughout the diocese and, in the case of Anselmo de Jalón, throughout the north of Spain, there were dozens of communities who had, as it were, a firsthand connection to the Limpias visions. Their prior exposure to the missionaries made the vision more credible for them and allowed them to share, however vicariously, in the vision excitement. Here, then, was a ready-made constituency for the pilgrimages.

There is another, similar lesson in the particular connection of Eraul to Montehano through the kinship of Raimundo Galdeano and P. Pastor María and in the relation of Cándido Galdeano to Piedramillera through his mother's kin. Kin ties among laypersons, and between laypersons and religious linked people across wide distances, and formed particular incentives to trust in these visions. Santiago Estebanell gave as one of his reasons for believing in the Limpias visions that the "town" believed. Limpias was a town of 1,500 persons, some of them well-connected to the regional and even national ruling class. The mayor of Madrid was the conde de Limpias; the mayor of Santander descended from Limpias. Once the home community was convinced, and fervently so, then their particular friends and relations would be alerted. Quite possibly Estebanell knew someone in the town well, someone whom he believed. From the "small world" experiments of Stanley Milgrim, we know just how thoroughly connected a modern nation-state is, and how quickly important messages can spread through the web.

So while the view from the shrine and from the published literature leads us to the ideological environment that made people receptive in general, the view from the village, from the "receptor cell" as it were, leads us to the personal connections that seem so important for the initial credibility of the events, and for an initial identification with the persons involved in them.

APPENDIX

APPENDIX TABLE 1

Total Spanish Pilgrims and Spanish Bishops at Lourdes, 1868–1936, as Reported in *Annales de Notre-Dame de Lourdes*[a]

Year	Spaniards in Groups	Bishops	All Organized Pilgrims	Year	Spaniards in Groups	Bishops	All Organized Pilgrims
1869		1		1904	N.A.	7	207,000
1870		2		1905	N.A.	4[b]	170,000 (est.)
1872		1		1906	5,000	5	162,000
1873	450	2		1907	3,092	0	186,000 (est.)
1876	3,171	4		1908	12,000[b]	5[b]	404,000 (est.)
1877		5		1909	5,430	4[b]	170,000
1878		4		1910	11,650	2	191,500
1879	1,500	1		1911	12,945	2	237,722
1880		1		1912	10,950	8	246,972
1881		1		1913	14,473	5	260,153
1882	150	2		1914	2,630	10	N.A.
1883	1,415	0		1917	0	2	N.A.
1885		2		1920	1,569	2	N.A.
1886		3		1921	5,625	3	N.A.
1887	2,687	12		1922	3,400	8	251,667
1889	600	2		1923	11,325	9	247,840
1890		1		1924	9,457	7	209,205
1891		2		1925	17,840	18	284,400
1893		1		1926	17,160	5	279,060
1894		5		1927	18,775	14	280,870
1895		2		1928	16,192	6	196,806
1896		1		1929	14,295	8	242,405
1897	700	2		1930	12,214	8	238,244
1898		1		1931	200	4	224,796
1899	1,300	2		1932	1,715	5	194,311
1900	1,510	10	158,000	1933	5,000	8	241,885
1901	1,750	0	243,000	1934	3,797	4	178,762
1902		2	170,000	1935	8,250	8	205,770
1903	300	3	154,000 (est.)	1936	1,200	3	187,499

N.A. = not available

[a] For total pilgrims I used the *Annales* statistical summaries. For Spanish pilgrims and bishops I made my own tallies from the monthly reports. For the years not given in this table (between 1868 and 1936) no Spanish pilgrimages nor Spanish bishops were reported in *Annales*. I am indebted to Bro. William Fackovec, Thomas Kselman, P. André Cabes, and M. le Économe Lalique of l'Oeuvre de N.D. de Lourdes for help in gaining access to the *Annales*.

[b] Incomplete.

APPENDIX TABLE 2
The Geography of Spanish Devotion to Lourdes, 1868–1936[a]

Diocese or Pilgrimage Area	Pilgrim-ages	Visits by Bishops	Total Group Pilgrims	% of Spanish Total	Year of First Pilgrimage	Year of Most Pilgrims	
Catalonia	54	56	83,000	35	1887	1928	(11,300)
Barcelona	43	14			1889		
Tarragona	7	7			1911		
Gerona	4	3			1908		
Vich	1	5			1908		
Urgel	—	8					
Tortosa	—	8					
Solsona	—	5					
Lérida	—	6					
Vitoria	28	12	75,000[b]	31	1904	1911	(8,200)
Pamplona	23	15	20,000	8	1908	1910	(2,200)
Valencia	22	12	14,000[b]	6	1899	1908	(2,800)
Oviedo	11	7	4,000	2	1901	1926	(700)
Madrid	11	5	2,000[b]	1	1908	1908	(700)
Valladolid	7	8	2,500	1	1910	1925	(800)
Zaragoza	8	2	2,500	1	1920	1920	(800)
Santander	5	5	3,000[b]	1	1908	1908	(1,000)
Others	53	127	36,000	15	1876	1913	(6,000 Jaimistas)
Total	219	249	241,000				

[a] Figures are lacking for 1904 and 1905 and incomplete for 1908.
[b] Includes 1908.

Appendix Table 3

Spanish Bishops Most Assiduous at Lourdes, 1868–1936,
as Reported in *Annales de Notre-Dame de Lourdes*

Bishop	Total Trips 1868–1936	Year Consecrated	Years Bishop by 1936	Years Per Trip
M. Múgica Urrestarazu	10[a]	1918	18	1.8
P. Melo Alcalde	9	1908	28	3.1
M. Irurita Almandoz	8	1927	9	1.1
F. Bilbao Ugarriza	7[a]	1924	12	1.7
J. López Mendoza y García	7	1891	32	4.6
A. Pérez Muñoz	6	1909	11	1.8
J. Guitart Vilardebó	6	1920	16	2.7
V. Comellas Santamaría	5	1920	16	3.3
F. Vidal Barraquer	5[a]	1914	22	4.4
J. Miralles Sbert	5	1914	22	4.4
R. Gandásegui Gorrochategui	5	1905	31	6.2
B. Nozaleda Villa	5	1890	37	7.4
P. Segura Saénz	4	1916	20	5.0
G. Aguirre García	4	1885	28	7.0

[a] Includes one trip organized and led before consecration.

APPENDIX TABLE 4
Missions Reported in the Diocesan Bulletin of Santander, 1910–1919

Year	CSsR	OFMCap	SJ	CP	OCD	OP	CMF	CM	?	Total
1910	4	2[a]	3	2	0	0	1	0	0	12
1911	6	0[a]	1	1	0	0	0	0	0	8
1912	5	4[a]	4	2	1	0	0	0	0	16
1913	4	4	3[b]	0	0	0	0	0	0	11[b]
1914	0	0[a]	2[b]	0	1	2	0	0	0	5[b]
1915	2	3	1	0	0	0	0	0	0	6
1916	3	1	3	0	0	0	0	0	0	7
1917	5	6[a]	3	1	0	0	0	0	0	15
1918	3	2	3	1	0	0	0	0	0	9
1919	0	6	2	0	0	0	0	1	1	10
Total	32	28[a]	25[b]	7	2	2	1	1	1	99[ab]

CSsR=Redemptorists; OFMCap=Capuchins; SJ=Jesuits; CP=Passionists; OCD=Discalced Carmelites; OP=Dominicans; CMF=Claretians; CM=Vincentians.

[a] The manuscript chronicle of the Capuchin house at Montehano mentions five additional missions in the diocese in the 1910–1912 period and two additional missions both in 1914 and 1917. If a similar degree of undercounting holds for other orders, then about one in four missions was not reported in the bulletin.

[b] From November 1913 through Lent 1914 Jesuits held missions in every parish of the *archiprestazgo* of San Vicente de la Barquera. The bulletin (1914: 124) published only two parish reports of this large group.

APPENDIX TABLE 5
Missionaries Most Called on, Diocese of Santander, 1910–1919

Missions	Name and Order	Base	Active in Diocese
15	Pablo de Salamanca, OFMCap	Montehano	entire period
12	Ramón Sarabia, CSsR	El Espino	1910–1912, 1916
12	Esteban Lasquibar, SJ	Santander	1911–
12	Paulino Turiso, CSsR	El Espino	1912–1917
9	Agat. de San Miguel, OFMCap	Montehano	1916–
8	Anselmo de Jalón, OFMCap	Montehano	1912–
8	Felix R. de Samaniego, CSsR	El Espino	1915–

APPENDIX TABLE 6
Place of Origin Given in Limpias Vision Register, 1919[a]

Month	Urban	Rural	Cantabria	Vizcaya	Asturias	Other
May	25	38	46	11	6	4
June	32	32	32	16	12	4
July	20	23	33	7	1	7

[a] Compiled from list in TMA, 93–99. Through July 20 only.

APPENDIX TABLE 7
Bishops Interested in Lourdes and Limpias (up to 1936) of Those Active in 1919

		Visited Limpias		
		No	Yes	Total
Visits to Lourdes	Never or only once	23	6	29
	More than once	10	12[a]	22
	Total	33	18	51

[a] Five bishops went to both Lourdes and Limpias more than once: Remigio Gandásegui Gorrochategui, Pedro Segura, Manuel González, Julián de Diego y García Alcolea, and Vicente Sánchez de Castro.

APPENDIX TABLE 8
Visionaries Named in the Texts of Six Apologetic Books

Author	Total	Priests or Male Religious	Laymen	Laywomen
T. Echevarría	70	18 (.26)	48 (.69)	4 (.06)
Andrés de P.	113	29 (.26)	69 (.61)	15 (.13)
Trenor	54	13 (.24)	30 (.56)	11 (.20)
Juan de Guernica	62	8 (.13)	45 (.73)	9 (.15)
T.M.A.	111	14 (.13)	64 (.58)	33 (.30)
Peña Santamaría	80	21 (.26)	57 (.71)	2 (.03)
Average	81	.21	.65	.15

APPENDIX TABLE 9
Gender of Limpias Seers

	Proportion of Named Seers		
	in complete list in *Los Frutos*	in selected list in *Los Frutos*	in texts of six apologetic books (averages)
Laywomen	.62	.09	.15
Laymen	.36	.77	.65
Priests or male religious	.02	.14	.21
Number named	335	44	81 (average)

APPENDIX TABLE 10
Proportion and Number of Limpias Pilgrims and Seers

Date	Franciscan Trips from Galicia	Priests or Religious	Laymen	Laywomen	Total
October 22, 1919	Pilgrims	.17 (81)	.18 (86)	.64 (308)	475
	Seers	.18 (5)	.32 (9)	.50 (14)	28
May 10, 1921	Pilgrims	.12 (70)	.25 (145)	.64 (379)	591
	Seers	.19 (5)	.22 (6)	.59 (16)	27
	Barcelona Trip Centro de Defensa Social				
June 24, 1920	Pilgrims	.08 (24)	.32 (100)	.60 (188)	312
	Seers	.10 (4)	.26 (10)	.64 (25)	39

APPENDIX TABLE 11
Religious Orders and Limpias, 1919–1926

Order	Number of Pilgrimages in Which Members of Order Were Present[a]	Authors of Books or Articles	Seers Mentioned in Print
Capuchins	34	8	11
Jesuits	23	3 (+3)[b]	1
Franciscans[c]	11	6	2
Carmelites	11	2	0
Passionists	11	1	1
Redemptorists	11	0	0
Salesians	7	1	3
Dominicans	6	1 (+1)	0
Vincentians	4	0	2
Sisters of the Poor	4	0	0
Augustinians	3	0	1
Sisters of Charity	3	0	0
Claretians[c]	2	3	0
Trinitarians	2	0	0
Bros. of Christian Doctrine	2	0	0
Dames of Catechism	1	0	0
Bros. of Christian Schools	1	0	0
Mothers of Sacred Hearts	1	0	0
Mercedarian Sisters[c]	1	0	0
Mercedarian Fathers[c]	1	0	0
Franciscan Sisters[c]	1	0	0
Fathers of Precious Blood[c]	1	0	0
Daughters of the Cross	0	0	2
Cistercians	0	0	2
Escolapians	0	1	0

[a] Includes groups under its spiritual direction. Not included are private visits by individual religious.

[b] ( ) authors opposed.

[c] No houses in diocese of Santander, according to *Anuario Eclesiástico 1919* (Barcelona: E. Subirana), 364–416.

APPENDIX TABLE 12
Missions of the Capuchins of Montehano in Navarra

Date	Location	Mission Leaders	Sources[a]
September 1918	Larrión	Agatángelo de San Miguel & Anselmo de Jalón	B,M
[March 1919 First visions in Limpias]		ASM & AJ	
September 1919	Zudaire	ASM & AJ	M
May 1920	Lezaún	ASM & AJ	B,C,M,R
[May 1920 First visions in Piedramillera]			
October 1920	Piedramillera	AJ & Ignacio de Ajanguiz	B,R
January 1923	Villatuerta	Pablo de Salamanca & Mariano de Guetaria	B,C,M,R
October 1923	Valle de Lana	ASM	B
April 1924	Acedo	ASM & Claudio de Viñayo	M
October 1929	Eulz (Allín)	ASM & Ildefonso de Armellada (from El Pardo)	B
?	Grocín[b]		C
1931?	Lizárraga[b]		C

[a] B=Diocesan bulletin, Pamplona; C=Cándido Galdeano; M=Chronicle of Montehano Capuchins; R=Raimundo Galdeano mentioned as donor.

[b] I could not find evidence of the missions at Grocín or Lizárraga, but both the diocesan bulletin and the Montehano Chronicle omitted some missions.

APPENDIX TABLE 13
Missions Reported in the Diocesan Bulletin of Pamplona, 1914–1933

Year	Religious Orders of the Missionaries[a]									Total
	OFMCap	CSsR	SJ	CMF	CM	CP	OFM	OCD	?	
1914	1	1	6	1	0	0	0	0	0	9
1915	1	1	5	3	0	0	0	0	0	10
1916	3	5	5	0	4	1	1	1	0	20
1917	2	4	0	2	0	0	1	0	0	9
1918	5	8	1	1	4	0	0	0	1	20
1919	2	7	0	3	4	0	1	1	0	18
1920	6	3	4	3	1	0	1	1	0	19
1921	7	7	4	0	2	0	0	1	0	21
1922	7	5	1	1	3	0	1	1	0	19
1923	11	7	5	1	0	0	0	1	0	25
1924	5	3	9	2	3	0	0	1	0	23
1925	6	7	4	3	2	0	1	0	0	23
1926	6	5	1	1	0	0	0	1	2	16
1927	10	5	4	4	2	3	1	1	0	30
1928	12	6	6	1	2	0	1	0	1	29
1929	2	2	1	0	0	1	0	0	0	6
1930	4	3	0	1	0	0	0	0	0	8
1931	6	10	5	1	0	1	1	0	1	25
1932	3	11	9	0	0	0	1	0	1	25
1933	4	8	11	2	0	1	1	0	1	28
Total	103	108	81	30	27	7	11	9	7	383

[a] OFMCap=Capuchins; CSsR=Redemptorists; SJ=Jesuits; CMF=Claretians; CM=Vincentians; CP= Passionists; OFM=Franciscans; OCD=Discalced Carmelites.

Notes

ABBREVIATIONS

A   *Annales de Notre-Dame de Lourdes*
ACM   Archivo del Convento Capuchino de Montehano (Cantábria)
ADP   Archivo Diocesano de Pamplona
BOEP   *Boletín Oficial Eclesiástico del Obispado de Pamplona*
BOES   *Boletín Oficial Eclesiástico del Obispado de Santander*
CE   *El Correo Español*, Madrid
D   (Diary) "El Santo Cristo de la Agonía de Limpias; Narraciones histori-
            cas y observaciones sobre dicha imagen"—Gabriel Fernández Somell-
            era, Archivo Parroquial, Limpias
DM   *El Diario Montañés* (Santander)
DN   *Diario de Navarra* (Pamplona)
DV   *Diario de Valencia*
E   Tomás Echevarría, *Los prodigios de Limpias*, 1919
ED   *El Debate* (Madrid)
EF   *El Eco Franciscano* (La Coruña)
EP   *El Pueblo*. Diario Republicano de Valencia
JLM   Fr. José López de Mendoza. Obispo de Pamplona
NA   National Archive, Washington, D.C.
PA   Pedro Arrastio, Regente de Piedramillera
PN   *El Pensamiento Navarro* (Pamplona)
SC   *La Semana Católica* (Madrid)
T   Leopoldo Trenor, *¿Qué pasa en Limpias?* 1920
TMA   [Teofilo Martínez Antigüedad], *Los frutos de una misión*, 1920

CHAPTER ONE

1. Charly Clerc, *Les théories relatives au culte des images chez les auteurs grecs, 2me siècle après J.-C.* (Paris: Fontemoing, 1915), 44–49. From Pygmalion to Pinocchio it was a secular tradition as well.

2. Agustín de Arques Jover, *Breve historia de Nuestra Señora del Milagro de Concentayna* (Madrid: Cano, 1805); William A. Christian, Jr., *Local Religion in Sixteenth-Century Spain* (Princeton, N.J.: Princeton University Press, 1981), 195–200, and "Francisco Martínez quiere ser santero; nuevas imágenes milagrosas y su control en las España del siglo XVIII," *El Folklore Andaluz* 4 (1989): 103–114, about a bleeding crucifix.

3. Roland Barthes, *Sade, Fourier, Loyola* (Paris: Editions du Seuil, 1971), 45–80.

4. Thomas A. Kselman, *Miracles and Prophecies in Nineteenth-Century France* (New Brunswick, N.J.: Rutgers University Press, 1983). For a sensitive study of "failed" apparitions in the Drôme in the context of secularization, see Bernard Delpal, *Entre paroisse et commune; les Catholiques de la Drôme au milieu du XIXᵉ siècle* (Valence: Editions Peuple Libre, 1989), 155–169.

5. The major French visions like those of Lourdes (see below) and La Salette were quickly reported in Spain. In the Biblioteca Municipal of Barcelona is abundant literature that testifies to Catalan devotion to La Salette: Duchaine, pbro. *Nueva relación de la aparición milagrosa de la Santísima Virgen a dos pastorcillos en una montaña de la Salette* (Barcelona: Hered. Vda. Pla, 1847), 16 pages; *Aparició milagrosa de María Santisima a dos pastorets en una montanya de la Salette partit de Corps* (Puigcerdà e Vich, J. Valls, 1847) 16 pages; R. Rousselot, *Manual de Peregrino à nuestra Señora de la Saleta, Distrito de Corps* (Isère) (Barcelona: Librería católica de Pous y Cia., 1861), 80 pages; another edition of the same work in 1863; and other devotional works on La Salette printed in 1861, 1867, and 1868. In 1883 in Barcelona there was a pious assocation and a magazine dedicated to the shrine. See Nazario Pérez, *Historia Mariana de España* 4 (Valladolid: Gerper, 1947): 221–222. Even "minor" visionaries, like Anne-Marie Coste, received attention, as with Fructuoso Morell, *Las apariciones de María Santísma a Ana-Maria Coste de Lyon (Francia)* (Barcelona: Imp. Península, 1884), an expanded version of a French pamphlet by L. de Cissey.

6. Herbert Thurston discusses the Italian cases of 1796, 1850, and others at Campocavallo in 1892, as well as French, Irish, German, and Maltese examples in "Limpias and the Problem of Collective Hallucination," *The Month* 136 (1920): 150–163, 235–246, 345–355, 386–398, 532–541, gathered in *Beauraing and Other Apparitions; an account of some borderland cases in the psychology of mysticism* (London: Burns, Oates and Washbourne, 1934). For Castel Petroso, Antonio M. Mattei, *Il Santuario dell' Addolorata a Castel Petroso* (Isernia: Grafica Isernina, 1982), which neglects to mention the negative judgment of the Holy Office on the visions. For recent studies of the 1796 episodes, Marta Pierini Francini, "Immagini sacre en Toscana: dal tumulto di Prato al 'Viva María,'" in Sofia Boesch Gajano and Lucia Sebastiani, *Culto dei santi, instituzioni, e classi sociali in età preindustriale* (L'Aquila-Roma: Japadre, 1984), 835–872; and Marina Caffiero, *La nuova era; miti e profezie dell' Italia in Rivoluzione* (Genoa: Marietti, 1991), 29–32, 61–62.

7. For Spanish accounts of these Italian episodes: *Extracto de una carta de Ancona de 27 de Junio de 1796, en la que se refiere el prodigio hecho en la dicha ciudad el día 25 del mismo mes por una imagen de María Santísima Señora Nuestra, pintada en un lienzo, y existente en la Iglesia Catedral, dedicada a San Ciriaco* (no place, printer, or date), 4 pages, and *Suplemento del día 19 de julio del ano 1796 de la continuacion de las maravillosas imagenes de la Ciudad de Ancona, y confirmacion*

de los portentos obrados por medio de ellas (Madrid, 1796), 4 pages, both in Biblioteca de la Real Academia de Historica; *Copia y relación del prodigioso, frecuentísimo abrimiento de ojos de una imagen en la iglesia de Maria Santissima . . . Ancona* (Málaga: Hered. de Francisco Martínez de Aguilar, 1796), 16 pages, cited in Andrés Llordén, *La Imprenta en Málaga* (Madrid: CSIC, 1972), 2 volumes. The Rimini and Prata cases are cited in DM, 28 July 1919, SC, 1 August 1919, and Juan de Guernica, *El Cristo maravilloso; la fe en lo de Limpias; nueva aportación de datos sobre los sucesos* (Buenos Aires: Imprenta y Casa Coni, 1920), 141–143.

8. The only cases of apparitions or image activations that attracted more than very local attention in Spain from 1800 to 1919 that I know of are as follows:

1837 Polán (Toledo). A painting of Nuestra Señora de la Piedad wept or bled in the context of Carlist tensions, a secularized monk who was the parish priest, and anticlerical hostility from the mayor, who would do his plowing on Sundays in front of the church. When the image was enclosed in a glass case, the secretions ceased. (Archive Diocesano de Toledo Vallejo 3: exp. 10.)

1850 La Solana (Ciudad Real). On May 25 María Antonia García Parra had her first vision of Nuestra Señora del Consuelo. She eventually entered a convent in Manzanares. The La Solana church at first had a painting illustrating her vision, which in 1855 was replaced by a statue. Devotion when I visited in 1977 was largely limited to the seer's family. See J. Alfonso López de la Osa, "Un capullo que se abre" and the seer's diary, edited by Carmen Velacoracho, and printed together by Editorial Aspiraciones, Madrid, 1952. There is also a novena issued by the same publisher in 1953, by Eusebio María Morales.

1886 Ochando (Segovia). From February to May a woman age 20 named Ruperta had daily visions to ever-increasing numbers of persons. The climax was May 8, when a great message was to be received. A French priest with a Spanish assistant confronted the girl in public, and then before municipal authorities. See. L.-J.-M. Cros, *Histoire de Notre Dame de Lourdes* (Paris: Beauchesne, 1926), 2:27–28.

1906 Chauchina (Granada). On April 9, Monday of Holy Week, Rosario Granados, age 65, was cured of suppurating sores on her leg during a vision of the Virgen de los Dolores. A convent of Capuchin nuns was founded as a result. In the convent archives is a three-page narration of the events by the parish priest Francisco Castro Izquierdo, along with his seven-page interrogation of the seer. A photocopy is in the archive of the Secretario de Cámara, Arzobispado de Granada. See also *Oración y Sacrificio; Boletín mensual órgano de la "Liga de oraciones y sacrificios" canónicamente fundada y adherida a la Adoración Diurna del Smo. Sacramento practicada con privilegio pontificio, por las RR. MM. Capuchinas, bajo los auspicios de Nuestra Señora de los Dolores, vulgo Del Espino* (Chauchina, Granada) 1: 4–5 (Abril y Mayo 1927) and Rafael María de Antequera, OFMCap., *Historia de la Aparición de Ntra. Sra. del Espino* (Chauchina, 1971). There was never a formal diocesan investigation of the cure or the vision.

For the case of Manzaneda (1903) and minor activations immediately preceding those at Gandía, Limpias, and Piedramillera, see below.

9. William J. Callahan, *Church, Politics, and Society in Spain 1750–1874* (Cambridge, Mass.: Harvard University Press, 1984), 231–241; Pedro María Ayala, *Vida documentada del Siervo de Dios, P. Francisco de Paula Tarín de la Compañía de Jesús* (Sevilla: Gráficas la Gavidia, 1951); José María Viñas, "San Antonio María Claret y la piedad de Cataluña," *Analecta Sacra Tarraconensis* 28:479–495.

10. For the demonstrations of 1906 and 1910, José Andrés Gallego, *La política religiosa en España 1889–1913* (Madrid: Editora Nacional, 1975), 295, 382, 389. Sor Patrocinio (María Josefa de Quiroga Capopardo, 1811–1891), known as La Monja de las Llagas, was a visionary and founder of convents who gained a certain political influence as a confidante of the royal family. See the ample bibliography on the subject, and Arturo González and Miguel Diéguez, *Sor Patrocinio* (Madrid: Editora Nacional, 1981).

11. For Madrid: "and we could expand this side of the matter more with a number of events that have occurred in modern times having to do with the Christ venerated in the parish church of St. Sebastian, in Madrid." (Juan de Guernica, *El Cristo maravilloso,* 143); For Cádiz: "In a village in the province of Cádiz, whose name at the moment escapes us, is venerated another image of Christ, which ten or twelve years ago sweated drops of blood, as people who saw it then and who are still alive can testify" (SC, 1 August 1919, 148); for Barcelona: "all of us in Barcelona remember the Church's prohibition of certain ceremonies in a famous shrine. At Limpias, on the contrary, the Church permits it." (Mariano Vilaseca, "Un juicio autorizado," DM, 8 July 1920, from *Gaceta de Cataluña.*) Elisa Kennelesky ("El Cristo de Limpias," *La Epoca,* 14 September 1919) cites the case of a moving image of a Niño Milagroso in a convent, without naming the diocese.

12. "About 1911 there was a lot of talk about certain manifestations, apparently miraculous, taking place in the Asilo del Niño Jesús de Praga in Seville, with an image of the Immaculate Conception of the Miraculous Medal. We will say nothing about them, as the Church authorities did not consider them well-enough founded to approve them. But we will note that a few years later, in 1916, P. Juan Cristóstomo Alonso, S.J., published a pamphlet, *La Virgen milagrosa en al Asilo del Niño Jesús de Praga,* with many cases of spiritual graces and marvelous cures obtained by this image, without mentioning the origin of the devotion to it." Nazario Pérez, *Historia Mariana de España* 5 (Valladolid: Gerper, 1949): 124, and 139, n. 3: "Of this image it was said that it opened its eyes, but the proofs did not convince Church authorities, according to what Cardenal Almaraz told us."

13. *Razón y Fe* 15 (July 1906): 403; Lorenzo L. Sanvicente, "Un milagro de la Virgen de los Dolores," who cites *Proceso diocesano sobre el hecho extraordinario acaecido el 20 de abril en el Colegio de los Padres Jesuitas* (Quito: Imprenta del Clero, 1906), xlviii + 79 pages; *Razón y Fe* 16 (September 1906): 178–187; Juan de Guernica, *El Cristo maravilloso,* 243–245; Camilo Ponce Enriques, "Un recente

favor extraordinario de la Dolorosa del Colegio de San Gabriel (Quito)," *La Estrella del Mar*, 8 May 1930, 252–253; "El año jubilar de la Dolorosa del Colegio," ibid., 24 October 1930, 600–601. See also "Milagro en Lorena," *La Hormiga de Oro*, 11 January 1908, 22. In Brin (Meurthe-et-Moselle) nearly all the congregation saw the image of a young man on the host displayed during mass on December 8, 1907. On the same page is an account of Pius X seeing the Virgin blessing him.

14. A 7 (1874): 102–103; some Carlist refugees came with the Perpignan pilgrimage of 1873, A 6 (1873): 144; A 13 (1880): 234; A 17 (1884): 362.

15. A 8 (1875): 268–269; A 13 (1880): 71–72; A 16 (1883): 90–92, 154–156.

16. A 20 (1887): 87–88, 142–143; A 22 (1889): 198; A 30 (1897): 195; A 32 (1899): 173–174; A 33 (1900): 199; A 34 (1901): 53, 182, 239; A 36 (1903): 79–80. Another way to get at early Spanish interest in Lourdes is through publications. In France there were booklets in Spanish printed as early as 1862. For publications in Spain, the collection of Léon Clugnet, now in the Marian Library of Dayton, Ohio, while it is by no means complete, contains 23 items published by 1900, as follows: 1871–1880 9 (Madrid 5, 1 each from Barcelona, Granada, Oviedo, and Tolosa); 1881–1890 7 (Barcelona 5, Madrid 2); 1891–1900 7 (Barcelona 3, Madrid 3, Córdoba 1).

17. A 38 (1905): 144–148; A 40 (1907): 200. For the upsurge of attention the 1904–1908 period, see the bibliography in El Conde de las Navas [Juan Gualberto], *Lourdes, impresiones de un incurable* (Madrid: Tipografía Ducazal, 1908).

18. The Nationalist pilgrimage had the support of López Mendoza of Pamplona, Gandásegui of Ciudad Real, and the Navarrese bishops Baztán of Oviedo, Ilundiáin of Orense, and Ozcoidi of Tarazona. Both Basque pilgrimages of 1911 had about four thousand participants. See A 43 (1910): 184–186; A 41 (1911): 139–140, 165, 170; and Engracio de Aranzadi, *Ereintza; siembra de nacionalismo vasco* [1935] (San Sebastian: Auñamendi, 1980) 284–313.

19. A 46 (1913): 4–5.

20. A 40 (1907): 59–64.

21. A 42 (1909): 7–8, 13.

22. A 44 (1911): 102–103, 139–140, 147, 201–202; A 45 (1912): 344–345; A 46 (1913): 85. Other cures (not a comprehensive list): nun from Málaga A 11 (1878): 119; girl from Loja A 21 (1888): 37–38; Catalan women A 57 (1924): 49–50, 65–69, and A 58 (1925): 50, 125–130, and A 60 (1927): 60–64; Basque woman and man A 61 (1928): 65–66; Valencian woman A 68 (1935): 142–143; and Barcelona woman A 68 (1935): 146–147.

23. Nazario Pérez, *Historia Mariana de España*, 4 (Valladolid: Gerper, 1947): 204.

24. P. Ortíz, S.J., cited in José María Azara, *Lourdes y el Pilar* (Zaragoza: Mariano Escar, 1906), 60. *Razón y Fe* 9 (1906): 389, approved: "Sr. Azara wants El Pilar to be another Lourdes and more than Lourdes. . . . This should be the aspiration of every good Spaniard.".

25. Nazario Pérez, *Historia Mariana* 5: 13–21, 117–118, 120, 138–140.

26. A 53 (1920): 113–118; A 54 (1921): 130; A 55 (1922): 126; A 67 (1934): 186.

27. Most pilgrims went to Basque shrines like Loyola; some parishes did not report where their pilgrims went. Compiled from Antonio Cillán Apalategui, *Sociología electoral de Guipúzcoa* (1900–1936) (San Sebastián: Sociedad Guipuzcoana de Ediciones y Publicaciones, 1975), 106–112.

28. A 42 (1909): 261.

29. I am indebted here to conversations with and unpublished writings of Susan Harding and Peter Brown.

30. For the location of large employers of industrial workers and miners in Santander province in the first decades of this century, see José Ortega Valcarcel, *Cantabria 1886–1986; formación y desarrollo de una economía moderna* (Santander: Librería Estvdio, 1986). For 1911 he gives 7,119 iron miners (about 1,500 in the mines close to Limpias around Castro-Urdiales, and the rest around Santander's bay) and 1,631 zinc miners, mostly around Torrelavega and to the west. The only other concentration of workers in large industries were in iron works in Santander and Torrelavega (1,400 in the two plants of Nueva Montaña in 1910), workers in the Santander tobacco factory, almost all of them women (about 900), and 300 workers in the Solvay chemical plant at Torrelavega. Of these groups, only the tobacco workers came to Limpias as such.

31. Sisinio Nevares, S.J. (Valladolid) to José Barrachina, S.J. (Rome), Asistente de España, 12 February 1920, in Quintín Aldea Vaquero, Joaquín García Granda, and Jesús Martín Tejedor, *Iglesia y sociedad en la España del siglo XX; Catolicismo Social (1909–1940)* 2 (Madrid: CSIC, 1987): 682.

32. Nazario Pérez, *Historia Mariana* 5: 3–4.

33. Santiago Díez Llama, *La situación socio-religiosa de Santander y el Obispo Sánchez de Castro (1884–1920)* (Santander: Institución Cultural de Cantabria, 1971) 125–126, 138. Benito Madariaga de la Campa, "La crítica de 'Electra' en la prensa de Cantabria," *Actas del Congreso Internacional de 'Fortunata y Jacinta' 1887–1987* (Madrid: Facultad de Ciencias de la Información, 1989), 325–335.

34. Juan Pablo Fusi Aizpurua, *Política obrera en el país vasco (1880–1923)* (Madrid: Ediciones Turner, 1975), 226–230; Andrés de Mañaricua, *Santa María de Begoña en la historia espiritual de Vizcaya* (Bilbao: Editorial Vizcaina, 1950), 468–474; Nazario Pérez, *Historia Mariana* 5:4–5.

35. *La Hormiga de Oro*, 20 February 1909, 131. The bombings took place February 7.

36. Joan Connelly Ullman, *The Tragic Week: A Study of Anticlericalism in Spain, 1875–1912* (Cambridge, Mass.: Harvard University Press, 1968).

37. National Archive, Diplomatic Branch [DB], Consular Reports [CR] Santander, 800. 1 October 1919, and 5 February 1920, by John H. Grant and Maurice Stafford, respectively.

38. The American consul reported from Santander on 14 August 1919, that "there is plenty of work here" NA DB CR 800 (John H. Grant).

39. NA DB CR (Bilbao) 800. 3 October 1923 (Henry M. Wolcott).

40. *El Pueblo Cántabro*, 3 May 1919, 3.

41. NA DB CR (Bilbao) 800 (Henry M. Wolcott).

42. María Encarnación Pérez Ruiz, Itziar Rubio Barcina, and Ana Ureta Basáñez, *Movilización obrera en Vizcaya, 1918–1923* (San Sebastian: Txertoa, 1986), 37; Ignacio Olabarri Gortazar, *Relaciones laborales en Vizcaya (1890–1936)* (Durango: Leopoldo Zugaza, 1978), 404, 498. I gratefuly acknowledge here the help of Ben Martin and his generously allowing me to consult his manuscript on the history of Spanish trade unionism.

43. Fr. S. M. Rodríguez Merino, "España: Los problemas cardinales de actualidad," *Razón y Fe* 19 (January–February 1919): 88–90.

44. Manuel Ballbé, *Orden público y militarismo en la España constitucional 1812–1983*, 2nd ed. (Madrid: Alianza, 1985), 297.

45. Joan A. Lacomba, *Crisi i revolució al Pais Valencià (1917)* (Valencia: Garbi, 1968), 141–150, 161–189; also Manuel Ballbé, *Orden público*, 289–296; 2nd especially Joan del Alcàzar, *Temps d'avalots al país valencià (1914–1923)* (Valencia: Diputació de València, 1989).

46. Luis Urbano, *Los prodigios de Limpias a la luz de la teología y de la ciencia* (Barcelona: Rosas y Espinas, 1920), 1, 3–4.

47. Leopoldo Trenor, *¿Qué pasa en Limpias? (Notas de la cartera de un vidente)* (Valencia: Tipografía Moderna, 1920), 12.

48. "Una información interesante; el hecho portentoso de Gandía," *Diario de Valencia*, 16 June 1918.

49. The *Asilo* was known as the "Casa del Beato," and its church was San Roque.

50. "Lo de Gandía: Hecho prodigioso?" DV, 13 June 1918.

51. Ibid.

52. I found nothing in *La Correspondencia de Valencia, El Mercantil Valenciano*, or *La Voz de Valencia. El Correo Español* broke the news in Madrid on June 11. It carried short notes on June 12, 13, and 22. *El Debate* gave a summary of the events on June 21. I found no mention in *El Siglo Futuro, ABC, Imparcial, Epoca, El Sol*, or *Heraldo de Madrid*.

53. "Milagro!! Suceso prodigioso—si que también sangriento," EP, 14 June 1918. The story begins with the following rhyme:

Fresca la sangre de Cristo
dicen está todavía
Lo dicen porque lo han visto,
tres muchachas de Gandía.

54. "El milagro de Gandía; dos réprobos, dos sangres—varias gotas y nungún milagro," EP, 21 June 1918. For Gandía in 1910, see Espasa-Calpe, *Enciclopedia* 25:681–685.

55. Dr. Darás is named by ED (25 June 1922) as one of the promoters of the

sixty-foot monument to the Sacred Heart erected overlooking Gandía. The town was first consecrated to the Sacred Heart 30 May 1920.

56. "El Milagro de Gandía; una figura interesante," EP, 23 June 1918. See also in EP: "Las víctimas del clericalismo. Secuestro de una señorita . . . ," 2 June 1903. "Las víctimas del clericalismo. El Secuestro de la Srta. Pilar Izquierdo . . . ," 3 June 1903. "El Mitín de Ayer," 4 June 1903. Enrique Brines, "A *La Voz de Valencia*," 5 June 1903. "El secuestro de la Srta. Pilar Izquierdo; carta de su hermano . . . Daniel Izquierdo Collado," 7 June 1903.

At this time *El Pueblo* was serializing Emile Zola, *La Verdad*. Perhaps because of commercial contacts resulting from the orange trade, Valencia was particularly keyed into French clerical/anticlerical struggles; cf. also, below, the activities of P. Corbató in relation to France, and Valencian pilgrimages to Lourdes. For more on the political tensions in Valencia in 1903 see Ramiro Reig, *Blasquistas y clericales; la lucha por la ciudad en la Valencia de 1900* (Valencia: Institució Alfons el Magnànim, 1986) 157–164, 290–298, 303–307. He does not mention this episode.

57. *Anuario Eclesiástico*, 1919 (Barcelona: E. Subirana), 402.

58. EP, 26 June 1918.

59. EP, 21 June 1918.

60. Ibid.

61. DV, 16 June 1918.

62. EP, 21 June 1918.

63. Ibid.

64. Conversations in Gandía, 5, 6 December 1983.

65. J. Luis Martín, "Los milagros," DV, 16 June 1918.

66. *Revista de Gandía* 19 (2 March 1918): 926. Odd issues of this weekly are in the Archivo Municipal de Gandía.

67. Ibid. 19 (6 June 1918): 939.

Queremos que los hombres errantes y perdidos
Que van huyendo ciegos del árbol de la Cruz,
No vivan por más tiempo en la impiedad sumidos
Ni cierran obstinados sus ojos a la luz.

68. Corresponsal, Pego, "El milagro de Gandía," EP, 18 June 1918 (sent 15 June). He goes on to cite pseudo-miraculous events in Pego that had not received wider media attention.

69. Odd issues of *Germinal* are in the Archivo Municipal de Gandía.

Chapter Two

1. Severiano de Santibáñez, *Manual escogido de ejercicios y cánticos religiosos que usan en sus misiones los RR.PP. Capuchinos. Le precede una breve instrucción acerca de lo que es la Misa y sus indulgencias y frutos* (Madrid: El Pardo, Imprenta de "El Mensajero Seráfico," 1915), 3–5. (Hereafter *Manual.*)

2. BOES 1917:149 (Somo).

3. Nemesio Otaño, "El canto de las mujeres en la Iglesia," *Razón y Fe* 61 (December 1921): 451–472.

4. *Manual,* 105.

¡Ea! Animosos, con bizarría,
De nuestros padres siguiendo en pos
Gritemos siempre a turba impía
A Dios queremos y sólo a Dios!

5. For seventeenth-century antecedents of this dramaturgy and the "hard" and "soft" roles in missions, see Giuseppe Orlandi, "Missioni parrochiali e drammatica popolare," *Spicilegium Historicum, Congregationis SSmi. Redemptoris* 22 (1974): 313–348.

6. BOES 1912:111–112, José María G. Toca.

7. Ibid., 111. Those attending included the priests and parishioners of Cabuérniga, Tudanca, Puentenansa, Cosío, San Sebastián de Garabandal, Obeso, and Celis.

8. BOES 1913:72, Juan Pellón Ruigómez, Arredondo.

9. BOES 1915:158, Ventura Fernández, Tudanca.

10. BOES 1917:150, José Prado, Cabárceno.

11. BOES 1917:149, José Prado, Cabárceno.

12. BOES 1912:111, José María G. Toca, Carmona.

13. BOES 1920:197, José Irigoyen, Lezaún.

14. BOES 1910:130, A. Gutiérrez Gómez, Cabezón de la Sal. On peasant resistance to Church-sponsored forgiveness, see David Warren Sabean, *Power in the Blood: Popular Culture and Village discourse in Early Modern Germany* (Cambridge: Cambridge University Press, 1984), 37–60.

15. Camilo de Grajal, Useras, 14 July 1989; Francisco de Bilbao, Madrid, 6 May 1989; BOES 1919:114; Andrés de Palazuelo, *Origen y desenvolvimiento de los sucesos de Limpias; reseña histórico-crítica del Santísimo Cristo de la Agonía venerado en la villa de Limpias* (Madrid: El Mensajero Seráfico, 1920), 70–71; BOES 1912:111–112.

16. ACM, "Necrología," No. 30. R. P. Anselmo de Jalón, signed by Leandro de Bilbao. Born 25 April 1872 Marcos Viguera, in Jalón (Logroño) (Andrés de Palazuelo gives date as 25 April 1871). Died 13 May 1945, at Montehano. According to Andrés de Palazuelo (*Origen,* 69), he became a priest 21 September 1894 and joined the Capuchins 1 January 1903.

17. Andrés de Palazuelo (*Origen,* 71), gives the following provinces: Navarra, Alava, Vizcaya, Burgos, Asturias, León, Valladolid, Avila, Lugo, La Coruña, Pontevedra, Orense, Zamora, Salamanca, Cáceres, and Toledo, omitting Santander.

18. Buenaventura de Carrocera, *Necrología de los Frailes Menores Capuchinos de la provincia del Sagrado Corazón de Castilla (1609–1943)* (Madrid: El Mensajero Seráfico, 1943), 321. He was born Vicente Baño Pérez 2 March 1867, became a

parish priest in the diocese of Mondoñedo 19 December 1891, entered the Capuchin Order 12 November 1911, and took solemn vows December 1915. He came to Montehano June 1916 and was its *guardián* (superior) 1922–1925, and *guardián* at Bilbao also in 1925. He died at El Pardo 28 December 1933. According to Enrique de Ventosa, Salamanca, 5 May 1989, he joined other Galician Capuchins in a failed attempt to set up a separate Capuchin province for Galicia in the mid-1920s. See also Andrés de Palazuelo, *Origen*, 72–73.

19. Enrique de Ventosa, Salamanca, 5 May 1989.

20. Camilo de Grajal, Useras, 14 July 1989.

21. ACM, "Crónica del Convento de Montehano" [1896–1927]. The chronicle proper does not begin until 1910, when there are rough notes for the earlier years. The pages are unnumbered. The citation here is from the entry for October 1918.

22. BOES 1919:114, Eduardo Miqueli (Limpias); Andrés de Palazuelo, *Origen*, 72–73; TMA, *Los frutos de una misión; El Santo Cristo de Limpias; narraciones completas y verídicas de los acontecimientos ocurridos en la villa de Limpia desde el día 30 de marzo de 1919* (Santander: La Propaganda Católica, 1919 [sic] [1920]), 35, iv. [Andrés de Palazuelo], "La importancia de una Santa Misión," DM, 8 April 1919. 1. Andrés de Palazuelo, *Origen*, 66–67.

23. Andrés de Palazuelo, *Origen*, 66–67.

24. Severiano de Santibáñez, "Diez días en Limpias," *El Siglo Futuro*, 17 August 1920. The zone around Limpias had been a center of Carlist activity in the nineteenth century. See Vicente Fernández Benítez, *Carlismo y rebeldía campesina; un estudio sobre la conflictividad social en Cantabria durante la crisis final del Antiguo Régimen* (Madrid: Siglo XXI, 1988), 43, 51. For earlier Limpias history, María del Carmen González Echegaray, "Limpias en la historia," *Altamira*, 1975, no. 1:295–335.

25. "On a daily basis the only persons attending mass were the sister of the parish priest, my family, and the odd woman from the barrio," Gabriel Fernández Somellera, "El Santísimo Cristo de la Agonía de Limpias; narraciones y observaciones sobre dicha imagen y sobre los prodigios obrados," 2. This is a combination diary and scrapbook in the parish archive of Limpias. For Miqueli's feelings about this see *Nuevo Mundo*, 4 July 1919, and Severiano de Santibáñez, "Diez días," *Siglo Futuro*, 28 July 1920. Miqueli told him in June 1920, "My parishioners, delighted with the chapel of the Vincentian Fathers, had forgotten their parish church."

26. [Andrés de Palazuelo] in DM, 8 April 1919. The following are the sources I have used for the events of March 30, 1919, roughly in order of their composition. I cite in subsequent notes only sources that provide unique details:

a. Eduardo Miqueli González to the bishop of Santander, written 2 April 1919, BOES 1919:113–116, and widely reprinted;

b. "La misión de Limpias, un milagro?" *Páginas domincales* (Santander), 6 April 1919, and DM, 7 April 1919;

c. [Andrés de Palazuelo], "La importancia de una Santa misión," DM, 8 April 1919.

d. The long articles in DM on April 9 and 10, based on the visit by José María Aguirre Gutiérrez on April 7;

e. An interview of Anselmo de Jalón in *La Atalaya* (Santander), 8 April 1919, reprinted the next day in DM;

f. Parish Archive of Limpias, "Declaración testifical del hecho maravilloso acaecido en esta villa de Limpias el día treinta de Marzo, Domingo, por el Smo. Cristo de la Agonía con ocasion de la misión en esta parroquia el año de mil novecientos diez y nueve." This is an eleven-page manuscript of the testimony given on April 10, 1919 by eight witnesses before the Limpias parish priest, Eduardo Miqueli González, and that of Marrón, Emilio Hidalgo Ungo. I photocopied this document in 1977. I am told that the original subsequently disappeared.

g. Pages 2 and 3 of the diary of Fernández Somellera (see note above).

h. The account in TMA 49–53, based on his interview with Anselmo de Jalón and Andrés de Palazuelo at Montehano not long after the first publicity.

i. "Cronica," ACM, July 1919. This account, slightly over two pages long, was written by Modesto de Azpeitia based on the oral version of one of the missionaries, who appears to have been Agatángelo de San Miguel.

j. An interview with Agatángelo de San Miguel by Tomás Echevarría, in *Los prodigios de Limpias, o sea, ensayo histórico, artístico, y teológico de su Santísimo Cristo de la Agonía* (Madrid: Editorial del Corazón de María, 1919), 128–138. Echevarría reprints in whole or in part items a, c, e above.

k. A letter of Miqueli to a Madrid priest, Angel Z. Cancio, dated 14 August 1919, BOEM 1 September 1919, and in Federico Santamaría Peña, *Los milagros del Santo Cristo de Limpias a la luz de la razón y de la teología* (Madrid: Imp. del Suc. de Enrique Teodoro, 1919), 15–16.

l. The long, detailed account published in 1920 by Andrés de Palazuelo, *Origen*, 66–120, based on information from his fellow Capuchins at Montehano.

27. TMA, 52.

28. This is the estimate of P. Agatángelo in E 137; P. Anselmo guessed "more than 50," TMA 51. Fernández Somellera named several seers.

29. TMA, 52–53. The coadjutor Emilio Veci checked and found no moisture on the other statues.

30. She was the daughter of Carolina del Rivero, who funded the mission, and the wife of the lawyer Ramón Carasa, also a seer that day. This couple had sponsored the hot chocolate for the children in the mission. Andrés de Palazuelo, *Origen*, 75.

31. On the suppression of this aspect by Miqueli, TMA, 52–53.

32. Andrés de Palazuelo, *Origen*, 109–117. One gets the impression that the Capuchins regretted the elimination of references to the "sweat."

33. NA DB (Mexico) 812.404/22, "The National Catholic Party"; Robert E. Quirk, *The Mexican Revolution and the Catholic Church 1910–1929* (Bloomington, Ind.: Indiana University Press, 1973), 50; Alicia Olivera de Bonfil, *Miguel Palomar y Vizcarra y su interpretación del conflicto religioso de 1926* (Mexico City: Instituto Nacional de Antropología, 1970), 15, 18. (I am grateful to Carlos Marichal for this reference). Fernández Somellera was still there in 1923 (DM, 15 December 1923).

34. ED, 9 July 1919; Andrés de Palazuelo, *Origen*, 66.

35. D, 3.

36. DM, 10 April 1919; "Cronica," ACM, July 1919.

37. E, 138; also ASM's interview with Asturian priests, reprinted SC 16 August 1919, 214, where he gives the date as June 2. He later claimed the date printed in the interview was incorrect (DM, 24 August 1919).

38. BOES 1919:115.

39. DM, 8 April 1919; Andrés de Palazuelo, *Origen*, 82.

40. DM, 21 April 1919. The visions recurred on Good Friday (18 April) and Easter (20 April), according to Miqueli, n. 26k above.

41. D, 1. "It was also said that a former sexton named [illegible] had seen the eyes of the Holy Christ move many years ago, and that in his house they laughed at him. Little credit is given to this story, for he is accustomed to drink a lot, and was frequently completely out of his mind."

42. P. López told the story to a number of persons: to Fernández Somellera (D, 1–2); to Florencio Amador Carrandi (a professor at Salamanca from Limpias), *El Cristo de Limpias; relatos de sus prodigios, investigación acerca de su historia, su origen, y su escultura* (Salamanca, 1919), 13–14 (reprinted in Andrés de Palazuelo, *Origen*, 62–63); and especially in a letter to TMA dated 16 March 1920 (TMA, 201–204). López later became superior at the Vincentian school, and in 1926 was made *visitador* of the Vincentians and the Hijas de la Caridad in Cuba and Puerto Rico (DM, 24 November 1926).

43. DM, 9 April 1919.

44. On more recent missions, Lawrence J. Taylor, "The Mission; the Ethnography of an Irish Religious Occasion," in T. Wilson and G. Curtin, eds., *Ireland from Below* (Galway: University of Galway Press, 1988); and my "Religious Apparitions and the Cold War in Southern Europe," in Eric R. Wolf, ed., *Religion, Power, and Protest in Local Communities* (Berlin: Mouton, 1984), 239–266.

45. William A. Christian, Jr., "Provoked Religious Weeping in Early Modern Spain," in John Davis, ed., *Religious Organization and Religious Experience*, ASA Monograph 21 (London: Academic Press, 1982): 97–114.

46. Ann Taves, *The Household of Faith; Roman Catholic Devotions in Mid-Nineteenth-Century America* (Notre Dame, Indiana: University of Notre Dame Press, 1986); Callahan, *Church and Society*, 233–235; John Lynch, "The Catholic Church in Latin America, 1830–1930," in Leslie Bethell, ed., *The Cambridge History of Latin America* 4 (Cambridge: Cambridge University Press, 1986): 541–546.

47. E, 130–131 (an account by Agatángelo de San Miguel); TMA, 36–37 (probably given him by Andrés de Palazuelo).

48. I have seen three related accounts of the Manzaneda events. The first to be written was probably the account in *La Luz de Astorga* published sometime after April 28, 1903. I saw similar versions in *La Hormiga de Oro*, 9 June 1906, 366–367, and Manuel Traval y Roset, *Prodigios Eucarísticos*, rev. ed. (Barcelona: Casals, 1958), 359–362. I am grateful to P. Tirso Cepedal, C.Ss.R., for providing two unpublished accounts: the favorable two-page entry in the (Latin) chronicle of the Redemptorist Community in Astorga; and the skeptical entry in the provincial chronicle in Madrid (1903: 297–299) written by Victoriano Pérez de Guerra.

Issues of the Astorga *El Ideal* ("Periódico Independiente. Libertad, Progreso, Moralidad, Trabajo") in the Hemeroteca Municipal of Madrid demonstrate the rarified situation in which the missionaries were moving. In the issues I saw (January to April 1903) of this somewhat irreverent gadfly, there were several references to the Redemptorists, mocking them for exorcising a country girl, for their evening lectures for women, and for the style of their oratory. By then the order had already been in Astorga for two decades. But, perhaps because of the French campaign against religious orders, and their own tenacious opposition to certain local customs and local freethinkers, they themselves were still, if not more than ever, an issue.

49. Orlandi, "Missioni parrochiali," 347.

50. Tirso Cepedal, "Ante un centenario frustrado, Nava del Rey (1879–1970)," *Boletín de la Provincia Española* (PP. Redentoristas) 16 (1979): 130–153.

51. Pedro R. Santidrián, ed., *Experiencias misionales; testamento misionero del P. Ramón Sarabia* (Madrid: El Perpetuo Socorro, 1959), 494.

52. Antonio Girón, *Sermones de Misión* (Madrid: El Perpetuo Socorro, 1932), 299–300. He also gives advice on the candle arrangement and (282–285) on how to rouse interest in the ceremony, solicit the candles, etc. In the literature the day of the Desagravio ceremony, the fifth day of the mission, is referred to as the "big day."

53. Vicente Alonso Salgado was named to Cartagena two months after the visions, on June 25, 1903. Mariano Cidad Olmos was due to replace him, but died in July before taking possession; his replacement, Julián Miranda Ristuer, was named in November, but not consecrated until February 1904. He in turn lasted only nine months before being named to Segovia. This discontinuity would have complicated any inclination on the part of the diocese to take the Manzaneda visions seriously. See Lamberto de Echeverría, *Episcopolgio español contemporáneo (1868–1985)* (Salamanca: Ediciones Universidad, 1986) [Acta Salamanticensia, Derecho, 45], 60, 62, 66.

54. Ottavia Niccoli, *Prophecy and People in Renaissance Italy*, trans. Lydia C. Cochrane (Princeton, N.J.: Princeton University Press, 1990).

55. J.-M. Curique, *Voix prophétiques ou signes, apparitions et prédictions mod-*

ernes touchant les grands événements de la chretienté au xix siècle et vers l'approche de la fin des temps*, fifth edition (Paris: Victor Palmé, 1872).

56. One of the voices of caution during the Limpias era was the English Jesuit, Herbert Thurston. For over forty years his articles in *The Month* gave a historical perspective on mystics, prophets, apparitions, and other sensational religious phenomena.

57. DM, 28 April 1919.

58. There was one major exception, his encouragement of the Catholic Farmers' Union from 1905 on.

59. Díez Llama, *La situación socio-religiosa*, 156, 162, 308–312. See also J. A. Gallego, *Política religiosa en España 1889–1913* (Madrid: Editora Nacional, 1975).

60. Diéz Llama, *La situación socio-religiosa*, 259. There were diocesan pilgrimages to Lourdes in 1910 and 1913 as well.

61. Demetrio Vicente, S.J. (Santander), to Sisinio Nevares, S.J. (Valladolid), 9 November 1919 in Q. Aldea Vaquero et al., *Iglesia y Sociedad*, vol. 2, 670–671.

62. "Declaración testifical," 1.

63. Aguirre Gutiérrez in DM, 27 May 1919, compared a Torrelavega boy visonary to Bernadette; Juan Bautista Ayerbe in *El Siglo Futuro*, 23 August 1919, asked if "Limpias was called to be the Lourdes of Spain"; Echevarría dedicated Chapter 12 of his book to "Lourdes and Limpias"; and for Federico Santamaría Peña in *Los milagros del Santo Cristo de Limpias*, Chapter 13, Limpias is "El Lourdes del siglo xx." The Liberal *El Cantábrico* (29 October 1919) argued for investment in roads and communications to facilitate the Limpias pilgrimages. "Look at the development of Lourdes in the last sixty years. What happened at Lourdes was less than what happened at Limpias, and today there is a Cathedral Basilica and an opulent city there." Juan de Guernica in the spring of 1920 wrote in *El Cristo maravilloso*, 27, that the "enthusiastic movement [at Limpias] is almost more than at Lourdes at the marvelous begining of the apparitions." At about the same time, the bishop of León wrote to Luis Urbano, "Would that [Limpias] were a Lourdes or greater, but it is necessary to keep doctrine sound and orthodox" (Urbano, *Los prodigios*, 2nd ed., x).

64. DM, 19 May 1919.

65. ED, 9 July 1919.

66. TMA, 93.

67. DM, 29, 30 April, 1, 2, 3, 4, 5, 6 May 1919. *El Pueblo Cántabro* [Santander, Maurista], 4, 5, 7 May 1919; *La Atalaya* [Santander, Datista], 5 May 1919; *El Debate*, 8 May 1919; and D.

68. According to DM, 6 May 1919, but the list of TMA for May 4 has only one signer. Is it incomplete? (TMA, 93).

69. DM, 28 April 1919.

70. DM, 9 May 1919. Fermin Gómez, Manuel Palacio, Manuel Llorente, Valentín Piedra, Federico Alvarez, Ramón Carasa, José Martínez, Juan Arrieta, Francisco Rocamora.

71. DM, 19 May 1919.

72. DM, 14 June 1919.

73. DM, 5 August 1919.

74. *El Pueblo Cántabro*, 29 April 1919.

75. Diéz Llama, *La situación socio-religiosa*, 257–259.

76. DM, 10 May 1919.

77. DM, 23 June 1919.

78. DM, 18 July 1919 for the Catechistic Pilgrimage.

79. DM, 10 June 1919.

80. D, 31 July.

81. *El Sol* (Madrid), 6 September 1919.

82. DM, 10 May 1919.

83. *Imparcial* (Madrid), 18 June 1919 (visit of reporter was 12 June 1919).

84. DM, 21 May 1919; DN, 3 August 1919.

85. In DM the first advertisement for "fotograbados . . . postales . . . placas de escayola con la imagen . . . estampas con oración para devocionarios" appeared on 5 May 1919. No doubt they were ready by the first Santander pilgrimage on May 4, if not before.

86. Archive, Arte Cristiano, S.A., Olot. I thank the Vayreda family for opening their books to me.

87. E, 327; PN, 22 April 1920.

88. *El Pueblo Cántabro*, 7 May 1919, and TMA, 93–101.

89. D, 5 July 1919; *El Siglo Futuro*, 23 August 1919; ED, 9 July 1919; E, 155. According to Adolfo Muñoyerro, CM., the parish priest in 1986, the books of testimony are not in the parish archive and were not there at the time of the two previous priests. If they were there in 1977, I was not allowed to see them. The total number of seers who had signed the books was occasionally reported, as follows:

20 July 1919—335 (my count from TMA, 93–101)
5 August 1919—400
29 August 1919—500+ DM, 29 August 1919
31 October 1919—850 TMA, 101
February 1920—930 Trenor, 276
22 July 1921—2,500 SC, 6 August 1921

The registers were still in use in 1925 (DM, 1 May 1925).

90. PN, 5 January 1920.

91. DM, 27 May 1919. Already on May 10 there was an article in DM titled "El Cristo de la Montaña."

92. DM, 18 July 1919.

93. From a pilgrimage program, "Adoración nocturna de Pamplona. Peregrinación Navarra a Limpias y Begoña" (October 13–15, 1919), in Fernández Somellera's diary/scrapbook.

94. For instance in the pilgrimage to Our Lady of Ujué—J. Clavería, *Historia documentada de la Virgen del santuario y villa de Ujué* (Pamplona: Gráficas Iruña, 1953), 71.

95. ED, 1 and 9 July 1919.

96. ED, 18 July 1919; DM 29 July 1919; DM 1 and 5 August 1919; DN, 5 August 1919.

97. DM, 5 July 1919; ED, 28 August 1919; ED, 31 August 1919; E, 179–180.

98. The archbishops of Lima, Granada, and Valencia (retired); the bishops of Pinar del Río (Cuba), Loja (Ecuador), Huesca, Madrid, and Salamanca; and the auxiliary bishops of Valladolid (Pedro Segura) and Málaga (Manuel González) DM passim; E, 181; T, 37–38. I have not found mention of the visit of the nuncio, Ragonesi, or of the bishop of Salamanca, Diego y García (in 1919), in DM. They are mentioned only in E, 181.

99. ED, 31 August 1919.

100. Bilbao was there 25 June 1919 (DM, 26). He gave a speech to the VOT congress there on 12 June 1921 (DM, 15). The Basque Integrist leader, Juan de Olazabal was at Limpias 6 September 1919 (DM, 6).

101. ED, 23 June 1920. Maura, however, endorsed Urbano's skeptical book in a letter dated 30 May 1920, as "muy saludable para poner en su lugar y medida las naturales exageraciones que oigo a menudo . . . ," *Los prodigios*, 2nd ed., xi. The Maurist *El Pueblo Cántabro* gave almost no coverage to the shrine after the first days.

102. *The Irish Catholic* (Dublin), 20 September 1919, and *Tidings* (California).

103. D, 29, 30 September 1919.

104. D, 31 December 1919.

105. DM, 21 November 1919.

106. D, 30 November 1919.

107. DM, 21 November 1919.

108. DM, 6 August 1919, and *El Siglo Futuro*, 23 August 1919.

109. DM, 10 October 1919.

110. DM, 9 August 1919.

111. DM, 28 May 1919; *El Mensajero Seráfico*, 1 July 1919, 307.

112. *El Santísimo Cristo de la Agonía* (Zaragoza: Tipografía Salvador Hermanos, 1919). I have not seen this. See DM, 9 March 1920.

113. E, 198.

114. EF, 15 September 1919, 514.

115. DM, 26 May 1919.

116. D, 6 July 1919.

117. DM, 24 August 1919.

118. E, 198. See also Urbano, *Los prodigios*, 124–127.

119. T, 32.

120. Widely reprinted: ED, 17 September 1919; DM, 1 October 1919; Urbano, *Los prodigios*, 115–116, etc.

121. T, 188–189.

122. Such conversions, rare as they were, were given inordinate attention. We read about a skeptical worker from Santander, José Pacheco (DM, 11 February 1920); the anticlerical photographer from Terrassa, Joaquín Sicart (DM, 14 August 1920); a hostile pianist (DM, 18 August 1920); a harlot from San Sebastián (and other cases, T, 88ff.); a husband who is an "espíritu fuerte" from Torrelavega (DM, 10 May 1919); a Swiss atheistic Socialist (ED, 1 July 1920); and a German Protestant, Carlos Glacer (Juan de Guernica, *El Cristo maravilloso*, 109–113, from DM). Most of these cases and others are discussed in E. Ugarte de Ercilla, "Los milagros de la gracia en Limpias," *Razón y Fe* 62 (1922): 5–18. See also H. Luis, "El Cristo de Limpias y sus enemigos personales," *El Correo Español*, 7 September 1920, and DM, 15 and 18 July 1923.

123. DM, 25 January 1920. By April, Switzerland and Germany led in letters of inquiry, DN 22 April 1920.

124. T, 276.

125. DN, 22 April 1920.

126. Severiano de Santibáñez, "Diez días en Limpias," 6–15 June 1920, *El Siglo Futuro*, 28 July, 3, 17, 26 August 1920.

127. The connection with Mexico was especially close. Much of Santander's emigration went there, and contacts were intense in 1918 and 1919 as many emigrants returned to Spain for political reasons. See Michael Kenny, "Twentieth century Spanish expatriate ties with the homeland; remigration and its consequences," in J. B. Aceves and W. A. Douglass, eds., *The Changing Faces of Rural Spain* (Cambridge: Schenckman, 1976), 106 and n. 16. In addition to Fernández Somellera there was a Mexican priest, Silvino Díaz, who assisted at Limpias from 1920–1922.

Through these contacts the devotion spread in certain parts of Mexico. One area was the Yucatan, focused on San Cristobal de las Casas (see below). Another was Morelia, where the diocesan bulletin reprinted many statements of thanks for cures. Many of the towns named were involved in the Cristero Rebellion a few years later, perhaps not coincidentally. (See DM, 28 November 1920; 31 December 1920; 5 August 1921; 17, 18, 19, 20, 21, January 1922; 13 May 1922; 30 August 1922.)

128. DM and ED passim. ED, 23 June 1920; DM, 9, 19 August 1920.

129. DM, 31 July 1920.

130. DM, 20 July 1920.

131. ED, 1 October 1920; ED, 23, 24 October 1920.

132. DM, 9 November 1920.

133. DM, 4 November 1920. The U.S. group was led by the bishop of Toledo, Ohio, who saw the image move.

134. José María Saénz de Tejada, *Bibliografía de la devoción al Corazón de Jesús (Ensayo)* (Bilbao: Editorial el Mensajero del Corazón de Jesús, 1952), 193–194. *El Mensajero Seráfico*, 16 February 1920, 81; 16 March-1–April 1920, 153–156; 16 April 1920, 172–173; 1 June 1920, 250–251.

135. Juan de Guernica, *El Cristo maravilloso*.

136. DM, 9 April 1920; DM, 27 December 1920; Andrés de Palazuelo, *Origen*, 233–235. Cubí had taught at the school that Trenor attended, T, 151–155.

137. DM, 5 June 1920.

138. DM, 24 August 1920.

139. DM, 2 February 1921.

140. DM, 10 September 1921 and DM, 27 August 1921, and passim.

141. Urbano, *Los prodigios*, 2nd ed., 180: "and the pilgrimages do not help much."

142. DM, 28 September 1921, and DM, 4 February 1922.

143. DM, 31 May 1921.

144. DM, 1921, passim.

145. Rafael López de Haro, *Ante el Cristo de Limpias* (Madrid: Biblioteca Nueva, n.d.—the text, p. 213, is dated September, 1921), 130–131. The book was first advertised in *El Debate*, 2 February 1922. It is written from a Liberal perspective, sympathetic to the Christ, but not to what its author sees as hypocritical aristocratic and bourgeois pilgrims. The book is dedicated to "mi amigo Angel Ossorio y Gallardo." In it are listed forty-four other works by the author, half of them "Novelas cortas" and seven of them "Novelas de la Carne."

146. Ibid., 132.

147. D, 21 June 1919.

148. *Imparcial* (Madrid), 18 June 1919.

149. Elisa Kennelesky, "El Cristo de Limpias," *La Epoca* (Madrid), 14 September 1919. See also, on the topic of binoculars, Juan F. Muñoz y Pabón, *El Santo Cristo de Limpias* (Sevilla: Sobrino de Izquierdo, 1919), 29–31; DM, 21 June 1919; and E, 240–242.

150. D, 26 September 1919.

151. D, 28 July 1919.

152. ED, 30 June 1920.

153. ED, 20 July 1921, and DM, 22 July 1921.

154. DM, 10 January 1923.

155. DM, 24 and 25 August 1920.

156. DM, 20 August 1921.

157. DM, 6, 10 August 1921; 9, 24 September 1921; 16 October 1921; 30 November 1921; 2, 4 December 1921; 18 May 1922; 3 September 1922. ED, 2 September 1922. In August and September 1923, Generals Navarro and Berenguer and their families prayed at the shrine, as did many soldiers who had been captives at Axdir, DM, 12 September 1923.

158. Urbano drew the parallel with Loublande in *Los prodigios*, 2nd ed., 191–199.

159. DM, 1 March 1921.

160. DM, 28 March 1922.

161. ED, 14 September 1922.

162. DM, 3 June 1923.

163. DM, 14 November 1922.

164. Ewald von Kleist, *Auffallende Erscheinungen an dem Cristusbilde von Limpias*, fifth ed. (Kirnach-Villingen, Baden: Vorlag der Waisenanstalt, 1932).

165. DM, 4 March 1922. DM claimed this number was for February 1922 alone, but that is unlikely. In all of 1924 there were only 2,085 foreign letters, and that represented an increase over 1923 (DM, 4 February 1925). Perhaps it represents the total for 1921, or even the total up to 1922 since 1919.

166. DM passim and 17 July 1926.

167. See Mary Lee Nolan and Sydney D. Nolan, *Christian Pilgrimage in Modern Western Europe* (Chapel Hill: University of North Carolina Press, 1989), Chapter 4.

168. DM, 9 July 1924.

169. Account Books 1964–1986, Arte Cristiana, S.A., Olot. In Levante, where the devotion feeds on that to the Santa Faz, a Verónica near Alicante, there have been two "activations" of images of the Christ of Limpias in the 1980s, at Ibi in the summer of 1984, and Denia in late March 1985. In both places images "wept tears of blood," that is, had some liquid on them. See *El País*, 4 April 1985, 14, and Choni Rodríguez, "Visiones fanáticas en torno al Cristo que lloró sangre en Denia," *Garbo*, 22 April 1985.

170. DM, 14, 15, 16, 18, 19, 29 November 1919; ED, 15, 16 November 1919; T, 39, 60–65, 101–102.

171. DM, 11–20, May 1920; ED, 12, 16 May 1920; ED, 25, 27, 30 June 1920.

172. Ramón Garriga, *El Cardenal Segura y el nacional-catolicismo* (Barcelona: Planeta, 1977), 77. Garriga had access to Segura's correspondence.

173. *La Época*, 14 September 1919.

174. Luis Urbano, "El Cristo que mueve los ojos," *Rosas y Espinas*, 1 August 1919; "Insistamos un poco, la razón y la fe," Ibid., 1 September 1919; reprinted in *Los prodigios*, 143–150. Urbano wrote prolifically, sometimes signing his articles X., L. Delmás, or D. Viñuelas. See *Index publicationem Prov. Aragoniae Ordinis Predicatorum* (typescript, Valencia: Archivo PP. Dominicos), 38–50. He was born 3 June 1882 and was killed in Valencia 21 August 1936. See "Artículos para el proceso informativo sobre la fama del martirio de los Siervos de Dios Jacinto I. Serrano y compañeros" (typescript, Valencia, 1957?, Archivo PP. Dominicos). His great rival, the Capuchin Andrés de Palazuelo, was killed in Madrid, 31 July 1936.

175. Urbano, *Los prodigios*, 90–91. Guisasola and Urbano coincided in Valencia for six months in 1913; Guisasola would have known of Urbano in any case from *Rosas y Espinas* and from his organization of the 500th anniversary of San Vicente Ferrer, 1919.

176. ED, 31 August 1920.

177. Urbano, *Los prodigios*, 2nd ed., 199.

178. See Chapter 1, n. 6, above.

179. Joseph A. Vaughan, "The Happenings at Limpias. Are the Marvels Narrated about the Crucifix at Limpias Objective Realities or Only Subjective Experiences?" *The Queen's Work*, 13, no.1 (January 1921): 1–3.

180. Manuel Rubio Cercas, "Explicación psicofísica de los que parecen prodigios de Limpias," *La Ciencia Tomista* 23 (January–February 1921): 20–34.

181. Ugarte y Ercilla's articles (see bibliography) were intended to be helpful for the official commission. He had previously written books on the Eucharist in Spain (1911), miracles in the Gospels (1914), Spiritism (1916), and Lourdes (1919), as well as a regular column in *El Mensajero del Corazón de Jesus*.

182. E, 181, *El Eco Franciscano*, 15 November 1919, 512.

183. DM, 28 August 1920.

184. SC, 9 October 1920.

185. DM, 19 April 1921.

186. DM, 9 July 1921; ACM, "Crónica," October 1921; Obituary, DM, 17 June 1923.

187. DM, 10 September 1921.

188. D, 16 June 1921. It was given to him by Silvino Díaz, the Mexican priest, DM, 17 January 1922.

189. It was claimed that Benedict XV had read Trenor, *Qué pasa*, and other books on Limpias, in DM, 9 February 1922.

190. I have found Lamberto de Echeverría, *Episcopologio español*, indispensable.

191. Urbano, *Los prodigios*, 2nd ed., v–xii.

192. Ibid., xi.

193. T, 40–55, and in most other books in favor.

194. The man quoted was age fifty in 1969, married, and not an assiduous churchgoer. A special diocesan commission checked the image soon after the first visions. Trenor, *Qué pasa*, 209–210, includes a letter by José M. Garrós, a sculptor who restored the image in 1898.

Chapter Three

1. It is useful to compare the Santander diocesan stance in regard to Limpias with that of Vitoria in regard to Ezquioga. A professor of the Santander seminary, Valentín de la Torre, was sent to Limpias in the summer of 1919 to observe the visions. There can be no doubt that his enthusiastically favorable analysis, delivered to the assembled diocesan hierarchy at the opening of the seminary term on October 4, 1919, had been previously cleared by Sánchez de Castro, who presided over the assembly. It was subsequently printed in full in *El Diario Montañés* (5, 6, 7, 8 October 1919). In contrast the Jesuit José Antonio Laburu was requested by the vicar general of Vitoria, Justo de Echeguren, to provide decisive arguments against the Ezquioga visions, and he delivered them in a very influential address at the Vitoria seminary on April 20, 1932.

2. *El Mensajero Seráfico*, 16 April 1920, 173.

3. DM, 18 April 1919.

4. Another official active in the cause was the Cathedral archivist, Santiago Camporredondo, who attempted to rebut Urbano in a pamphlet entitled, *El Santo Cristo de la Agonía; ligero estudio sobre los prodigios que se le atribuyen* (Santander: Librería Católica de Vicente Oria, 1919). It is mentioned in DM, 8 October 1919.

5. EF, 1919, 529–541, and 1921, 271–279.

6. DM, 28 April 1919; DM, 13 May 1919, and Antonio del Campo Echeverría, *Limpias; Descripción de esta villa—arte—geografía—historia—El Santo Cristo de la Agonía* (Santander: Tipografía F. Fons, 1919), 37.

7. TMA, 71–73.

8. TMA, 73–74.

9. TMA, 241–242, from DM June 1919.

10. T, 35.

11. E, 218–219.

12. *El Eco Franciscano*, 15 November 1919, 529–541; 1 June 1921, 271–279; 1 July 1919, 321–322; *Cataluña al Santísimo Cristo de la Agonía de Limpias* (Barcelona: Editorial Barcelonesa, 1920), 51–116, 143–153.

13. Cf. EF, 15 September 1919, 529, "Many more than those who signed saw the movements of the venerated image, but they did not put it down for lack of time or because they did not consider it necessary."

14. *Cataluña*, 82 (Jaime de Moner, abogado y propietario).

15. Ibid., 104.

16. Urbano, *Los prodigios*, 127.

17. Ibid., 21.

18. Obituaries, DM, 7 September 1926; 10 September 1926.

19. DM, 12 May 1919, along with José Posse, reporter for *La Gaceta del Norte* of Bilbao. Another DM reporter, López Recio, saw the Christ move 27 May 1920; TMA, 237–240.

20. He was assisted by the pharmacist in Limpias, Emilio Temiñé, who also sent information to *La Semana Católica* in Madrid.

21. The Arri family first visited Limpias in mid-June, 1919 (DM, 18).

22. One focus there was the Marist School in Montilla, where the nuns distributed estampas. DM, 29 April 1920 and 5 May 1921.

23. The Guardian of Salamanca was José María de Solórzano and that of El Pardo was Alfonso de Escalante, both from villages near Limpias. Antonio María de Torrelavega (Pedro Ceballos Pérez, 1880–1961) was a Capuchin brother at Torrente. From a wealthy, noble family, both he and his sister were seers at Limpias, and he defended Limpias in *Diario de Valencia*. His order, Spain's youngest for men, was Religiosos Terciarios Capuchinos de Nuestra Señora de los Dolores, founded in 1889 by Luis Amigó y Ferrer. See Juan Antonio Vives Aguilella, *En la Casa del Padre* (Madrid: Rel. Ter. Caps., 1988), 265–268.

24. María de Echarri, "Action de graces à Notre-Dame de Lourdes," A 44 (1911): 393–395. She had been to Lourdes in 1907.

25. For devotion in Cuba, see *La Montaña* (La Habana). DM, 10 September 1919, reprints one article. The interest in Cuba for Limpias is reflected in Fernando Caamaño, *Recorriendo España (Guía del Viajero)* (Habana: La Prueba, 1923), 48–51. Numerous conversions resulted from the preaching about Limpias by the bishop of Pinar del Río in La Habana after his visions in 1919. See L. Urbano, *El milagro* (Madrid: Bruno del Amo, n.d. [1928?]), 210–211.

26. DM, 22 July 1920. See also Chapter 2, n. 127, above.

27. DM, 8 May 1920. She hired someone to copy out testimonies to take to Peru from the registers.

28. SC, 12 November 1921, 625.

29. DM, 8 July 1921. The reporter was José María Pareja of *La Gaceta de Cataluña*.

30. DM, 7 July 1921; SC, 26 August 1922, 238 for distribution to Melilla.

31. Capuchin seers included: Agatángelo de San Miguel, Baltasar de Lodaces, Ambrosio de Santibáñez, Celestino María de Pozuelo, Constantino de la Vega, León de Santibáñez, Benito María de Ojedo, Doroteo de Macendo, Paulino María de Cervatos, Francisco María de Santibáñez, and Antonio María de Torrelavega. In addition another seer, Edilberto Herrero, joined the order as a result of his visions.

32. P. Buenaventura de Ciudad Rodrigo, in particular.

33. See Chapter 2, n. 186.

34. See Alessandro de Ripabottoni, *Molti hanno scritto di lui (Bibliografia su p. Pio da Pietrelcina)* (San Giovanni Rotondo: Edizioni Padre Pio da Pietrelcina, 1986), 2 vols., 384, 824. The first two pamphlets on P. Pio anywhere were printed in Spain in 1921 by Fray Peregrino de Mataró, who in his *Breve noticia biográfica del Rdo. P. Pío de Pietrelcina* (Barcelona: Imprenta de Fidel Giró, 1921), 9–11, states that he first heard about P. Pio in June 1919 and that the first article in Spain was a translation from *Le petit messager de Saint François* printed November 1919 in the Capuchin *Revista Antoniana*. It was written by a French Capuchin in Rome, Bernardino de Apremont. Laureano María de las Muñeca's article, "El siervo de Dios P. Pio de Pietra-Elcina" was printed in *El Mensajero Seráfico* 1 May 1920, 226–229.

35. Severiano de Santibáñez, *Manual*, 66–67.

36. Patricio Espinosa (22 October 1919) and Angel Diéguez (10 May 1921).

37. Cipriano de San Agustín (5 August 1919).

38. The Superior José Pujol saw the image move 12 May 1919; so did Tómas Nervi (5 March 1920) and an Italian Salesian in late August 1922.

39. Ana Yetano, *La enseñanza religiosa en la España de la Restauración* (Barcelona: Antropos, 1988), 1–99.

40. Díez Llama, *La situación socio-religiosa*, 188–189. On the Redemptorist foundation in Santander, Raimundo Tellería, *Un Instituto Misionero; La Con-*

gregación del Santísimo Redentor en el segundo centenario de su fundación (1732–1932) (Madrid: El Perpetuo Socorro, 1932), 411–417.

41. Ullman, *The Tragic Week*, 36–38. For the growth of the orders in general in this period, and the resentment they provoked in the working class, see Frances Lannon, *Privilege, Persecution and Prophecy, The Catholic Church in Spain, 1875–1975* (Oxford: Oxford University Press, 1988), Chapter 3.

42. DM, 28 June 1924.

43. DM, 20 July 1920.

44. Enrique de Ventosa, Salamanca, 5 May 1989.

45. Pedro Nolasco de Medio, *Las visiones ante el Cristo de Limpias* (Oviedo: Imp. La Cruz, 1923). Much of this work was printed in DM, 17, 19, 20 April 1923. For his death, *El Santisimo Rosario* (Vergara) 1928, 427–428.

46. Note the insistence of Juan G. Arintero (O.P.) that a Jesuit be involved in the propagation of the new devotion of Amor Misericordioso in the mid-1920s: "se necesita un grupito de téologos . . . uno de ellos a toda costa Jesuita." Cited by M. L. Fariñas Windel, "Apostol del Amor Misericordioso," *Vida Sobrenatural* (Salamanca) 17:98 (February 1929), 103–122, 113, in an issue entirely dedicated to the memory of Arintero. Arintero visited Limpias in August 1919 (DM, 17 August 1919), and was in touch with Urbano on the subject (Urbano, *Los prodigios*, 122–124). He had been Urbano's teacher.

47. DM, 19 May 1919; DM, 13 July 1919; a canon of Barcelona, Mariano Vilaseca, went a little farther, writing in July 1920 that "it would be rash to *doubt* it (DM, 8 July 1920 from *Gaceta de Cataluña*).

48. DM, 15 August 1920.

49. For Vaughan and Thurston, see above. Huberto Gründer, "A propósito de lo de Limpias; movimientos aparentes de objetos fijos," *Razón y Fe* 60 (July 1921): 351–362.

50. Urbano, *Los prodigios*, 35–36.

51. López de Haro, *Ante el Cristo*, 114–115.

52. *Cataluña*, 76. Similarly at Ezquioga in 1931 some seers saw Mary first as one devotion and then as another.

53. T, 56–60, reprints excerpts from an article about Limpias by Manuel González written 25 September 1919 and published in the association's magazine, *El Granito de Arena*. Melilla, where there were Limpias-like visions in 1922 (See Chapter 4), fell under his jurisdiction as bishop of Málaga. I have not seen J. Campos Giles, *El Obispo del Sagrario abandonado; biografía del Excmo. Sr. D. Manuel González García* (Palencia, 1950).

54. DM, 5 May 1919.

55. DM, 11 June 1919.

56. DM, 3 June 1919; D, 1 June 1919.

57. DM, 11 July 1919.

58. DM, 28 September 1919.

59. DM, 14 July 1920.

60. Domingo Benavides, *El fracaso social del catolicismo español; Arboleya-Martínez 1870–1951* (Barcelona: Editorial Nova Terra, 1973), 275.

61. Urbano, *Los prodigios*, 133.

62. This article was in Fernández Somellera's scrapbook with the notation, "Humanidad, 24 August 1919." It would appear to be from *La Humanidad*, "órgano de la Juventud de la Izquierda Liberal" (the party of Santiago Alba). The Hemeroteca Municipal de Madrid has only the first issue of this newspaper, dated 15 May 1919; the type is the same as the clipping of the article above. Trenor, *Qué Pasa*, 14, refers to a similar article he read in the last week of August in an illustrated magazine. Fernández Piñero was a journalist who worked first in Seville, and then in Madrid for *Nuevo Mundo*. In 1922 he published a novel, *Memorias del legionario Juan Ferragut* (Madrid: Mundo Latino).

63. DM, 2 July 1919.

64. DM, 11 September 1919; the last paragraph is from DM, 12 September 1919.

65. This song has been sung to me on several occasions. The last two lines are from a version gathered by Scott Sherman in Bilbao, 1987, personal communication.

66. See descriptions in *El Debate*, 31 May 1919; *Estrella del Mar*, June 1920; Ramón Garriga, *El Cardenal Segura*, 72–73; and above all José María Saénz de Tejada, *La consagración de España al Sagrado Corazón de Jesús* (Bilbao: El Mensajero del Corazón de Jesus, 1940), 80 pages.

67. DM, 28 April 1919.

68. SC, 16 August 1919, 214–215; E, 307. The interview originally appeared in a weekly magazine of Onis (Asturia), 27 July 1919. I am informed by the Cronista of Cangas de Onis, Celso Diego Somoano, that the magazine was probably *El Candil*, but he has been unable to locate a copy of the original issue. A censored version was printed in *El Mensajero Seráfico*, 1 October 1919.

69. 7th ed., Toulouse, 1872, cited in H. Thurston, *The War and the Prophets* (London: Burns and Oates, 1915), 3.

70. See n. 68 above.

71. DM, 5 September 1919.

72. Santamaría Peña, *Los milagros*, 9.

73. ED, 15 August 1919.

74. ED, 20 July 1921.

75. E, 319.

76. Santamaría Peña, *Los milagros*, 138.

77. See above Chapter 2, n. 122.

78. Daniel Palomera, parish priest of Nra. Sra. de la Consolación, on 8 June 1919 in DM, 10 June 1919.

79. *La Atalaya*, 5 May 1919.

80. ED, 1 July 1920.

81. ED, 20 July 1921.

82. ED, 15 August 1919.

83. T, 68 from DM, 5, 6, 7, 8, October 1919, Valentín de la Torre, "Los prodigios de Limpias, a la luz de la crítica histórica."

84. Manuel Llerena, "La devoción del Espíritu Santo y un prodigio de Limpias," *El Siglo Futuro*, 19 July 1920.

85. SC, 1 November 1919, 565 from *El Granito de Arena.*

86. Trenor wrote *El amo de casa* (Valencia: Librería Religiosa Belenquer, 1918) and *El apóstol del Amo de casa, Segunda parte de El amo de casa. Una jornada del P. Mateo Crawley en Valencia* (Valencia: Librería Religiosa Belenquer).

87. SC, 13 March 1920, 338.

88. *El Mensajero Seráfico*, 16 April 1920.

89. *El Carbayón* (Oviedo), 18 July 1919—"El caso de Limpias. Las exigencias de la Razón y las exigencias de la Fe," cited in Urbano, *Los prodigios*, 35–36.

90. Benavides, *El fracaso;* M. Arboleya Martínez, *Otra masonería; El Integrismo contra la Compañía de Jesús y contra el papa* (Madrid: Mundo Latino, 1930).

91. DM, 1 March 1921; E, 326–327.

92. Julio Romero Garmendia, "El Cristo de Limpias, Sufre," *El Cantábrico*, 21 September 1919.

93. Emma, "Gloria al Smo. Cristo de Limpias," DN, 28 October 1920. For more on dress and dress codes, a preoccupation of the entire ecclesiastical hierarchy, SC, 28 June 1919, 821–822; SC, 1 August 1919, 143–144; "Reglas que deben observar las señoras, señoritas y niñas en las manera de vestir," SC, 18 October 1919, 502–503; DM, 30 August 1923.

94. E, 319.

95. José Rubio Martínez arrived at Limpias sometime before 14 August 1919 (DM, 15 August). His visions were circulated by word of mouth and published informally (SC, 22 November 1919, 659–660) before the Augustinian librarian of El Escorial, P. Migúelez, persuaded him to sign them in the Madrid monarchist daily *ABC* on 30 December 1919 (reprinted in T, 140–145). His assertions were particularly scorned by Urbano, *Los prodigios*, 95–96, who no doubt recognized in them the ghost of his fellow Dominican from Valencia, P. Corbató.

96. Pedro Valls, Pbro., *El apocalipsis en 1918* (Madrid: Librería Internacional de Adrián Romo, 1915), 18 (52 pp.).

97. See Walter Hamisch Espíndola, "El P. Manuel Lacunza (1731–1801); su hogar, su vida y la censura española," *Historia* (Inst. de Historia, Universidad de Chile) 8 (1969):157–234, and Marina Caffiero, *La nuova era; miti e profezie dell' Italia in Rivoluzione* (Genoa: Marietti, 1991), 56, 82. Part Three of Lacunza's work, edited by Adolfo Nordenflicht, was published in Madrid by Editorial Nacional in 1978. Caro Baroja comments on this strain, which he considers "impoverished," tracing it back to its medieval roots in *Las formas complejas de la vida religiosa; religión, sociedad y carácter en la España de los siglos XVI y XVII* (Madrid: Akal, 1978), 247–265.

98. Cristino Morrondo Rodríguez, *Estudios bíblicos-milenarios; la proximidad de la catástrofe del mundo y el advenimiento de la regeneración universal* (Jaén: Mora y Alvarez, 1922) and *Jésus no viene, Jésus vendrá; catástrofe y renovación* (Jaén: El Pueblo Católico, 1924). See also Francisco Tiburcio Arribas (1815–1876), *El misterio de iniquidad o conjuración satánico-humano contra Jesucristo . . .* second ed. (Madrid: 1873); Toribio Martín de Belaustegui, *El fin de las naciones y la conversión de los judíos* (Barcelona: Editorial Poliglota, 1922), and articles by José Ramos, CMF, in *La ilustración del Clero* in 1915 and 1923. See also Richard L. Kagan, *Lucrecia's Dreams: Politics and Prophecy in Sixteenth-Century Spain* (Berkeley: University of California Press, 1990), 86–113.

99. Julio Echeverría Larráin, *Predicciones privadas acerca de algunos acontecimientos modernos* (Santiago de Chile: Carnet Social, 1932), 82 pp.

100. José Domingo María Corbató (Benlloch, 9 May 1862-Valencia, 23 May 1913), alias Máximo Filiberto, fought in his youth with the Carlists, and in 1879 took the Dominican habit. About 1889 he was expelled, allegedly for theft, and became a journalist. But his publication, in 1894, of *León XIII, los Carlistas, y la monarquía liberal* (2 vols., Valencia: Manuel Alufre) led to his expulsion from Spain. In Paris about 1900 he became convinced that he himself was the great monarch, and in 1903 he returned to Valencia, having founded the Militia of the Cross, whose members he called "crucíferos." Beginning that year he published a series of works about the new order, including a two-volume, *Apologia del Gran Monarca* (Valencia: Biblioteca Españolista, 1904, 489+484 pp.), in part a compendium of nineteenth-century French prophecies. His identity as the great monarch was partly based on these Integrist French sources, including L'Abbé Curicque, partly on the letters of St. Francis de Paula, and partly on the IV Book of Esdras, published in 1569 by Casiodoro de Reina. In Valencia he published, at times without Church permission, a number of journals that spread his ideas, including *Luz Católica, La Señal de la Victoria* (1903–1907), and *Tradición y Progreso* (1912). His booklet, *El Inmaculado San José* was placed on the Index in 1907 (Boletín Oficial Eclesiástico de Valencia 15 March 1907), and he was suspended from saying mass in January 1908. He had followers, especially among parish clergy, sprinkled throughout eastern Spain, and many of them were convinced that he was indeed the great monarch and that when he died he would be resurrected. They were mistaken. But in some form the crucíferos continued to exist, and emerged again in the 1930s among the believers in Ezquioga.

The best place to find out about him is in the library and archive of the Dominican Fathers, Calle Cirilo Amorós 54, Valencia, where there are copies of most if not all of his books, and manuscripts of his autobiography, "Mi historia íntima," a statement of self-defense written in 1896, and a 500-page, unpublished biography, "El Padre Corbató o las pasiones políticas del siglo XIX," by P. Manuel García Miralles, completed in 1969. Judging from those in attendance at his funeral, he seems to have had some following among Capuchins (García Miralles, 482).

101. Domingo de Arrese, *Profecías de la Madre Rafols* (Barcelona: Eugenio Subirana, 1939, Año de la Victoria), which considers 1940 to be the start of a new age; the fifth edition of Rafael Pijoan, *El siglo XX y el fin del mundo según la profecía de San Malaquías* (Barcelona: La Hormiga de Oro, 1941); and Enrique López Galua (Arcipreste-párroco de Ribadeo), *Futura grandeza de España según notables profecías*, 2nd ed., augmented (La Coruña: Imp. Moret, 1941).

102. For instance, J. H. Lavaur, "Cómo llega en los actuales momentos, el fin del imperio alemán, pronósticado por varias profecías célebres, precisas y concordantes . . . ," trad. Juan García Valladolid (Madrid: Bally-Baillière, n.d.), 62 p. Even the sedate *Études* had a series of articles from 20 September to 20 December 1915 entitled, "Le Destin de L'Empire Allemand et les oracles prophétiques." See also the case of Claire Ferchaud, above; Herbert Thurston, *The War and the Prophets; Notes on certain popular predictions current in this latter age* (London: Burns and Oates, 1915); and Marc Bloch, "Réflexions d'un historien sur les fausses nouvelles de la guerre," *Revue de synthèse historique*, 1921. I am grateful to Carol Fink for this reference.

103. BOES 1919:115 (written 2 April 1919).

104. TMA, iv.

105. Enrique de Ventosa, Salamanca, 5 May 1989.

106. Fernando Maria de Santiago, "Los extraordinarios sucesos de Limpias," *El Mensajero Seráfico*, 1 July 1919, 305–307.

107. A. G. de C., "A Limpias!" DM, 28 May 1919. Gutíerrez de Cossío, who was consul of Honduras in Santander, went to Limpias July 13, had the vision, and described it in "Por Deber," ED, 24 July 1919; DM, 2 August 1919, and widely reprinted. He was an influential figure in the diocese, the organizer of the 1913 pilgrimage to Lourdes.

108. *El Mensajero Seráfico*, 16 March 1921, 166. The quotes are from preparatory material for the National Congress in 1921. Less belligerent is José de Calasanz de Llevaneras, *Regla de la Venerable Orden Tercera fundada por N.P. San Francisco reformada por N.S.P. León XIII meditada y explicada según el espíritu de N.S. Patriarca y N. Smo. Padre* (Sevilla: El Adalid Seráfico, 1914), 121 + 5 pp.

109. J. A. Ferrer Benimeli, *El contubernio judeo-masónico-comunista* (Madrid: Istmo, 1982), 31–126.

110. Severiano de Santibáñez, *Manual*, 122–123.

111. Sáenz de Tejada, *La consagración*, 33–35.

112. ACM Crónica, passim. With the possible exception of the Dominicans, the relations of the Capuchins of Montehano with other orders were quite friendly. Capuchins preached in Jesuit houses, and Jesuits came to Montehano to visit, as did the Trinitarians of Bien-Aparecida and the Vincentians of Limpias. Capuchins were asked to preach the sermon of the Miraculous Medal, a Vincentian devotion, at the school at Limpias. And at the annual fiesta of the Porciuncula at Montehano, a Salesian played the organ.

113. Saénz de Tejada, *La consagración*, 12–40.

114. See n. 68, above.

115. DM, 24 August 1919.

116. DM, 22 April 1921 (from *Diario de Galicia*). Diéguez saw the image move 10 May 1921; EF, 1 June 1921, 277.

117. José Maria Aguirre Gutiérrez, "Nuestra impresión, palabras de un misionero," DM, 26 September 1919.

118. DM, 27 May 1920.

119. Kselman, *Miracles and Prophecies*, 90–94. Again Lourdes had for some Capuchins a particular eschatological significance. Father Marie Antoine, the author of pamphlets about prophecies, was an assiduous and very popular preacher in southwestern France. He accompanied many pilgrimages to Lourdes, and his sermons were reported with great relish in the *Annales*. They appear in their colloquialness, verve, and spontaneity to have been like those of Saint Vincent Ferrer. Referred to in the 1870 volume as "le moine populaire de Toulouse," he preached at Lourdes from at least that year to 1905. By 1889 he was referred to as "l'apostol populaire des pèlerinages." In his thinking, the apparitions at Lourdes and the miracles there were not simply a supernatural fixture, but rather part of an active, developing divine plan. See A 3 (1870): 14–16; and 22 (1889): 138. Not long before his death he was rebuked by Bishop Schoepfer for hearing confessions at Lourdes without first obtaining permission—A 40 (1907): 28–32. The movements of Marian images in the Papal States in 1796 were interpreted similarly; see Caffiero, *La nuova era*, 29–32, 61–62.

120. Fr. B. de E., "Advenimiento del Reino de María," *El Mensajero Seráfico*, 16 May 1920, 229–231. He dedicated the article to the Hijas de María of Grado, reorganized by Capuchins in 1919. He may have taken the text from Curicque, *Voix Prophetiques*, 2, 470–480. The link between the visions at Lourdes, the Sacred Heart, and the social reign of Jesus Christ was drawn as well in the Lourdes *Annales* of 1917, perhaps influenced by the visions of Claire Ferchaud—"Le 25 mars et le Règne social de Jésus-Christ," A 50 (1917): 1–12.

121. We read in the report of the mission in Cabezón de la Sal in 1910, that "Freemasonry was penetrating in shacks as well as palaces." In the report of Guarnizo, the priest wrote that the enemies of Christ were active in the district, "subtly inculcating in the simple countrypeople the poison of their ideas hostile to the religion of their parents." During this mission by Redemptorists in 1912, the anticlercals put out *Hojitas Cuaresmales* (Little Lenten Leaflets) to counteract the sermons. The chief ideological rival seems to have been the teacher in the lay school. BOES 1910:129 and BOES 1912:106–109.

This antagonism to missionaries, in the countryside as well as in larger towns, dated from their arrival in the 1870s. See examples in Cepedal, "Ante un centenario frustrado," and his "El Espino, misionero," in *Espino, Aniversario 1882–1957* (Burgos, Montepío diocesano, 1957), 60–67, where he cites the case of a village (which in fact was in Cantabria) in which in December 1900, when the citizens were asked to adorn their balconies for the mission procession, one man hung out issues of *El Liberal*, and then sat behind them with his shotgun in case the missionary should object.

122. Vicaría general del Obispado, "Ecos diocesanos; Sentencia penando el no descubrirse ante el Santo Viático," DM, 31 May 1922, 1. The man was denounced to the court by the vicar general, José María Goy.

123. "Habla un padre de la Compañía de Jesús," DM, 13 July 1919, from the "Telefonemas" section of *El Mensajero del Corazón de Jesús*, July 1919.

124. Domingo Blanco, "Ante el Cristo milagroso de Limpias; la revelación de un fraile misionero; desfile de más de veintecinco mil peregrinos," *El Imparcial* (Madrid), 18 June 1919.

125. Written 22 October 1919; EF 15 November 1919:530.

126. Written 22 October 1919; EF 15 November 1919:531. Abellás was *canonigo magistral* of Lugo.

127. See below, Chapter 4, n. 50, for the vision statements of Galician and Catalan pilgrims to Limpias.

Chapter Four

1. DM, 26 September 1919 and 27 May 1920. He appears to have told Echevarría that he knew *before* Limpias that Christs would soon move all over the peninsula.

2. ADP Piedramillera, Pedro Arrastio (hereafter PA) to José López de Mendoza (hereafter JLM), 14 May 1920. Pedro Arrastio Aguirre was born in Vera in 1877 and died in Pamplona in 1960.

3. DN, 19 August 1919 and 28 August 1919; SC, 20 September 1919, 313.

4. It was a priest from Estella, Corpus Garín, who wrote a chronicle of the October 1919 pilgrimage in PN (3, 5, 8, 9 and 13 January 1920), subsequently published as a pamphlet (BOEP 1920: 90).

5. DM, 21 April 1920.

6. José Irigoyen, "Misiones en Lezaún," BOEP 2 July 1920:196.

7. For more on the social and political context of this zone, see María Cruz Mina, "Elecciones y partidos en Navarra (1891–1923)" in José Luis García Delgado, *La España de la Restauración: política, economía, legislación y cultura* (Madrid: Siglo XXI, 1985), 111–129; Angel García-Sanz Marcotegui, *Navarra, conflictividad social a comienzos del siglo XX* (Pamplona: Pamiela, 1984); and Emilio Majuelo Gil, *Luchas de clases en Navarra (1931–1936)* (Pamplona: Institución Príncipe de Viana, 1989).

8. Conversations with townspeople, Piedramillera, 13 August 1982. On the widespread projection of evil on towns to the south, see Julio Cara Baroja, *Etnografía histórica de Navarra* 2 (Pamplona: Ed. Aranzadi, 1972): 393–395.

9. Figures are for 1923 from the *Anuario Estadístico de España* (Madrid: Suc. de Rivadeneyra, 1933), 664.

10. For more on vocations, see Epilogue, n. 8.

11. DN, 11 June 1920, Lodosa; also DN, 12 May 1921, Viana; DN, 13 May 1921, Lodosa.

12. Valeriano Ordóñez, *Santuario de Codés* (Pamplona: Diputación Foral, n.d.) [Navarra: Temás de Cultura Popular, 343], 22–24.

13. The closest shrines to Christ were relatively local ones at Calatorao (Zaragoza), Ambas Aguas (Rioja), Lezo (Guipúzcoa), and the more reknowned Cristo de Burgos in the Cathedral.

14. Juan de Guernica, *El Cristo maravilloso*, 140, cites the Javier case.

15. Ordóñez, *Santuario de Codés*, 26.

16. Roberto Sáenz Serra, *Los picados de San Vicente de la Sonsierra* (Barcelona: 1977). Penitents carry heavy crosses to the Navarrese shrines of Roncesvalles and Ujue in Holy Week.

17. Piedramillera, 13 August 1982. María Muneta was born in 1910. I have been told that one of the first seers was María Ganuza, now deceased.

18. About the bells, see DN, 10 December 1920.

19. CE, 28 May 1920 and 22 June 1920.

20. ADP Piedramillera, PA to JLM, 14 May 1920.

21. This letter is lost; its contents have been inferred from the other correspondence.

22. ADP Piedramillera, JLM to PA, c. 18 May 1920.

23. ADP Piedramillera, PA to JLM, 18 May 1920.

24. ADP Piedramillera, Miguel Atienza to JLM, from Acedo, 29 May 1920. Miguel Atienza Martínez was born in Corella in 1883. He was the parish priest of Acedo from 1914 to 1921, and that of Monreal from 1921 until he died in 1935.

25. The register in the parish archive of Piedramillera is untitled. The text begins: "A.M.D.G. Autorizado por el Excmo é Iltmo. Sr. Obispo de la Diócesis Fray José López de Mendoza, comienzo á tomar información de algunos de los hechos mas salientes observados por personas fidedignas en el Santo Cristo de esta parroquia de Piedramillera (Navarra)." (Hereafter "Register.") After the last testimony on 23 February 1921 on page 20, on pages 21–25 there is the sworn promise by village men, "before the glorious and miraculous Holy Christ," during a mission in 1945 by two Vincentian fathers not to blaspheme and to defend the Christ aganst blasphemers. There are 102 names, of which 4 are of illiterates. There were evening classes for adults in the village in November 1920 (DN, 10 December 1920).

26. Urbano, *Los prodigios*, 201–204. I have not seen Urbano's article, "Otro Cristo comienza a moverse," in *Rosas y Espinas*, November 1920.

27. The decline of devotion from outside the village can be followed in the "Libro de Cuentas 1915–" and the "Libro de Fabrica 1923–" in the parish archive of Piedramillera, in which alms given to the Christ are recorded. The drop in 1922 and 1923 was quite rapid. Before the visions there was no separate entry for alms to the Christ.

1920	4000	pesetas (May 11–December 31).
1921	3863	
1922	982	
1923	482	
1924	101	
1925	191	
1926	223	
1927	112	
1928	88	
1929	52	
1930	17	
1931	44	

28. Pedro Arrastio, "Misiones en Piedramillera," BOEP 2 November 1920:315–316.

29. DN, 10 December 1920. Victorina de Larrinaga, Viuda de Basabe, was "fervent and wealthy," a "Basque queen" who in addition to her many philanthropic causes supported the Nationalist newspaper *Euzkadi*, according to Alfonso C. Saiz Valdivielso, *Triunfo y tragedia del periodismo vasco (1900–1939)* (Madrid: Editora Nacional, 1977), 113. Engracio de Aranzadi ("Kizkitza"), wrote her obituary in *Euzkadi*, April 1932.

30. DN, 14 May 1921. The Jesuit who preached, P. Miqueleiz, had accompanied the April 1920 Navarre trip to Limpias (DN, 20 April 1920). The accounts for the anniversary are in the Libro de Cuentas, 31.

31. Libro de Cuentas, 31.

32. Lambea's family in Mañeru told me (July 1988) that he never mentioned the Christ of Piedramillera to them.

33. See n. 27, above.

34. Conversations with townspeople, Piedramillera, 13 August 1982.

35. ADP Piedramillera, PA to JLM, 8 June 1920 (misdated 8 May 1920).

36. Register, 7 (my numbering).

37. CE, 22 June 1920.

38. Urbano, *Los prodigios*, 97–104.

39. ADP Piedramillera, Miguel Atienza to JLM, 29 May 1920.

40. BOEP 2 July 1920:196–198; 2 November 1920:315–316.

41. ADP Piedramillera, Juan Azanza to JLM, Eraul, 25 May 1920. The sentences interpolated in brackets are in the Arrastio version, PA to JLM, 25 May 1920, and Register, 1.

42. ADP Piedramillera, PA to JLM, 25 May 1920.

43. Ibid.

44. Edilberto Herrero to Emilio Temiñé, Bilbao, 1 March 1920, in Andrés de Palazuelo, *Origen*, 336–338 and (abridged) in SC, 13 March 1920, 338–339.

45. Register, 2–3.

46. Dionisia Ocariz y Lana, c. 11 November 1920, b. Aramendia, resident in Piedramillera (Register, 16).

47. Domingo García y Díaz, visions on 30 May 1920 and 20 June 1920 (Register, 8).

48. F. Latasa, "Viana, El Santo Cristo de Piedramillera," CE, 22 June 1920. "Rorro" was temporarily cured of rheumatism as a result.

49. Andrés de Palazuelo, *Origen*, 337.

50. For Limpias the only complete vision sequences for which a similar evaluation could be made are those of the three Franciscan Galician pilgrimages (70 seers) and the Catalan pilgrimage of 1920 (39 seers). In the Galician pilgrimages there were 12 priests or religious, 16 laymen, and 42 laywomen who were seers. The Galicians' descriptions of the visions are less complete than at Piedramillera, probably because at Limpias no one was asking the seers details about what they saw and there was a line of people waiting to testify, whereas at Piedramillera testimonies were taken by the parish priest, and there was never more than one or two taken on a given day.

One similarity between those few Galician seers who mentioned both that the Christ was looking at them and what his expression was and the seers at Piedramillera is that in both cases the women have a more intimate relation with Christ. Three Galician women saw Christ looking at them in a positive way (smiling, with approval, benignly), and two saw him looking at them sadly (with eyes full of tears, with eyes in agony). Christ looked at two other women in response to their prayers—at one, without expression recorded, when she said good-bye, and at another, in agony, when she asked for forgiveness. Three laymen saw Christ look at them, but did not record his expression, although it made one of them feel happy. A priest wrote, "I asked him directly a favor, and he granted it to me. I use the word directly, because until then I had made my requests through his Most Holy Mother and the saints to whom I am devoted, for I always considered I had no right to speak to Him, since I had offended him so much" (EF, 1924, 281).

In regard to the glances at the congregation in general, the situation is different, for the congregation is an organized pilgrimage, of which each seer feels a part, not, as at Piedramillera, a heterogeneous body of visitors with which the seer may not identify at all. At Limpias three seers (a layman, a priest, and a woman) saw Christ give his blessing to the Galician group (two of them when a priest had asked for a farewell blessing). Another woman said, "He looked on all of us [by which I assume she means the pilgrimage] with mercy in his eyes." Only one woman, who felt called by him, said Christ objected to the congregation with his eyes, but even so he looked at them benevolently. A layman, two priests, and a woman saw him look at the congregation, but did not note his expression.

The bulk of the recorded visions from the Galician trips are descriptions of the image in agony and dying (two priests mentioned how similar it was to humans they had seen die in their parishes), sometimes dying a number of times, or simply of eyes and/or mouth moving. Two visionaries appear to have been affected by postcard or souvenir images, for they saw the Christ's head alone, surrounded as if by a cloud, without the body or the cross. A quarter of the seers specified that they saw the Christ move during the mass. (Texts: EF, 15 November 1919, 529–531; EF, 1 June 1921, 276–279; EF, 1 July 1921, 321–322; EF, 15 June 1924, 280–281.)

The experience of the Catalan (largely Barcelona) pilgrims was similar to that of the Galicians, but we know more details. About an eighth of the 312 Catalans drew up statements about their visions, almost all of them at their leisure once they had returned home, and their testimony runs to sixty-five printed pages. While most of the visions are of a Christ in agony, here too there were described a number of glances, directed at the group as a whole, seen by eight seers; at the Catalan priests who preached, seen by six seers, including one of the priests as he was speaking; and at the seers themselves (seen by nine seers).

All but three of the twenty-three glances described were either loving/happy looks or neutral stares. The three serious glances (one hard and frightening, one severe, and one tragic) were directed at individual seers. In terms of the glances observed or received, there was no difference between seers who were men or women.

As with the Galicians, most supposed that the glances at the group as a whole were in approbation or blessing of the pilgrimage—for instance, they were seen when the group entered, when it departed, and when it communed. The seers also implied that the glances at the preachers (the Christ appeared to be listening intently to the sermons), showed his approval of what was being said. Except for the three persons who received serious looks, those receiving glances experienced it as a blessing and were pleased.

Several seers addressed questions to the Christ as he watched them, and he answered positively with his glances. A poor semiliterate elderly woman from Bañolas wanted to know if her parents and siblings were in heaven, and if the souls in purgatory would go there. An elderly, infirm, retired naval mechanic from Barcelona wanted to know if his sins had been forgiven and if his past general confessions had been complete. The preacher wanted to know whether the sinner for whom the entire expedition was praying would be converted. For all the seers it was a time of great emotional intensity. Several said they felt emotions they had never felt before. (*Cataluña*, 78–79, 87–91, 103–116.)

Much like Bishop López y Mendoza of Pamplona, the priest who organized the expedition reassured them in his sermons that, whether the glances they received were loving or severe, they came from a loving God who wanted to help and comfort them.

The difference in the glances and those who saw them between the Piedramillera seers and those of the Galician and Catalan pilgrimages at Limpias point to two quite different constituencies. On the one hand there were Navarrese villagers of every stripe, drawn to the Piedramillera church by the news of a miracle; and on the other hand there were self-recruited, grouped believers, who paid for a trip of several hundred kilometers to Limpias because of their belief, not only in Catholicism but also in the Limpias visions. This kind of Limpias pilgrim was spiritually prepared for visions by days of prayer, special hymns, and sermons. Each went to the shrine not only as an individual but also as an emissary for his or her place and region.

51. *Estadísticas básicas de España 1900–1970* (Confederación Española de Cajas de Ahorros), cited in M. Cruz Mina, "Elecciones," 112; Majuelo Gil, *Luchas de clases*, 36.

52. One of the men I talked to in August 1982 had been making charcoal near Aránzazu when the first visions took place.

53. Archivo Parroquial de Limpias, "Declaración testifical," 7: Miguel Goñi Lacunza, thirty-eight, married, resident in Limpias.

54. Casto López de Goicoechea, "Misiones en Oroz-Betelu," BOEP 1 April 1920:92; See also BOEP 1917:396 (Unzué): "Here we have three causes of laxness: the influence of the railroad employees; the workers in the Carrascal quarry; and the constant coming and going of emigrants who in the New World lose or forget their religious practices, and even their religious ideas." Such observations go back at least to the 1880s (García-Sanz Marcotegui, *Navarra, conflictividad social*, 85).

55. F. Latasa, "Viana," CE, 22 June 1920; similarly, the Estella correspondent wrote (CE, 28 May 1920), "The Lord wants to give doubters concrete proof of his infinite mercies."

56. About López de Mendoza: A. Manrique in *Diccionario de historia eclesiástica de España* 2: 1342; Tomás Rodríguez, "El Ilmo. y Revmo. Sr. Dr. Fr. José López, Obispo de Jaca," *La Ciudad de Dios* 1891:5–13; M. F. Migúelez, "El Rvmo. P. López, fallecido Obispo de Pamplona," *La Ciudad de Dios* 1923:280–298; G. de Santiago, "Excmo. e Ilmo. D. Fr. José López Mendoza y García," *Archivo Histórico Hispano-Agustiniano* 1923:210–222; and Victor Moreno, "El *Diario de Navarra* y el Obispo Fray José López de Mendoza," *Príncipe de Viana* 47, Anejo 5 (1986) [I Congreso de Historia de Navarra de los siglos 18–19 y 20]: 449–454.

57. ADP Piedramillera, JLM to PA, 8 p., unsigned rough draft, undated, c. 18 May 1920.

58. Urbano, *Los prodigios*, 2nd. ed., vii–viii. Urbano sent out the first edition of his book at the end of March 1920 (I have a copy dedicated by him, dated 30 March 1920), which would have given time for López de Mendoza to respond before the Piedramillera visions began May 11.

59. Ibid., 204.

60. I found nothing on the Mañeru episode in the Pamplona Diocesan archives. In Mañeru older residents remembered vaguely that a child saw a crucifix move its head, and some thought it might have been a boy who later entered a religious order, but all agreed that "it came to nothing." The crucifix, at the back of the church, is accorded no special devotion now. The only mission at that time was held by Claretians from Pamplona December 13–21, 1919. From my brief visit to Mañeru in July 1988, one thing was clear. In sharp contrast to Piedramillera, whatever it was that happened in 1920 with the Christ in the parish church of Mañeru was not memorable. (Interviews with the parish priest José María Azurmendi, and Román Santisteban [b. 1897] and Miguel Fernández de Ezquide [b. 1906] on 31 July 1988; and BOEP 1 January 1920.)

Mañeru was even closer than Piedramillera to the front line of social conflict. There had been political turmoil between Liberals and Carlists in adjacent Cirauqui, and in Mañeru itself in 1915 there had been a demonstration of men, women, and children, shouting "Death to the mayor, the rich, and the priests." Seven houses, including those of the mayor and his lieutenant, were stoned. See García-Sanz Marcotegui, *Navarra, conflictividad social*, 36, 82, and the forthcoming study on Cirauqui by Jeremy McClancy.

There was another sort of riot there on September 19, 1920, to protest the transfer of the parish priest, Heriberto Morilla. Bishop López de Mendoza sent a stern letter to the village on September 25, 1920, warning them he would shut down the parish church if they did not accept the new priest. The protest in part seems to have been because of Morilla's zeal for social questions, and most likely had nothing to do with visions of the moving crucifix. See "El Obispo de Pamplona a los Habitantes de Mañeru," Roncesvalles, 25 September 1920, 3 p. ms., ADP, Mañeru.

According to Canon Agustín Arbeloa (who is from Mañeru), with whom I spoke in Pamplona July 27, 1989, Morilla had been in favor of parceling out a communal plot of land among the inhabitants, something the richer citizens opposed. Many inhabitants went by burro to the episcopal palace to see the bishop on the matter, but had to settle for the vicar general.

61. Joseph Vaughan, "The Happenings at Limpias," *The Queen's Work* (January 1921), 2.

62. DM, 26 May 1922, p. 1. The only reference to the episode in the progressive Melilla daily, *El Telegrama del Rif*, was on May 23, 1922, p. 3, a somewhat jocular verse by "P. Pillo," entitled, "Un Cristo milagroso en Melilla." The Novena was from May 13 to May 21, was dedicated to the Capuchin devotion of the Divine Shepherdess, and preached in part by a Capuchin from the house in Córdoba, Antonio de Ubeda. I am indebted to Vicente Moga Romero, director of the Biblioteca Municipal de Melilla, for this reference. Note in the verse the emphasis upon *ellas*, the predominance of women seers.

EPILOGUE

1. Information otherwise unattributed in this epilogue is from a conversation with Cándido Galdeano in Eraul on July 31, 1988.

2. For the relation of Raimundo Galdeano with P. Pastor María de Eraul, see ACM, "Crónica del convento de Montehano" (1896–1927) for May 1920: "Del 8 al 17 dieron una misión en Lezaún (Navarra) los PP. Anselmo y Agatángelo, encargados por un pariente del P. Pastor." P. Pastor was born Cecilio Echarri Galdeano 22 November 1861; he took the habit in 1881 in Fuenterrabia; made his solemn profession in 1885. He was consejero provincial 1895–1920, and ministro provincial 1910–1913. He died at El Pardo on 20 December 1930.

3. ACM Crónica, March and April 1917.

4. BOEP 1918:345–346 (September 14–22). In ACM Crónica the mission was given as "the villages around Eraul." Larrión is the adjacent village.

5. The orders that came in from these adjacent provinces were the Jesuits, the Franciscans, and the Capuchins.

6. BOEP 1916:78–79.

7. This Capuchin, who, like P. Bernardino was not a close relative of Raimundo Galdeano, died in July 1989, age 92. The close tie between the inhabitants of Eraul and the Capuchins can be seen from the fact that P. Bernardino persuaded fourteen youths from the village to go down to Estella to work "as an alms" leveling out the plaza in front of the monastery. I spoke with one of these men in Eraul July 25, 1989. He thinks it was about 1919.

8. As in Piedramillera, Mañeru and Eraul supplied many religious. From Mañeru in this century, the males became Redemptorists, and the females, Redemptorist Oblates. The most favored orders for men in Eraul were Augustinian Recollects and Capuchins; and for women, Sisters of Charity. Villagers in all three villages stress the importance of particular priests in channeling these vocations. Particularly salient in Navarra were those priests who established *preceptorías*, beginning schools. In 1916 the new curate of Abárzuza, near Eraul, established a free preceptoría. When Bruno Lezaún died in 1961 at the age of 83, it is said that more than 100 priests and male religious, and over 500 nuns had found their vocations at this school. The convent that he established in Abárzuza eventually employed Juan Galdeano, the seer at Piedramillera from Eraul, as a gardener. See José Ricart Torrens, "Don Bruno Lezaún, sacerdote navarro, apóstol de las vocaciones sacerdotales, y religiosas (1877–1961)," *Vida sobrenatural* 45:391, 223–232. See also Lannon, *Privilege, Persecution*, Chapter 3, and Antón M. Pazos, *El clero Navarro 1900–1936* (Pamplona, Eunsa, 1990).

9. BOEP 1920:93–94, 158–160. The overall frequency of missions in the entire northwestern quadrant of Navarre is patent from the diocesan bulletins. This was especially true in areas like La Barranca where there was an added incentive to preserve Catholic agricultural life from the ravages of socialism in adjacent factory towns. See the report of Yabar in BOEP 1921:153.

10. According to Cándido Galdeano, this mission was held in the winter; on his return to Eraul, Raimundo's horse slipped in the snow climbing a mountain pass and died.

11. For the Lizárraga visions of 1931–1932, see Amado de Cristo Burguera y Serrano, *Los hechos de Ezquioga ante la razón y la fe* (Valladolid: Casa Martín, 1934) and his *De Dios a la creación; de la creación al arte; del arte a Dios* 2 (Valencia: Tipografía del Carmen, 1931): 622–638; and for Ezquioga in general, William A. Christian, Jr., "Tapping and Defining New Power: The First Month of Visions at Ezquioga, July 1931," *American Ethnologist* 14 (1987): 140–166.

Bibliography

PRIMARY SOURCES FOR THE STUDY OF THE
EVENTS AT LIMPIAS, 1919–1926

Archives

Archivo Convento Capuchino de Montehano
Archivo de La Provincia del Sagrado Corazón de Jesus de Castilla, Convento de
    Jesús de Medinaceli, Madrid
Archivo Parroquial, Limpias
Archivo Fotográfico Marugán, Ampuero
Archivo P.P. Dominicos, Valencia

Apologetic Books and Leaflets

The many items I have not seen are marked with an asterisk. Most of the non-
Spanish items are from a list drawn up by Fernández Somellera.

Ackermann, August. *Die Wunder von Limpias oder der heilige Christus von der
    Todesangst von Limpias.* Einsiedeln: Druck and verlag von M. Ochsner, 1920,
    96 p.
Amador Carrandi, Florencio. *El Cristo de Limpias; relatos de sus prodigios; investi-
    gación acerca de su historia, su origen y su escultor.* Salamanca: Imp. El Salman-
    tino, 1919 (before November). There was also an edition in Bilbao in 1920.
Andrés de Palazuelo, *Origen y desenvolvimiento de los sucesos de Limpias; reseña
    histórico-crítica del Santísimo Cristo de la Agonía venerado en la villa de Limpias.*
    Madrid: El Mensajero Seráfico, 1920, 401 p. (Published about April 20, 1920.)
———. *Nuevos estudios críticos sobre los sucesos de Limpias.* Madrid: El Mensajero
    Seráfico, 1923, 128 p. (Published as articles in *El Mensajero Seráfico* previously.)
*Arendt, Léon. *Le Christ de Limpias.* Bruxelles: La Lecture au Foyer; Paris: Tequi.
Bericht über das Wunder-tätige Christus-Bild in Limpias. Karlsruhe, Baden:
    Kunstverlag Schlevter.
Campo Echeverría, Antonio del. *Limpias; descripción de esta villa-arte-geografía-
    historia-el Santo Cristo de la Agonía.* Santander: Vda. de F. Fons, 1919, 49 p.
*Camporredondo, Santiago. *El Santo Cristo de Limpias; ligero estudio sobre los
    prodigios que se le atribuyen.* Santander: Imp. y Lib. Católica de Vicente Oria,
    1919. (Available October 8, 1919.)
*Cataluña al Santísimo Cristo de la Agonía de Limpias; recuerdo y homenaje de la
    primera peregrinación catalana, 1920.* Barcelona: Imp. Editorial Barcelonesa,
    1920, 153 p.

*Despertador divino. ¿Qué quiere el Santísimo Cristo de Limpias? Rome: Imp. del
    Instituto Pio IX por los artesanillos de San José.

Echevarría, Tomás. Los prodigios de Limpias; o sea, ensayo histórico, artístico y
    teológico de su Santísimo Cristo de la Agonía. Madrid: Editorial del Corazón de
    María, 1919, 387 p. (October 1919.)

El Eco Franciscano. Número consagrado a conmemorar el éxito de la pere-
    grinación gallega al Santo Cristo de Limpias que tuvo lugar de 20 al 25 octubre
    último. 36:627 (15 November 1919).

*Espinosa, Alberto. El Cristo de la Agonía. Santander: La Atalaya, 1919. (DM, 31
    August 1919.)

Fernández Bernales, Aurelio. Historia del Santísimo Cristo de Limpias. Santander:
    Librería Religiosa Benito Hernández, 1919, 16 p.

Garín, Corpus. El Santo Cristo de Limpias. Impresiones de un viaje y de la lectura
    de un libro. Bilbao: Imp. del Ave María, 1920. First published in El Pensa-
    miento Navarro.

Geijo, Jenaro G. El Cristo milagroso. (May 1920) Santander: La Ideal. Repub-
    lished Bilbao: Artes Gráficas Sta. Casa de Misericordia, 1968, 48 p.

*González Gallego, Serapio. Crónica de la primera peregrinación gallega al Santu-
    ario de Limpias. El Ferrol: Imp. y Estereotipia El Correo Gallego, 1920. (Cf.
    Iris de Paz, 4 April 1920, 215.)

*Hoppe, Alfred. Auffallende Ereignisse an dem Kreuzesbilde der hl. Christus von der
    Todesangst. Steyr (Austria): Rudolf Zeilberger.

*———. Unsere Reise nach Lourdes und Limpias, 1923. Steyr (Austria): Rudolf
    Zeilberger, 1923.

Index Publicationem Prov. Aragoniae Ordinis Predicatorum. Valencia: Archivo P.P.
    Dominicos, typescript.

Juan de Guernica. El Cristo maravilloso; la fe en lo de Limpias; nueva aportación
    de datos sobre los sucesos. Buenos Aires: Imprenta y Casa Editora Coni, 1920,
    252 p. (Probably not issued until 1921.)

Kleist, Ewald von. Auffallende Erscheinungen an dem Christusbilde von Lim-
    pias. Fifth edition. Kirnach-Villingen (Baden): Verlag der Waisenanstalt, 1922,
    200 p.

*———. Récit des apparitions merveilleuses constatées au Christ de Limpias. Trans.
    Joseph Gruss. Colmar: Société alsacienne d'imprimerie et d'édition Alsatia,
    1921.

———. Wonderbare verchijnselen aan het Christusbeeld van Limpias. 's-Herto-
    genbosch: De Katholieke Illustratie, 1921.

*———. The Wonderful Crucifix of Limpias. Trans. E. F. Reeve. London: Burns,
    Oates and Washbourne.

*Lacalle Apellániz, Jaime. El Cristo de Limpias y su Romancero. Santander: Imp.
    El Correo.

López de Haro, Rafael. Ante el Cristo de Limpias; Novela. Madrid: Biblioteca
    Nueva, n.d. [1922—ED, 7 February 1922], 213 p.

M[artínez] A[ntigüedad], T[eófilo]. *Los frutos de una misión; el Santo Cristo de Limpias; narraciones completes y verídicas de los acontecimientos ocurridos en la villa de Limpias desde el día 30 de marzo de 1919.* Santander: La Propaganda Católica, 1919 (sic) [by August 1920, see *El Siglo Futuro,* 17 August 1920].

*Medio, Pedro Nolasco de. *Las visiones ante el Cristo de Limpias.* Oviedo: Imp. La Cruz, 1923. (Summarized in DM, 17, 19, 20 April 1923.)

The Miraculous Crucifix of Limpias. Clyde, Mo.: Benedictine Convent of Perpetual Adoration.

Muñóz y Pabón, Juan Francisco. *El Santo Cristo de Limpias.* Sevilla: Imp. y Lib. de Sobrino de Izquierdo, 1919, 39 p. (by November 1919).

*Paulovics, Sándo, ed. *Szentévi magyar zarándoklatok. Visszaemlékezések a jubleumi év eseményeire olasz, francia és spanyol földön. Róma - Lourdes - Limpias -Szentföld.* Budapest: Stepaneum, 1928, 291 p.

Pía-Unión de San Miguel Arcángel. *Guía del peregrino; Peregrinación a los santuarios de Limpias, Begoña, y Pilar de Zaragoza.* Barcelona: Manuel García, 1920, 24 p.

*Ramos Díez, Demetrio. *Los milagros del siglo XX.* Buenos Aires: Librería Santa Catalina, 1921. (2d ed., 1922.)

*Reviczky, Aladár. *A Limpiasi Csoda.* Esztergom (Hungary): Papnevelde, Kapató Reviczky Aladárnál.

*Ricardo de Azpeitia. *Doce meses de agonía.* Barcelona (Sarriá): Librería Salesiana, 1920, 80 p. (*Razón y Fe,* April 1921, 510).

Santamaría Peña, Federico. *Los milagros del Santo Cristo de Limpias a la luz de la razón y de la teología.* Madrid: Imp. del Suc. de Enrique Teodoro, 1919, 138 p.

El Santísimo Cristo de la Agonía. Zaragoza: Tipografía Salvador Hermanos, 1919. (DM, 9 March 1920; SC, 13 March 1920.)

Seis meses de agonía . . . El Cristo de Limpias. Gijón: Edición de Páginas Escolares, October, 1919, 34 p. (*El Mensajero Seráfico,* 1 October 1919 cites.)

Thurston, Herbert. *Beauraing and other Apparitions; an account of some borderland cases in the psychology of mysticism.* London: Burns, Oates, and Washbourne, 1934. Limpias section first published in *The Month,* 1920.

*Tóth, János. *Limpias kilenced.* Sopron (Hungary): Tóth Nyomda, 1928, 100 p.

Trenor, Leopoldo. *¿Qué pasa en Limpias? (Notas de la cartera de un vidente).* Valencia: Tipografía Moderna, 1920, 296 p.

Urbano, Luís. *Los prodigios de Limpias a la luz de la teología y de la ciencia; estudio crítico.* Barcelona, Madrid, Valencia: Ediciones de "Rosas y Espinas," 1920, 152 p. (Out by late March.)

―――. Idem. Segunda edición aumentada notablemente. 1920, 207 p.

―――. *Cuestiones apologéticas de hoy. El Milagro. Conferencias predicadas en la iglesia de San Ginés, de Madrid, en la cuaresma de 1928.* Madrid: Bruno del Amo, n.d. [1928?].

Vendel, János, S.J. *A Limpiasi csodás feszület.* Budapest: Korda Részvénytársaság, 1921, 48 p.

*Das Wundertätige Crucifix in Limpias. St. Gallen: Verlag Freiderich Gegen-
bauer.

Magazine Articles

This list includes the major polemical articles, especially from the more scholarly
journals, but not all articles from all magazines.

Andrés de Palazuelo. "¿Maravillas del arte?" El Mensajero Seráfico 1921:95–97,
    164–167, 182–183, 214–217, 243–245.
———. "Ecos de Limpias." El Mensajero Seráfico 1921:358–360.
———. "¿Discromatopsia o daltonismo?" El Mensajero Seráfico 1921:391–393.
——— "¿El mono-ideismo en acción?" El Mensajero Seráfico
1921:449–450, 470–472.
———"El cambio de color en el Cristo y la explicación que de él nos da uno que
    vió sin ver." El Mensajero Seráfico 1921:298–300 (sic) [498–500], 327–328 (sic)
    [527–528], 359–360 (sic) [559–560].
———. "Nimiedades que dan chispas de luz para que vean los que no ven." El
    Mensajero Seráfico 1921:386–388 (sic) [586–588], 409–411 (sic) [609–611].

[These articles were gathered in his 1923 book, Nuevos estudios.]

Buenaventura de Ciudad Rodrigo. "Algo sobre el Cristo de Limpias." El Mensa-
    jero Seráfico 1919:328–330.
Echevarría, Tomás. "Relación verídica de lo acontecido con el Santísimo Cristo
    de Limpias." El Iris de Paz 29 June 1919:508–510; 6 July 1919:12–13; 13 July
    1919:29–31.
Fernando María de Santiago. "Los extraordinarios sucesos de Limpias." El Men-
    sajero Seráfico 1 July 1919:305–307.
Fernández, Ramón. "Galicia ante el Santísimo Cristo de Limpias." El Eco
    Franciscano 15 November 1919:507–514.
Figueiras, José. "Crónica de la tercera peregrinación gallega a Limpias." El Eco
    Franciscano 15 June 1924:268–280.
———. "La peregrinación gallega a Limpias." El Eco Franciscano 15 November
    1919:506–507.
Getino, Luís G. Alonso. Reviews of Urbano, Los prodigios. La Ciencia Tomista.
    1920:396; 1921:296.
González y García, Manuel [Obispo de Olimpo—Auxiliary of Málaga]. "Mi
    visita a Limpias." in Trenor, 57–60, from El Granito de Arena. Written 25
    September 1919.
Gründer, Huberto. "Movimientos aparentes de objetos fijos (a propósito de lo de
    Limpias)." Razón y Fe July 1920:351–362.
Juan de Guernica. "Basilica nacional eucarística de expiación." El Mensajero Será-
    fico 16 February 1920:81; 16 March–1 April 1920:153–154; 16 April 1920:172–173.
———. "De la Basilica de Limpias." El Mensajero Seráfico 1 June 1920:250–251.

————. "Limpias, Lourdes, Quito." *El Mensajero Seráfico* 1 and 16 November 1920:410–413.

Léon de Santibáñez. "Una visita al Smo. Cristo de Limpias." *El Mensajero Seráfico* 16 March–1 April 1920:141–144.

Manterola, Martín. "Después de la Peregrinación. Gratitud." *El Eco Franciscano* 1 June 1921:249–250.

————. "Impresiones. Voto de Gracia." *El Eco Franciscano* 15 September 1919:517–522.

Mariño, A. "Apostillas a la cuestión de Limpias." *El Eco Franciscano* 15 November 1919:542–546.

————. "Un libro de actualidad, *Los prodigios de Limpias*." *El Eco Franciscano* 15 June 1920:282–288.

Naval, Francisco. "El Santo Cristo de Limpias. Cuestiones artísticas." *El Iris de Paz* 22 February 1920:107–109.

————. "El Santo Cristo de Limpias. Cuestiones científicas." *El Iris de Paz* 29 February 1920:121–123.

————. "El Santo Cristo de Limpias. Cuestiones ascético-místicas." *El Iris de Paz* 7 March 1920:137–138.

Nebreda, Eulogio. Review of Echevarría, *Los prodigios de Limpias*. *El Iris de Paz* 9 November 1919:377–378.

Quílez y Faura, Antonio. "Apuntes de un viaje a Limpias." *La Semana Católica* 30 August 1919:274–277; 6 September 1919:307–309.

Rubio Cercas, Manuel. "Explicación psicofísica de los que parecen prodigios de Limpias." *La Ciencia Tomista* 1 February 1921:20–34.

Ruíz y Rodríguez, José Manuel (Obispo de Pinar del Río, Cuba). "Carta Pastoral." 11 September 1919. Printed in part in Trenor, 40–55; TMA, 85–93; and DM, 19 September 1919:1.

Thurston, Herbert. "Limpias and the Problem of Collective Hallucination." *The Month* August 1920:150–163; September 1920:235–246; October 1920:345–355; November 1920:387–398; December 1920:533–541. Later published in *Beauraing and other Apparitions* (1934).

Toribio, Alejandro. "Después de la peregrinación a Limpias; gratitud obliga." *El Eco Franciscano* 15 June 1924:266–267.

Ugarte de Ercilla, Eustaquio. "Ante el Santo Cristo de Limpias." *Razón y Fe* March 1921:273–286.

————. "El misterio de Limpias." *Razón y Fe* June 1921:137–151.

————. "Las visiones de Limpias y las experiencias de comprobación." *Razón y Fe* November 1921: 273–285.

————. "El Santo Cristo y las curaciones de Limpias." *Razón y Fe* December 1921:431–451.

————. "Los fenomenos de Limpias" (reviews of Urbano, Juan de Guernica, and Ricardo de Azpeitia). *Razón y Fe* December 1921:510.

————. "Los milagros de la gracia en Limpias." *Razón y Fe* January 1922:5–18.

Ugarte de Ercilla, Eustaquio. "¿Alucinaciones colectivas en Limpias?" *Razón y Fe* February 1922:137–152.

———. "Ante el Santo Cristo de Limpias (no son alucinaciones colectivas)." *Razón y Fe* April 1922:435–453.

Urbano, Luis. "La emoción del pueblo; el Cristo que mueve los ojos." *Rosas y Espinas* 1 August 1919. (Also *Los prodigios*, 143–148.)

———. "Insistamos un poco.—La razón y la fe." *Rosas y Espinas* 1 September 1919. (Also *Los prodigios*, 148–150).

———. "Los prodigios de Limpias a la luz de la teología y de la ciencia." *La Ciencia Tomista* September–October 1919:153–171.

———. Idem., part 2. *La Ciencia Tomista* November–December 1919:301–317.

———. Idem., part 3. *La Ciencia Tomista* January–February 1920:41–52. (Gathered in *Los prodigios*.)

*———. "Otro Cristo comienza a moverse." *Rosas y Espinas*, 1 November 1920.

Vaughan, Joseph A. "The Happenings at Limpias; Are the Marvels Narrated About the Crucifix of Limpias Objective Realities or Only Subjective Experiences." *The Queen's Work; a Magazine of Catholic Activities* January 1921:1–3.

Newspaper Articles

This is a rather arbitrary sampling of signed newspaper articles, based on the information they provide or the originality or sharpness of the opinions they express. My list of items in *El Diario Montañés* takes up thirty single-spaced pages alone (1919–1926), and virtually every Catholic newspaper carried some articles on the events.

Aguirre Gutiérrez, José María. Articles in *El Diario Montañés*.

Amador Carrandi, Florencio. "El Cristo de Limpias." *El Debate*, 18 August 1919, 3.

[Andrés de Palazuelo]. "La importancia de una Santa Misión." *El Diario Montañés*, 8 April 1919, 1.

Anievas, Manuel de. "De Limpias; el Santo Cristo de la Agonía." *El Siglo Futuro*, 26 August 1919, 1.

Arrarás, Joaquín. "El Cristo que mueve los ojos." *El Sol*, 6 September 1919, 5.

Ayerbe, Juan Bautista. "El Santo Cristo de Limpias; relato de un testigo." *El Siglo Futuro*, 23 August 1919, 1. (His visit was about 6 August 1919.)

———. "Los acontecimientos de Limpias." ED, 20 July 1921, 3.

Balbontín, Adolfo. "Impresiones de un creyente español en Limpias." DM, 6 August 1920, 2, from *ABC* (Madrid).

Blanco, Domingo. "Ante el Cristo milagroso de Limpias; la revelación de un fraile misionero; desfile de más de veinticinco mil peregrinos." *El Imparcial*, 18 June 1919, 3.

Cea-Bermudez y Ziburu, Francisco. "Los prodigios del Santo Cristo de Limpias a la luz de la ciencia." *La Semana Católica*, 31 July 1920, 143–148, from *Diario de Habana*.

"Clementa." See Pérez de Miranda, Micaela.

Cueva, Jorge de la. "Por tierras cántabras." ED, 21 June 1919, 3; 26 June 1919, 3; 28 June 1919, 3; 1 July 1919, 3; 5 July 1919, 3; 9 July 1919, 3.

Diéguez, Angel. (title not known.) DM, 22 April 1921, 2 from *Diario de Galicia*.

Echarri, María de. "El Maestro nos llama." ED, 24 September 1919, 3.

———. "Lo que me ha pedido El Cristo de Limpias." ED, 14 November 1919, 3.

———. "Mi enhorabuena." DM, 3 December 1919, from *El Diario Regional* (Valladolid).

Emma. "Gloria al Smo. Cristo de la Agonía de Limpias." *Diario de Navarra*, 28 October 1920, 2.

Garín, Corpus. "Impresiones de un viaje y de la lectura de un libro." *El Pensamiento Navarro*, 3, 5, 7, 8, 9, 13 January 1920, 1.

G[utierrez] de C[ossío], A[ntonio]. "A Limpias!" DM, 28 May 1919, 2.

Gutierrez de Cossío, Antonio. "Por deber." ED, 24 July 1919, 3.

Irigaray, A. "La peregrinación navarra al Santo Cristo de Limpias." PN, 22, 23 April 1920, 1.

Kennelesky, Elisa. "El Cristo de Limpias." *La Epoca*, 14 November 1919, 1.

Lerena, Manuel F. "La devoción del Espíritu Santo y un prodigio del Santo Cristo de Limpias." *El Siglo Futuro*, 19 July 1920, 2.

Mangado. "Peregrinación navarra al Santo Cristo de Limpias." DN, 20, 21, 22, 23 April 1920, 2.

Minguijón, Salvador. "El testigo que no cree." ED, 23 September 1919, 3.

———. "Los hombres ante el prodigio." ED, 30 October 1919, 3.

Miqueli, Eduardo. "En Limpias." *Boletín Oficial Ecclesiástico del Obispado de Santander* 1919, 113–116.

Monte-Cristo. "El Santo Cristo de Limpias." *El Imparcial*, 5 August 1919, 3.

Ortega Munilla, J. "De mi veraneo." DM, 28 August 1920, 2 from *ABC*.

Pérez de Miranda, Micaela ("Clementa"). "Testimonio de una riojana." DM, 5, 6 September 1919, 2 from *Diario de Rioja*.

Romero Garmendia, Julio. "El Cristo de Limpias, sufre." *El Cantábrico*, 21 September 1919, 1–2.

Rubio Martínez, José. "Carta al P. Miguélez." *ABC*, 30 December 1919, in Trenor, 140–145.

Ruíz de Pombo, Soledad. "El Cristo de Limpias." ED, 15 August 1919, 3.

Severiano de Santibáñez. "Diez días en Limpias." *El Siglo Futuro*, 28 July, 3 August, 17 August, 26 August 1920, 2. (He was there 6–16 June 1920.)

Siso Cavero, Francisco. "La peregrinación madrileña; un día en Limpias." ED, 30 June 1920, 4.

Torre, Valentín de la. "Los prodigios de Limpias, a la luz de la crítica histórica." DM, 6, 7, 8, October 1919, 1–2.

Vilaseca, Mariano. "Un juicio autorizado." DM, 8 July 1920, 2.

Index

Pueblo Cántabro, El (Santander), 174n.101
Puentenansa (Cantabria), 167n.7
Puente San Miguel (Cantabria), 55
Puerto Rico, 170n.42
Pueyo, El (Navarra), 143
Pujol, José, SDB, 180n.38
purgatory, 191n.50
Puy, Our Lady of (Estella), 121

Quietists, 7
Quito (Ecuador), 9

Rafols Bruna, María, prophecies falsely attributed to, 110
Ragonesi, Francesco (Nuncio), 63, 77, 79, 174n.98
railroads and shrines, 10, 13, 14, 16, 50, 53, 55–57, 192n.54
Ramales (Cantabria), 16, 97–98
Ramos, José, CMF, 110
Razón y Fe (Madrid), 9, 19, 78, 96, 110
Redemptorist Oblates, 96, 121, 194n.8
Redemptorists: in Cantabria, 29, 35, 152; and Limpias, 93, 155; at Manzaneda, 46–50; in Navarra, 128, 142, 157; opposition to, 186n.121
red scare, 19, 27
**Reig y Casanova, Vicente, 80
Reinosa (Cantabria), 56, 83
relics, 7, 121
Religiosos Terciarios Capuchinos de Nuestra Señora de los Dolores, 179n.23
religious orders: and Limpias, 90–98, 155; and Lourdes, 10; and missions, 29–30, 142, 152, 156–57; seers from, 85–88, 154, 155; and social work, 93–94
Renan, Ernest, 105
reproductions of images, 59, 67, 173n.85
republicans, 17, 22, 26–27
Rerum Novarum, 17
Revista de Gandía, 27
ridicule: of Church, 26, 78, 137–38; of seers, 43–44, 59, 100–102, 170n.41
Rif War, 74, 138–39, 176n.157
Rimini (Italy), 8
Rioja, La, 122
Rivero, Carolina del, 37–38, 169n.30

roads for pilgrims, 55, 67, 172n.63
Rocamora, Francisco, 172n.70
Romanones, Conde de, 74, 108–9
Rome, 8, 10, 70, 75, 79
Romero, P., CSsR, 46–50
Romero, Pedro, 110
Roncesvalles (Navarra), 188n.16
Rosary, 30, 38, 51, 90, 108, 128
Rosas y Espinas (Valencia), 177n.175
*Rubio Cercas, Manuel, 25, 28, 78
*Rubio Martínez, José, 109, 183n.95
Ruíz de Pombo, Soledad, 104–6
Russia, 19, 32

Sabbath, work on, 31, 51, 161n.8
Sacred Heart Fathers, 112
Sacred Heart of Jesus: consecration to, 17, 102, 108–9, 113, 119; enthronement of, 97, 102, 107, 112–13; in French visions, 74, 77–78, 186n.120; and Gandía, 27, 165–66n.55; and Jesuits, 96, 112, 115; at Limpias, 37; as political symbol, 4, 9; in sermons, 48; Social Reign of, 97, 112–15
Salamanca, diocese of, 63, 67, 80, 89–90, 174n.98
Salesians, 17, 93, 155, 185n.112
Saltacaballos, 16
Salvat y Deu, Consuelo, 96
Samaniego, Felix R. de, CSsR, 152
**Sánchez de Castro, Vicente Santiago, 51–52; and Bien-Aparecida, 54; and Limpias, 52–53, 69, 82–83, 97, 153, 179n.1; and Lourdes, 52, 153, 172n.60; and religious orders, 93–94
*Sancho, José, 21–26
San Cristobal de las Casas (Chiapas, Mexico), 89, 175n.127
Sangüesa (Navarra), 142
San Juan de Dios, order of, 70
San Martín de Manzaneda (Orense), visions, 46–50
San Miguel de Aralar (Navarra), 121
San Salvador del Valle (Vizcaya), 16
San Sebastián (Guipúzcoa), 63, 69
San Sebastián de Garabandal (Cantabria), 167n.7